DR. DAVID JEREMIAH

THE COMING ECONOMIC ARMAGEDDON

What Bible Prophecy Warns about the New Global Economy

FaithWords

New York Boston Nashville

Published in association with Yates & Yates, LLP, www.yates2.com

Unless otherwise indicated, Scriptures are taken from the New King James Version®. Copyright © 1982 by Thomas Nelson, Inc. Used by permission. All rights reserved.

Scriptures noted NIV are taken from the HOLY BIBLE, NEW INTERNATIONAL VERSION®. Copyright © 1973, 1978, 1984 by International Bible Society. Used by permission of Zondervan. All rights reserved.

Scriptures noted KJV are taken from the King James Version of the Bible.

Scriptures noted The Message are taken from *The Message*. Copyright © 1993, 1994, 1995, 1996, 2000, 2001, 2002. Used by permission of NavPress Publishing Group.

Scriptures noted NLT are taken from the *Holy Bible*, New Living Translation, copyright © 1996, 2004, 2007. Used by permission of Tyndale House Publishers, Inc., Carol Stream, Illinois 60188. All rights reserved.

FaithWords
Hachette Book Group
237 Park Avenue
New York, NY 10017

www.faithwords.com

Printed in the United States of America

First Edition: October 2010

10 9 8 7 6 5 4 3 2 1

FaithWords is a division of Hachette Book Group, Inc.
The FaithWords name and logo are trademarks of Hachette Book Group, Inc.

Library of Congress Cataloging-in-Publication Data

Jeremiah, David, 1941–
    The coming economic Armageddon : what Bible prophecy warns about the new global economy / David Jeremiah.—1st ed.
        p. cm.
        ISBN 978-0-446-56594-3 (regular edition)—ISBN 978-0-446-57415-0 (large print edition)   1. Financial crises—Forecasting.   2. Economic history—21st century.   3. International economic relations.   4. End of the world.
I. Title.
    HB3722.J47 2010
    261.8'5—dc22

2010022310

To the friends of the Turning Point radio and television ministry who have stood with us during these financially difficult days. Because you have interceded for us, interacted with us, and invested in what God is doing through us, we have been able to continue reaching out to this ever-changing world with the never-changing Word of God.

Contents

Acknowledgments   vii
Introduction: The Spreading Virus of
Global Debt   ix

Chapter 1. The Fall of the American Economy   1
Chapter 2. The New World Order   27
Chapter 3. The New Global Economy   51
Chapter 4. From Crisis to Consolidation   77
Chapter 5. Satan's CEO   103
Chapter 6. "The Mark of the Beast"   131
Chapter 7. Financial Signs of the End Times   155
Chapter 8. The Collapse of the Global Financial Market   183
Chapter 9. God's Ultimate New World Order   211
Chapter 10. Keep Your Head in the Game
            and Your Hope in God   239

Notes   265
About the Author   293

Acknowledgments

This is my first book with FaithWords and I am delighted to be working with the visionary people who lead this company. Publisher Rolf Zettersten has a rich background in Christian media, and it has been a joy to get to know him and sense his passion for this project. I am also very thankful to work with an old friend, editor Joey Paul.

Sealy Yates is my literary agent, and he and his firm, Yates and Yates, have given great council and direction as we have dreamed together about the message of this book. Sealy has a profound understanding of the publishing business and he brings it all to the table each and every time we work together.

I want to thank my wife, Donna, for her encouragement. She alone knows how many times I hit the wall with this assignment. She prayed for me and helped me keep going when I was feeling overwhelmed by the enormous implications of this book.

My son, David Michael, is the vice president of Turning Point and the designer and director of the launch strategy for all of our books. With each release he helps us become more focused on the possibility of reaching the world through the printed message.

During the early days of the writing of this book, Cathy Lord, my research assistant, told me that God was relocating her and her husband to Cincinnati, Ohio. Because of her commitment to *The Coming Economic Armageddon*, she made several round-trips back to San Diego. Cathy, thank you for your sacrifice and your determination to see this project through. I would have been lost without you!

I also want to thank Beau Sager, who joined our literary team this year. Beau, it's good to have you on board. Thanks to William Kruidenier and Rob Morgan for their research and helpful suggestions. It has again been my pleasure to work with Tom Williams, who added his many creative talents to this project. Thanks, Tom. Diane Sutherland continues to be the best administrative assistant, and she coordinates so much of what happens when we publish a book. With Diane on the Turning Point side of my life and Barbara Boucher on the Shadow Mountain Church side, I manage to stay organized and focused on the important things God has called me to do. Diane and Barbara, thank you!

This will be the fourth book we have released since we began to make the publication of a new book the focus of our entire ministry. The creative genius behind our efforts belongs to Paul Joiner. Paul, I never cease to be amazed at the ideas God gives to you and your ability to make them come alive. We are so blessed to have you at Turning Point!

Most of all I thank my Lord Jesus Christ for calling me to be His servant. I know in my heart that there is no higher calling!

David Jeremiah

San Diego, California

October 2010

The Spreading Virus of Global Debt

G reece sneezes and Portugal catches a cold. Portugal coughs and Spain falls ill. Spain runs a fever and Italy comes down with the flu."[1] They call it *financial contagion*...the corrupting, fast-spreading influence of debt on the world economy.

This debt virus has infected an economic system that is teetering on the edge of bankruptcy. Greece is not its only victim. Belgium and Iceland were among the first to succumb. The Greek strain, however, is the most viral, and it is spreading its sickness among the other nations in the euro zone. There is great concern that this fear-based epidemic is filtering into the United States. Some argue that it is already here.

The most noticeable evidence of financial contagion is the continued borrowing of money by governments for the purpose of living beyond their means. In May 2009, representatives of the European Union (EU) and the International Monetary Fund (IMF) held late-night and early morning sessions hoping to stabilize world markets by earmarking nearly $1 trillion for further bailouts. In a statement released to the world press, the leaders said, "Each one of us is ready, depending on the situation of his country, to take the necessary measures to accelerate consolidation and to ensure the sustainability of public finances."[2]

As global financial earthquakes continue to increase in frequency and intensity, many are beginning to wonder if we are on the threshold of Armageddon!

Armageddon. It's a ten-letter word—four vowels and six conso-
nants—worth a minimum of fifteen points in a game of Scrabble.
Often misspelled and mispronounced, it is just as often misapplied.
According to the dictionary, *Armageddon* has been a recognized word
in the English language since the 1300s. It can refer to three things: the
place of a future "final and conclusive" war between good and evil; the
name of that specific battle; or a massive conflict or confrontation.[3]

Of course, as Christians know, the word *Armageddon* is from
the Bible, designating the world's final, climactic battle that will be
fought on the plains of Megiddo.

Drawing its power from that biblical imagery, in today's common usage the word refers to any event of cataclysmic proportion,
such as that experienced by the major stock-trading boards at the
end of 2008. Geoff Colvin, a senior editor at *Fortune*, declared in
an article that October: "This isn't Armageddon." But by spring of
2009 many thought perhaps it was. Allan Roth wrote in a recent
CBS Market Watch blog that until March 9, 2009, when the financial market made a turnaround, he thought that "Armageddon was
clearly upon us as capitalism was declared dead and buried with
the Great Depression ahead." In his review one year later, with U.S.
stocks up significantly, he wrote, "Hope has indeed come back...in
the good times since Armageddon."[4]

President Obama adapted the word and dubbed the record snow-
falls that crippled Washington, D.C., in early 2010 as *Snowmaged-
don.* In the hectic hours leading up to the 2010 vote on the American
healthcare bill, House Minority Leader John Boehner referred to
that critical period in American history as "Armageddon," conclud-
ing that the proposed bill will "ruin our country."[5]

I chose to use that word in the title of this book because it pictures the catastrophic conditions that will prevail on the earth in the
end times and because many of those conditions are beginning to
be visible today. For the past three years, I have devoted my study
to the identification and understanding of these prophetic attributes.

Somewhere in the middle of my investigation, I began to notice a financial thread running through the center of these end-time events, and it wasn't long before I could see how that thread pulled things together.

The ten chapters of this book are about these end-time occurrences and the financial warnings that are pointing us toward the Armageddon of the Bible. While that Armageddon is still in the future, the trembling of our financial foundations is a call for us to "awake out of sleep; for now our salvation is nearer than when we first believed" (Romans 13:11).

There is something about catastrophes of "biblical proportions" to which we seem to gravitate. The title of Mark Moring's article in the March 2010 edition of *Christianity Today* declared, "It's the end of the world, and we love it."[6] Moring points out that the growth in theater revenue since the current recession began is not surprising; it follows a trend that began in the hard times of the Great Depression of the 1930s. In 2009 a record $10 billion was spent at the box office, and attendance was up 4.5 percent despite the record high unemployment rate, which led to drastic cuts in many other areas of consumer spending. The movies that garnered record attendances included end-of-the-world offerings such as: *Transformers: Revenge of the Fallen*, *2012*, *Terminator Salvation*, and *The Road*. The trend continued in the early months of 2010 with *The Book of Eli* and *Legion*. Several others of a similar genre are scheduled for release later in the year.

And let's not forget that the best-selling Christian fiction series of all time was the twelve original volumes of the Left Behind series by Tim LaHaye and Jerry Jenkins, which sold more than 63 million copies over a period of fifteen years.

Why is there so much interest in entertainment that majors on the apocalyptic themes of the Bible? Moring suggests that "in a fear-filled world where war, terrorism, and economic collapse bring the question of death and the afterlife to the fore, the film industry has delivered more stories to fuel the question—though not always providing answers."[7]

I believe that much about the future of this world has been revealed to us in the prophetic pages of the Bible. In the following chapters we will explore together the answers we find there.

We begin with a look at the state of the American economy, which is still deteriorating and threatening to collapse. Although there are glimmers of hope, unemployment is at near-record highs in most of the country, and in my home state of California, it continues to rise.

In October 2009, according to the Labor Department's report, the National Unemployment Rate had risen to 10.2 percent, more than doubling the rate when the financial crisis began to be evident in December 2007. The unemployment report issued in June 2010 indicated that the seasonably adjusted unemployment rate in the country was down slightly to 9.7 percent. But in California it was still above 12 percent, and there was little hope for any major move downward.[8]

Since percentages tend to be very impersonal, let's look at this statistic in another way. These cold numbers translate into the fact that nationally more than 17 million real people—sisters, brothers, neighbors, maybe you—are unemployed and looking for work. As of the end of May 2010, 46 percent (6.8 million) had been unemployed for more than twenty-seven weeks. Add to that another 8.8 million workers who had become "involuntary part-time workers" since their hours were cut. Another 2.2 million had given up looking for work in the four weeks previous to the Bureau of Labor Statistics report and were not included in the unemployed figure. The total unemployed in May 2010 was 17.2 million.[9]

According to my calculations, that means there are 26 million would-be full-time workers in our country today in some degree of financial distress related to unemployment. That "more than 49 million Americans—one in seven—struggled to get enough to eat" was only one indication of the severity of the recession in the

United States.[10] More than 11 million homes nationwide are now "underwater"—that is, worth significantly less than the mortgage owed on them. According to the Federal Reserve, the collapsing housing market has produced a $7 trillion loss in value from late 2006 through the end of 2009.[11]

The overflow of unemployment pain reaches even beyond immediate families into the community at large where increased unemployment has added to the already burgeoning crisis in Social Security and Medicare. It is projected that in 2010 Social Security programs alone will "pay out more in benefits than they receive in payroll taxes."[12] Unemployed workers do not contribute to Social Security or Medicare programs, which means the number of recipients is rising while the number of contributors is falling.

Social entitlement programs inevitably lead to bigger government, which means more government oversight of private industry, especially in the financial sector. In the aftermath of the subprime mortgage and credit upheaval, which epicentered in the United States, the Federal Reserve, the Senate, and the Treasury Department have each pursued greater regulatory powers. Their published motive is to shield Americans from lending abuses by enacting caps on salaries and perks within the banking industry. Such bills have been passed in both houses of Congress and are waiting to be reconciled.

While most of us are understandably concerned with the impact of the American financial crisis, we cannot ignore the global economic meltdown that seems to be herding us in the direction of a new world order and a one-world government.

The idea of a one-world government is as old as the book of Genesis and as current as the United Nations. The world is looking for someone who can say, "We saved the world from disaster"—someone with more credibility than Fed Chairman Ben Bernanke, who made that claim in the summer of 2009.[13]

Our world is ripe for globalization. When the Cold War ended with a widespread thaw in hostilities, the nations and their economies began the process of trying to conglomerate from separate national-istic entities into one heterogeneous unity.

That process has been about as easy as incorporating iron into clay. Sure, it can be done, but not without the manipulation of basic structures, and even then the results can only be temporary. No com-bination of nations will ever be able to form a strong, stable world government—at least, not one that will last for very long.

Not that they aren't trying! Politicians, economists, scientists, and futurists have long sought such a supranational unity. The eight-year struggle to ratify a reform charter/constitution for the European Union is a good example of the difficulty inherent in combining twenty-seven separate national identities into one coherent unit. The European Union was finally successful in adopting a constitu-tion-type government with the approval of the Treaty of Lisbon in November 2009. Its implementation on December 1, 2009, opened the door for a stronger and more centralized government in Europe.

Despite the acceptance of this treaty, however, there is one linger-ing issue: the euro crisis. Joachim Starbatty, a German professor of economics, has written that the unity between the member nations of the European Union is now looking less like unity and more like illusion. Greece is the current focus of the discussion of restructur-ing the euro because of her precarious financial condition. Professor Starbatty further suggests that the euro, as it is presently configured, is "headed toward collapse" and that Germany may take the lead in withdrawing from the current euro structure, bringing with them other nations with strong money, and together creating a new com-mon currency.[14]

The aftermath of such a move could include a "new, more powerful euro [that] could easily supersede the dollar as the global safe-haven currency."[15] According to Starbatty's article, while there might be some immediate gains to be made by a restructured European currency, the long-term impact could be "global economic instability" and the "pos-sibility of a catastrophic plunge in faith in the [U.S.] dollar."[16]

As I write this, the world is still in the early stages of recovery from the major recession that began in 2007. Recent recessions have lasted no longer than eleven months, but the effects of this one have already lasted nearly three times that long.[17]

Reversing a promise by global leaders in April 2009 to end the recession, only China, France, Germany, and Japan were into the recovery stage by the end of that year. Today Canada, Italy, Greece, Great Britain, and the U.S. are still struggling to check the downward trend of the economy.[18] Great Britain's expected "probable" recovery from the recession in the last quarter of the year was met with the announcement of "an unprecedented sixth consecutive quarter decline."[19]

On the same day that announcement was made, former Federal Reserve Chairman Paul Volcker referred to the American version of the recession as "deep and potentially lengthy" and labeled it "the Great Recession."[20]

According to a *Washington Post*–ABC News poll, Americans agreed with Volcker's assessment. Eighty-three percent did not think the recession was over, and three-quarters were "worried about the direction of the nation's economy." Fifty-seven percent thought the actions taken by the government either had no effect or had actually made it worse.[21]

Historically, it has been the economy of the United States that has recovered earliest and has been able to pull "the rest of the world out of its funk."[22] This time around, it is hoped that China will lift the U.S. out of recession. If neither of these two nations can rise to the challenge, there seem to be few options left on the horizon.

Could we be standing today on the edge of a recession from which no one economy, no one nation, no one union will be able to extricate the world? The Bible predicts that such an era is coming. Fueled by the world's economic convulsions, the only answer will seem to be the unification of the nations under one economic system and one world ruler.

One would expect such a process to begin with the gradual consolidation of wealth and power, both nationally and globally. Today as we witness the merging of banks and the centralization of financial regulations, we cannot help but wonder if the Antichrist is waiting in the wings, ready to make his entrance onto the stage of this desperate world.

When he finally appears, the world will embrace him. He will have all of the answers to the pressing problems of mankind. He will be the ultimate financial czar—Satan's CEO, and he will deceive the world with a promise of stability and order. When the whole world is singing his praises, he will unveil his master plan for the destruction of all those who refuse to fall down and worship him.

In those final months of his evil reign, no one will be able to buy or sell without his special identification mark implanted in his or her forehead or hand. Using the technology that is already powerful enough to accomplish his plan, the Antichrist will control the financial destiny of every nation and every individual.

From his center in the ancient rebuilt city of Babylon, the Antichrist and his partner, the False Prophet, will regulate the commerce of the world until Almighty God brings it all to an end "in one hour" (Revelation 18:10, 17, 19).

Then there will at last emerge the ultimate one-world government and a one-world economy that will be the fulfillment of the long-desired utopia. The Bible assures us that a golden age of unprecedented peace and prosperity is coming. What the Antichrist will have failed to do with his militaristic and computer surveillance, Jesus Christ will do by His omniscience, omnipotence, and omnipresence. For one thousand years Jesus Christ will preside over an idyllic age of peace and prosperity.

With these events facing the world, we ask the question posed in a book title by the late revered apologist Francis Schaeffer: How should we then live? In light of all that is happening and all that is going to happen, how should we organize our schedules and live our lives? I have called the last chapter of this book, "Keep Your Head in the Game and Your Hope in God." This is the instruction that God has etched upon my own heart. In these desperate days, this is my prayer for you!

CHAPTER 1

The Fall of the American Economy

Bernard Madoff will go down in history as Wall Street's most notorious criminal. He systematically cheated investors out of $65 billion, far eclipsing the 1980s insider-trading scandals involving junk-bond financiers Michael Milken and Ivan Boesky. Among the thousands of Madoff's victims were a number of Hollywood celebrities such as Kevin Bacon and Kyra Sedgwick. Zsa Zsa Gabor and her ninth husband lost almost $10 million. Director Steven Spielberg and DreamWorks executive Jeffrey Katzenberg lost money they had invested for their Wunderkind Foundation.

Other celebrities who fell victim to Madoff included CNN's Larry King, former baseball great Sandy Koufax, Jane Fonda, and John Robbins of the Baskin-Robbins ice cream family. Also affected were prominent New York financial figures, some of the country's leading Jewish charities, Jewish patriot Elie Wiesel, thousands of elderly retirees who lost their life savings and, oh yes, Madoff's own sister, whom he scammed out of $3 million.[1]

Madoff took money from investors and then used their money to pay out profits to earlier investors. As long as the new money kept coming into the system, it worked like a charm. His investors prospered, and he promised to continue the bountiful flow with a steady stream of 12 to 20 percent returns. Impossible? Of course! But Madoff delivered on his promises. When asked how he did it, he would answer with some gobbledygook about his "split strike conversion strategy." If pressed too hard he would get angry and refuse

1

to answer. His clients should be grateful for his wizardry and quit looking for the levers behind the curtain.

Some of his investors assumed he was cheating, but they did not press for details for fear of killing the goose that was delivering golden eggs. As investment advisor Suzanne Murphy said, "It was a great con. The best cons are when you keep the pigeons happy, right? And the pigeons were happy because they were getting good returns."[2]

"Madoff did not have to put ads in the *Wall Street Journal*," wrote financial analysts William Bonner and Addison Wiggin. "Customers were banging on his door begging him to let them in. His oldest friends would come up to him and practically beg him to take their trust funds.... Madoff's charm was that he out-foxed the foxes and out-scammed the scammers.... In the history of high-stakes gambling, he out-did them all. Like a Robin Hood with Alzheimer's, he stole from the rich. If only he'd remembered to give to the poor, he'd be a hero to everyone!"[3]

Bernie Madoff was arrested, pleaded guilty to eleven federal offenses, and in June of 2009 was sentenced to 150 years in prison. "Once worth...millions, Madoff now lives austerely at a North Carolina federal prison. According to court papers, he eats pizza cooked by a child molester, sleeps in the lower bunk in a cell he shares with a 21-year-old druggie, and spends his time with a former Colombo crime boss and a spy for Israel."[4]

The Origin of the "Ponzi Scheme"

Eight decades before Bernie Madoff's crimes, Charles Ponzi (March 3, 1882–January 18, 1949) held the record as the greatest swindler in American history. The term *Ponzi scheme* is a widely known description of any scam that pays early investors with ill-gotten funds from later investors. Ponzi's scheme began shortly after the end of the

First World War at the start of the Roaring Twenties. He promised his clients a 50 percent profit within forty-five days or a 100 percent profit within ninety days. In the end, Ponzi was charged with more than eighty counts of mail fraud. He spent three and a half years in a federal prison before he was deported and moved to Rio de Janeiro, where he died in a charity hospital in 1949.

One would think Bernie Madoff wins hands down as the number one Ponzi perpetrator of all time. But if you compare his scheme to what is going on today in America's system of finance, Bernie Madoff is an amateur! Financing and administering massive entitlement programs, wars, and runaway big government have sunk our nation into a quagmire of deficits, debts, and inflation. And our government seems to see no way out except to continue the policies that created the problem—to spend and borrow at an ever-increasing pace until the entire system falls on its face, exhausted from trying to outrun itself.

This national Ponzi scheme was predicted twenty centuries ago in the New Testament letter of James and figures prominently as a sign of the coming economic Armageddon. In this chapter we will look at the causes, effects, and meaning of how Madoff-like greed and fiscal irresponsibility are contributing to the coming fall of the American economy.

The Ponzi Scheme of Social Security

One of the earliest triggers of financial instability in America was the inception of Social Security. In 1935, during the presidency of Franklin Roosevelt, the Social Security Act was passed into law. According to its architects, Social Security would rid our nation of all the evils associated with "old age" and make it possible for every American who lived to age sixty-five to have some kind of retirement income.

Within four years of passing the Social Security Act, Congress amended the program to include survivor's insurance. In 1965

Medicare benefits were added. By 2008 Social Security and Medicare had swollen to a massive entitlement consuming more than $1 trillion—one-third of the federal budget.[5]

Today Social Security functions as an unfunded entitlement program. While it is true that the government has raked in more in Social Security payroll taxes than it has paid out in benefits, that money is not protected in a trust fund, as many are led to believe. The government uses the Social Security funds to pay for other programs. There is no Social Security Trust Fund.

Social Security operates exactly like the schemes of Charles Ponzi and Bernard Madoff. New contributors to the program fund the promises made to the older contributors. American workers who have faithfully paid their Social Security tax each year are relying on an empty federal purse to fulfill its promise to them. And today, according to most economists, we are about to enter the perfect storm.

As *New York Times* economics reporter Edmund Andrews writes:

> The nation's oldest baby boomers are approaching 65, setting off what experts have warned for years will be a fiscal nightmare for the government. "What a good country or a good squirrel should be doing is stashing away nuts for the winter," said William H. Gross, managing director of the Pimco Group, the giant bond-management firm. "The United States is not only not saving nuts, it's eating the ones left over from the last winter."[6]

In a recent *USA Today* article, Richard Wolf detailed some of the other problems facing Social Security:

- Payroll Social Security taxes "flattened out in 2009 because of rising unemployment and expected pay raises that largely disappeared."

- "The number of retired workers who began taking benefits increased by 20 percent; those taking disability jumped by 10 percent."
- "Monthly benefits were raised 5.8 percent because of a spike in energy prices the year before."[7]

Social Security has become one of our most ominous unsustainable programs leading to unending deficits. Richard Lamm, former governor of Colorado, summed it up like this: "Christmas is a time when kids tell Santa what they want and adults pay for it. Deficits are when adults tell the government what they want and their kids pay for it."[8] The next generation is paying for this generation's Social Security. How long before the system collapses under its own ever-increasing weight?

War and National Defense

In 2008, 41.5 percent of all the military expenditures in the entire world belonged to the United States. We spent more on national defense than China, Japan, Russia, Europe, and several other nations combined. In 2009 our defense budget was $642 billion, second only to Social Security at $677 billion. Our defense costs were 36 percent of the total income from taxes in fiscal year 2009.

Economist Joseph Stiglitz, a Nobel laureate, and his coauthor, Linda Bilmes, wrote a book about the costs of our current war, including its hidden costs. The book's title, *The Three Trillion Dollar War*, summarizes its conclusion. Many who praised the book said its only failure was underestimating the cost by at least another trillion.[9]

Joel Belz, executive director of *WORLD* magazine, put these astronomical figures into focus: "Wherever you stand on increasing our forces in Afghanistan, you'll have to concede that war is expensive. In round numbers, by some estimates, it costs us a million dollars per soldier per year to send someone to Iraq or Afghanistan."[10]

Clearly, the cost of war and national defense is another drain on our national economy and a contributing factor to our growing deficit.

The Growth of Big Government

The size of the United States government began to balloon during the presidency of Franklin Roosevelt as his New Deal attempted to address the misery of the Great Depression. According to a recent State Department report,

> The rise of the United States as the world's major military power during and after World War II also fueled government growth.... Greater educational expectations led to significant government investment in schools and colleges. An enormous national push for scientific and technological advances spawned new agencies and substantial public investment in fields ranging from space exploration to health care.[11]

And it's not just the federal government that continues to grow. According to the same report, between 1960 and 1990, "the number of state and local government employees increased from 6.4 million to 15.2 million."[12]

Today the United States government is our nation's largest employer. The December 2009 total payroll for federal government employees rang up at $15,471,672,417! In 1900 only one in twenty-four Americans worked for the government. By 1948 government employment rose almost 500 percent to one in eight.[13] In 2009 there

6

were nearly two million federal employees, and that number is projected to rise by 15.6 percent in fiscal year 2010. It's no wonder that more than a third of Americans polled by Gallup would prefer the "perceived 'safeness' and typically generous benefits" of a federal job.[14]

A *USA Today* analysis on December 11, 2009, showed that at least one sector of the job market had been thriving during the previous eighteen months—the one your tax dollars pay for. The paper analyzed the two million federal workers tracked by the database of the Office of Personnel Management, which excludes the White House, Congress, the postal service, intelligence agencies, and uniformed military personnel. Its findings: 19 percent of federal workers make more than $100,000 per year (before overtime and bonuses), compared to 14 percent when the recession began. The average federal worker's pay is now $71,206, much higher than the average private sector worker's pay of $40,331. "There's no way to justify this to the American people," Rep. Jason Chaffetz (R-Utah) told the paper. "It's ridiculous."[15]

More than ridiculous, the uncontrolled growth of big government is also a major contributor to our rapidly escalating deficit.

National and Private Debt

In 2009, the *New York Times* reported, "With the national debt now topping $12 trillion, the White House estimates that the government's tab for servicing the debt will exceed $700 billion a year in 2019, up from $202 billion this year....Just one of the wrenching challenges facing the United States after decades of living beyond its means."[16]

I wish I could tell you that $12 trillion is the whole story, but it is not; it is only the "visible debt," the tip of the iceberg. In his book

The Dollar Meltdown, Charles Goyette paints the larger picture in vivid detail:

> The debt is not really just $12 trillion! By any commonsensical definition of the term "debt," something owed, the real debt is larger. If you have paid into Social Security for a lifetime and you believe your promised benefits are a debt of the government; if you believe the government should make good on promises of veteran's health care; if your bank has been paying insurance premiums to the FDIC and you expect that in the event of a run on the banks, loss coverage is a debt of the government; if you have been paying the government for medical coverage which you will expect to be there when the need arises; if you believe that government "guarantees," tossed around like confetti lately, are real promises upon which institutions and individuals should rely; then you will agree the government's debt is much larger than the $12 trillion on the books. All of these expectations represent unfunded liabilities; promises the government has made, but for which no provision to pay has been made. The bulk of the iceberg is below the waterline, the visible "national debt" is just a fraction of our government's liabilities.[17]

Fiscal economists use a term that designates the cause and magnitude of our debt: *infinite horizon discounted value.* While this term represents a highly complicated formula that determines the value of all promised benefits—current and future—in terms of our present-day dollars going forward into the infinite future, its simple meaning is: the gap between promised Social Security and Medicare benefits accruing to every American with a registered Social Security number and the actual income from taxes in a given year. It is an approximation based on life expectancy in actuarials. For Social Security alone that gap is $17.5 trillion!

Unfortunately, Social Security is not our greatest problem. Medicare is many times worse. Our current Medicare program has three separate centers of coverage and funding. Medicare Part A covers hospital stays. Medicare Part B covers doctor visits. The most recent addition to the Medicare programs, Part D, which covers prescriptions, took effect in 2006.

The current unfunded liability for Medicare Part A is $36.7 trillion; for Part B it is $37 trillion; and for Part D it is $15.6 trillion. The total liability of all three unfunded Medicare programs is $89.3 trillion. This is five times as much as the unfunded Social Security bill.

Add the unfunded liability of all three parts of Medicare to the unfunded liability of Social Security and you come up with a figure of $106.8 trillion. Now add to that our national debt of $12 trillion, and the bottom line totals $118.8 trillion. That amounts to a debt load of $383,000 per person, or $1,532,000 per family of four.[18]

Charles Goyette summarized the problem with this enormous debt load:

America's debts at any level—$12 trillion...won't be paid. They will simply be rolled over again and again until America's creditors are unwilling to loan any longer. The nation is in the same position as someone who has taken a cash advance from his Visa card to meet his mortgage payment, and then has taken out a new MasterCard credit line to pay his Visa bill. Credit card debt juggling may appear to work in the short run, but it is a road to financial ruin. And just as compound interest is said to be the investor's best friend, it is the debtor's worst nightmare, as debt growth becomes exponential.[19]

Incidentally, as of June 1, 2010, the national debt had grown to $13 trillion—a disconcerting new record.[20]

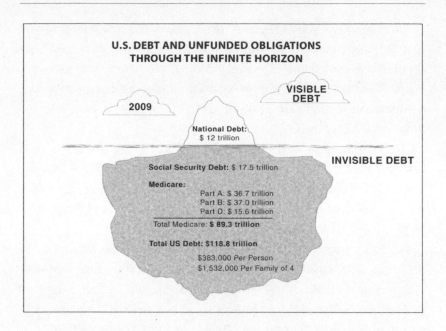

So far we have been addressing only the debt itself. But what about the interest on all that debt? If you have a mortgage on your home, you have probably experienced a reaction similar to mine when you received your year-end interest statement. Isn't it discouraging to see the disparity between the amount consumed by interest compared to how little is applied against the principal? If you think you have reason to be discouraged, consider the U.S. government's fiscal year-end interest statement. According to the White House Office of Management and Budget, $904 billion came into the Treasury through our tax payments at the end of the fiscal year on September 30, 2009. The interest on our national debt was $383 billion. This means that the cost of interest on the debt represented more than 40 cents of every dollar that came in from individual income taxes.[21]

Another disconcerting problem with our enormous debt burden is the parties to whom we owe it. In 1952 we owed most of our national debt to ourselves—to individual investors and American financial institutions. In fact, less than 5 percent of U.S. Treasury bonds were in foreign hands. According to the Department of the Treasury, at the end of the 2009 financial year, nearly 50 percent of our nation's public debt was owned by foreign governments and financial institutions. The rate of foreign ownership of American debt securities is increasing at an alarming pace; it is now triple what it was in 2001. Here is a partial list of the nations that hold our debt and the amount they owned as of the end of 2009:[22]

China	798.9
Japan	746.5
United Kingdom	230.7
Oil Exporting Countries	188.4
Caribbean Banking Centers	169.3
Brazil	156.2
Hong Kong	142.0
Russia*	122.5

*Russia owned no U.S. debts as of 2007. She is now the eighth-largest foreign holder.

This money has been borrowed by issuing IOUs, which are called bonds or Treasury notes. We use that borrowed money to pay our government's current bills. Until our debt is repaid (which it likely never will be), we pay interest on those IOUs. According to the Congressional Budget Office's forecast for this decade, the government expects to incur $9 trillion in new debt. More than half of that amount ($4.8 trillion) will be applied to interest payments.[23]

One financial professional has determined that the interest on the national debt accrues at the rate of $41 million an hour. That's $690,000 a minute, and $11,500 per second! Remember, that's just the interest. These payments do not touch the principal.[24]

Even a small increase in the interest rate has a big impact. As Edmund Andrews explains, "An increase of one percentage point in the Treasury's average cost of borrowing would cost American taxpayers an extra $80 billion this year—about equal to the combined budgets of the Department of Energy and the Department of Education."[25]

When you move past the nation's debt to the private debt of its citizens, the picture does not get any prettier. Bonner and Wiggin tell us, "Household debt rose from $7.8 trillion in 2002 to nearly $14 trillion in 2008."[26] That debt cannot possibly be paid off in one generation, so it is passed on, in some cases to people who have yet to be born.

Here we are, supposedly the wealthiest nation in the world, and we are over our heads in debt. Shouldn't a nation with our wealth be known for lending instead of borrowing? That seems to have been God's perspective when He said to the nation of Israel: "For the LORD your God will bless you just as He promised you; you shall lend to many nations, but you shall not borrow; you shall reign over many nations, but they shall not reign over you" (Deuteronomy 15:6; also see 28:12). Solomon reinforces this principle in Proverbs 22:7: "The borrower is servant to the lender."

Wise King Solomon hit the nail squarely on the head. The lender always holds power over the borrower. This principle does not bode well for the future of America. With our out-of-control borrowing, we have placed our financial well-being in the hands of foreign countries that have no love for us.

The Cancer of Inflation

Since 1934 people have been playing Monopoly. The world's best-selling board game, it is now played in 103 countries and in thirty-seven languages.[27] Unfortunately, many world governments, including our own, are currently playing Monopoly as well. To see what I mean, look at this section of the rules for the game: "The Bank collects all taxes, fines, loans, and interest, and the price of all Monopoly properties which it sells and auctions. The Bank never 'goes broke.' If the Bank runs out of Monopoly money, *it may issue as much more as may be needed by merely writing on any ordinary paper*" (emphasis added).[28] These are exactly the rules our government plays by in managing the U.S. monetary supply. In his 2009 book, *The New Economic Disorder*, economist Larry Bates writes:

> Today in America, we are living in a fool's paradise. We seem to believe we've found the secret that eluded the ancient alchemists: we believe we can slap ink on paper and somehow it will turn to gold. The money manipulators have successfully created the illusion of prosperity through the most massive creation of debt and paper money that has ever occurred in history. That debt bubble is about to burst again; [and] when it does, all those...investments your friends, and maybe even you, think are safe—CDs, and bonds, and mutual funds—will be in deep, deep trouble. And that's just the tip of the iceberg about to ram us.[29]

When the dollar loses its status, the U.S. will have to begin offering IOUs with increasingly higher interest rates to attract lenders, which means interest payments will take an even larger share of the U.S. budget. Those higher rates will cause consumer interest rates to rise in proportion. This means the cost of borrowing for homes and cars will get more expensive, partly as a result of the high rates themselves, and partly because rising interest rates will trigger inflation as the economy needs more dollars to meet the rising cost of borrowing.

Many economists foresee a period of massive inflation ahead as the economy begins absorbing the billions of dollars of stimulus money the Fed has printed. If you insert more printed dollars into the economy, the value of existing dollars is decreased, meaning the price of everything goes up.

Larry Bates removes any ambiguity from the meaning of inflation:

Despite what politicians and money manipulators would like you to believe, inflation is not rising prices. That is only a symptom of inflation, just as sniffles are the symptom of a cold. Knowledgeable people are well aware that inflation is an increase in the supply of money—period. Nothing more and nothing less. The more money the Federal Reserve prints and pumps into our economy, the higher prices will be driven up.[30]

Hyperinflation robs money of its value. During the inflationary period of the 1920s in postwar Germany, the government printed so many marks that they were being used to light fires. Erwin Lutzer tells a story of a woman who filled her wheelbarrow with German marks and left them outside a grocery store as she shopped—confident that no one would steal the worthless currency. She returned to find a pile of marks but no wheelbarrow.[31]

We can learn much about the impact of inflation from history. Economist Constantino Bresciani-Turroni, writing of the summer of 1923 when Germany's financial crisis was heating up, said, "The state's need of money increased rapidly. Private banks, besieged by their clients, found it impossible to meet the demand for money."[32] In an attempt to stabilize the economy, German economists were urging the government to print less money. But their cries were in vain because, as Bonner and Wiggin explain in their review of Bresciani-Turroni's work, "officials were in roughly the same situation as Ben Bernanke and Barack Obama today, 'More,' said they. They feared the economy might fall into trouble unless they made more cash and credit available."[33] So they printed more money, just as we have done and are doing. But according to Bresciani-Turroni, printing more money simply forestalled Germany's problem and increased its severity:

At first inflation stimulated production…but later…it annihilated thrift; it made reform of the national budget impossible for years…it destroyed incalculable moral and intellectual values.

It provoked a serious revolution in social classes, a few people accumulating wealth and forming a class of usurpers of national property; whilst millions of individuals were thrown into poverty. It was a distressing preoccupation and constant torment of innumerable families; it poisoned the German people by spreading among all classes the spirit of speculation and by diverting them from proper and regular work, and it was the cause of incessant political and moral disturbance. It is indeed easy enough to understand why the record of the sad years 1919–1923 always weighs like a nightmare on the German people.[34]

Inflation also played a part in the fall of the Roman Empire, as Bonner and Wiggin explain:

Rome wasn't built in a day, nor was its money destroyed overnight. In AD 64, in Nero's reign, the aureus was reduced by 10 percent of its weight. Thereafter, whenever Romans needed more money to finance their wars, their public improvements, their social welfare services and circuses, and their trade deficits, they reduced the metal content of the coins [called "clipping coins"]. By the time Odoacer deposed the last emperor in 476, the silver denarius contained only 0.02 percent silver.[35]

From then until now, "every central banker in the world has taken the devil's bait, creating money, out of thin air, as if no one were looking. As if it had not been tried before. As if they could get away with it and people really could get something for nothing!"[36]

Deficits, debts, and inflation all add up to economic chaos because shortsighted leaders tend to address the problem by creating more deficits, debts, and inflation. As a result, for the first time in my lifetime, the word *trillion* is being tossed around like a common denominator. Just how much is a trillion? It's a million million; a thousand billion. It's a one followed by twelve zeroes. An illustration might help us grasp this incomprehensible number. I'll start with

15

a hundred-dollar bill because the U.S. Treasury hasn't issued bills larger than that since July 14, 1969.[37]

The Federal Reserve issues new one-hundred-dollar bills to your bank in banded packages of one hundred bills each. Each package equals $10,000. One hundred such stacks equal one million dollars. A measly one million dollars doesn't look very impressive; you could easily stuff it into a shopping bag. A hundred million looks a little more respectable. It stacks into a neat cube shape that fills a standard industrial pallet. One billion dollars fills ten pallets of hundred-dollar bills. A trillion dollars would fill ten thousand pallets of hundred-dollar bills—enough to fill the floor of a fair-sized warehouse.[38]

If you're still having trouble getting your mind around a trillion, here's an analogy from *WORLD* magazine that might help: "To get an idea of how massive this amount is, think of it in seconds. Going back in time 1 million seconds would take you back 12 days. One billion seconds would take you back 30 years and one trillion seconds would take you back 32,000 years."[39]

The fact that our government, economists, and the media are beginning to think in terms of trillions instead of billions is not a good sign. It tells us that the economy is being filled with Monopoly money, and the government's giant Ponzi scheme is ballooning ever more rapidly in order to keep from collapsing.

The Specter of Bankruptcy

What will happen when the government's giant Ponzi scheme catches up with itself? According to a 2009 article in the *Wall Street Journal*, "If the government were ever to default on its promise to pay periodic interest payments or to repay the debt at maturity, the United States economy would plunge into a level of chaos that would make the Lehman bankruptcy look like a nonevent."[40]

I agree with those who say it seems very unlikely that our nation will ever be able to pay off her debts. Social Security, Medicare, Medicaid, and any new health benefit program require more funding than our current tax structure can support. Even if the tax rates are increased—as we have been assured will happen—there simply is not enough money to buy our way out of debt. If these assumptions are accurate, our nation is headed toward bankruptcy.

If the United States were to go bankrupt, it would morally default on everything it owes by simply saying, "We no longer acknowledge our debts." The government would simply reset the value of our currency by declaring the worth of a dollar with no real value to back it up. Taxes could go as high as 70 percent of one's income. If history repeated itself, revolution would follow!

While we may not live to see our nation in bankruptcy, most economists believe that the government's monetary policies have taken us beyond the possibility of our economy ever being as stable as it once was. In a recent *USA Today* editorial titled "There Is No Normal Anymore," James P. Gannon expressed what many of us feel about America's current economic instability:

> That statement [There is no normal anymore] ... goes a long way toward explaining why so many Americans are angry, confused and worried today. Polls show that 58 percent of Americans think the country is on the wrong track, suffering an economy that's sick.... They want things to get back to normal but increasingly feel that there is no normal any more.... Only Americans who lived through the Great Depression of the 1930s can remember a time of greater stress. In the midst of a so-called recovery, the economy is still shedding tens of thousands of jobs monthly, with the national unemployment rate already at 10 percent. In the past, a 4–6 percent unemployment rate was considered normal, but that now seems like a distant dream because it takes job growth of about 100,000 a month just to keep the unemployment rate from rising further—given the expected growth of the labor force. So normal unemployment could be years off.

There is nothing normal about an economy in which the federal government takes over giant automakers, bails out too-big-to-fail banks, buys up nearly all mortgages, keeps short-term interest rates at zero and prints over a trillion new dollars. As the national debt passes $12 trillion and the White House projects $9 trillion more in deficits over the next 10 years, the value of the dollar sinks and the price of gold—America's best fear gauge—rises past $1,100 an ounce.[41]

We long for a return to normalcy, but it seems impossible to get there from where we are. The future is beginning to be clear; barring some dramatic reversal, our nation is facing certain bankruptcy or some equivalent financial meltdown.

Today's Economic Meltdown in Biblical Prophecy

You may be surprised to learn that the Bible predicted the future that is our present reality. James, the half brother of our Lord, the son of Mary and Joseph (see Galatians 1:19), wrote a startling description of the economic conditions of "the last days."

Come now, you rich, weep and howl for your miseries that are coming upon you! Your riches are corrupted, and your garments are moth-eaten. Your gold and silver are corroded, and their corrosion will be a witness against you and will eat your flesh like fire. You have heaped up treasure in the last days. Indeed the wages of the laborers who mowed your fields, which you kept back by fraud, cry out; and the cries of the reapers have reached the ears of the Lord of Sabaoth. You have lived on the earth in pleasure and luxury; you have fattened your hearts as in a day of slaughter. You have condemned, you have murdered the just. (James 5:1–6)

Although James wrote his letter to the Christian church, these first six verses of chapter 5 are addressed to wealthy nonbelievers. In doing this, James "employs a rhetorical device known as *apostrophe*, a turning away from his real audience to address some other group."[42]

James was not indicting these people simply for having wealth. The Bible makes it clear that it is not wrong to have wealth: "The blessing of the LORD makes one rich, and He adds no sorrow with it" (Proverbs 10:22). The Bible contains many notable examples of godly, wealthy people, such as Job, Abraham, David, Solomon, Nicodemus, Mary, Martha, Lazarus, Joseph of Arimathea, Barnabas, and Philemon.

James gives us two distinct reasons for his condemnation. First, he considers the sins of wicked wealthy people to be especially grievous because they are being committed "in the last days." Why would this make a difference? In his commentary on the book of James, Homer Kent explains: "The 'last days' was a designation for messianic times, which began with Christ's first coming (Acts 2:16–17; 1 Timothy 4:1–2; 2 Peter 3:3; 1 John 2:18). These rich men were oblivious to the momentous days in which they were living. They did not understand that the 'last days' had already begun and that Christ's second coming could be at any moment."[43]

Pastor and teacher John MacArthur doesn't pull any punches in addressing the foolish audacity of amassing wealth in the end times:

> James sharply rebuked them for hoarding their wealth without regard for God's timetable, the flow of redemptive history, or the reality of eternity. How utterly unthinkable to amass and hoard wealth as the day of judgment draws near. Those who do so "are storing up wrath for themselves in the day of wrath and revelation of the righteous judgment of God, who will render to each person according to his deeds."[44]

As James said in verse 5, these indulgent rich people were merely fattening themselves for slaughter—a vivid metaphor for the judgment they were bringing on their heads.

The second reason for James's indictment of the wicked wealthy was their utterly self-centered use of their wealth. These people were so consumed with providing comfort and security for their own lives that they even withheld rightful wages from their workers and condemned just people. Nothing mattered but themselves. Someone has said that God will not condemn a man for being wealthy, but He will ask him two questions: first, "How did you gain your wealth?" and second, "How did you use your wealth?"

While God does not condemn having money, He does speak out against those who "trust in riches." "He who trusts in his riches will fall" (Proverbs 11:28). As Jesus Himself said, "How hard it is for those who trust in riches to enter the kingdom of God!" (Mark 10:24).

Global economist Wilfred J. Hahn shows us that the actions and attitudes toward wealth that James condemns are certain signs of the last days:

> The entire prophecy found in James 5:1–6 lists at least six financial or economic signs of the last days. I have counted almost 50 such general signs following years of Bible study. They include hoarding, accumulation of wealth, wage inequities, different classes of workers, luxuries and indulgence (consumerism at its peak!), conditions of economic brutality.... Most significantly the edifice of wealth is then turned into a curse as it is corroded and proven illusory.[45]

It doesn't take a rocket scientist to see that these signs of corrupted wealth are rampant in modern America. There's no question about it; we are living in the end times. And we can be sure that James's prediction of riches disintegrating into corrosion and misery is every bit as certain as his accurate prediction of today's economic abuses. In fact, it has already begun to happen.

Eroding Wealth

When we think of wealth, we think of stocks and bonds, bank accounts, and real estate holdings. But James writes of wealth in terms that would have been understood in his own culture. He speaks of corrupting riches, moth-eaten garments, and corroded gold and silver (see James 5:2–3). James points out to the wealthy that they are storing up wealth that is not enduring but eroding.

Nothing describes the current plight of our nation like the term *eroding wealth*. The December 7, 2009, issue of *Time* magazine carried the cover story, "The Decade from Hell." *Fortune* magazine editor Andy Serwer wrote the lead article and framed the first decade of the new millennium with these words: "Book-ended by 9/11 at the start and a financial wipe-out at the end, the first 10 years of this century will very likely go down as the most dispiriting and disillusioning decade Americans have lived through in the post–World War II era."[46] As the following facts show, it was actually the last three years of that decade that sent our nation spinning out of control.

- In 2008, U.S. households lost an estimated 18 percent of their net worth. This $11.2 trillion loss was the biggest since the Federal Reserve began tracking household wealth after World War II.[47]
- From the end of 2006 through March 2009, the total value of household real estate tumbled from $21.9 trillion to $17.9 trillion.[48]
- From August 2007 to October 2008, an estimated 20 percent, or about $2 trillion, vanished from Americans' retirement plans.[49]
- Unemployment reached a record 10.2 percent, and here in California, where I live, it has risen past 12 percent. The number of Americans living below the poverty level rose to 13.2 percent compared to 11.3 percent at the start of the decade. The number

of Americans without health insurance rose to 15.4 percent compared to 13.7 percent in 2000. National defense spending increased from $294 billion in 2000 to $642 billion in 2009. The price of oil tripled. The price of gold quadrupled. The U.S. Federal budget deficit gap tripled to a record $1.8 trillion.[50] U.S. public debt grew 31 percent to account for 53 percent of our gross domestic product (GDP) and reached a record high $1.4 trillion.[51]

- As of May 2010, the U.S. government had run a budget deficit for nineteen consecutive months. In fact, 2009 was the first year in twenty-nine years of record keeping in which the U.S. government ran a deficit *every* month.[52]
- The biggest single-day point loss ever in the Dow occurred on September 29, 2008, when the Dow slumped 777.68 points, or approximately $1.2 trillion in market value.[53]
- Some of our biggest and most "secure" institutions either failed or were bailed out by the government. The names are familiar: Lehman Brothers, Merrill Lynch, Fannie Mae, Freddie Mac, Washington Mutual, Wachovia, and AIG.[54]

Even Bill Gates and Warren Buffett felt the effects of the decade's wealth erosion. It is estimated that the two of them lost a collective $43 billion in 2008. But don't feel too sorry for them. They still managed to enter 2009 with a combined estimated worth of $77 billion. According to *Forbes* magazine, Gates and Buffett were not the only billionaires to have a rough year. The number of billionaires dropped from 1,125 in 2008 to 793 in 2009.[55]

The enormous erosion of wealth in the century's first decade shows clearly that the gleam from the American dream has dimmed. We feel alarm not only because of the extent to which these events are affecting us, but also because of their rapid acceleration. Many are beginning to wonder if there is any force strong enough to reverse our headlong slide into national chaos.

In the Sermon on the Mount, Jesus warned of the illusory nature of earthly treasures and pointed the way to real wealth: "Do not lay up for yourselves treasures on earth, where moth and rust destroy and where thieves break in and steal; but lay up for yourselves treasures in heaven, where neither moth nor rust destroys and where thieves do not break in and steal. For where your treasure is, there your heart will be also" (Matthew 6:19–21).

Erupting Wickedness

The wealthy people James addresses were guilty not only of the hoarding of wealth, but also of the sinful acquisition of it. By deliberately withholding pay from their hired laborers, they were getting rich at the expense of "the little guy." Many Old Testament passages condemn this wicked practice: "Woe to him who builds his house by unrighteousness and his chambers by injustice, who uses his neighbor's service without wages and gives him nothing for his work" (Jeremiah 22:13; see also Deuteronomy 24:14–15 and Leviticus 19:13).

This is exactly what we see happening today as many who pursue wealth disdain honest labor or service in favor of manipulation and ruthless power. We've all heard of businessmen justifying a deal that ruins a mom-and-pop company with the cold-blooded phrase, "It's just good business." That kind of economic nastiness has become common practice in our time.

As Andy Serwer points out, the living symbol of our present economic sordidness is "prisoner No. 61727-054, a.k.a. Bernie Madoff, [who] rots away in a Butner, N.C., jail cell, doing 150 years for orchestrating the biggest Ponzi scheme in the history of humanity."[56]

At his sentencing hearing, Madoff spoke honestly for perhaps the first time in a long time:

I cannot offer you an excuse for my behavior. How do you excuse betraying thousands of investors who entrusted me with their life savings? How do you excuse deceiving two hundred employees who spent most of their working life with me? How do you excuse lying to a brother and two sons who spent their lives helping to build a successful business? How do you excuse lying to a wife who stood by you for fifty years?[57]

The list of offenses in Madoff's confession shows him to be the archetypal symbol for the wicked wealthy James predicted would characterize the end times. Madoff's sole interest was himself. He ruthlessly exploited the little guy. He put his trust in his riches— riches he had gained by depriving others of their rightful money. His riches eroded and left him in misery.

Bernie Madoff is also a fitting symbol for what our own government is doing to America. As I will explain in the next two chapters, the eroding wealth and erupting wickedness of our nation are marching us headlong toward a new world order and its global economy.

America's Puzzling Absence in Biblical Prophecy

In an earlier book, *What in the World Is Going On?*, I devoted an entire chapter to the question, "Does America have a role in Bible prophecy?" The simple answer is no.

Indeed, no specific mention of the United States or any other country in North or South America can be found in the Bible. One reason may be that in the grand scheme of history, the United States is a new kid on the block. As a nation, it is less than 250 years old—much younger than the nations of Bible times that are featured in biblical prophecy.[58]

In that chapter I set forth three other possible reasons for America's absence in biblical prophecy. Some believe our nation will be incorporated into the European coalition of nations. Others suggest that by the time the Tribulation period arrives, America will have been invaded by outside forces and will no longer be a superpower. Perhaps the decay that is so rapidly eating away at our moral foundations will have destroyed us from within.

Up until the writing of this book, I considered the Rapture of the church to be the most plausible explanation for the Bible's silence about America's future. My reasoning went something like this:

> If the Rapture were to happen today and all true believers in Jesus Christ disappeared...America as we know it could be obliterated....Not only would our country lose 25 percent of her population, but she would also lose the very best, the "salt and light" of the nation....It would be like a reverse surgical operation—one in which all the healthy cells are removed and only the cancerous ones are left to consume one another.[59]

What if none of the reasons I have listed explain why America is a nonplayer in the final events of history? What if there is another explanation so obvious that students of prophecy have failed to notice it? What if this once-great nation, because of its inability to repay its trillions of dollars of indebtedness, is so weakened as to be absorbed into the new world order and its global economy, thus losing its sovereignty and separate identity?

What Should We Do?

I know that many readers will be disturbed by this chapter's dire assessment of our nation's economic future. Warnings by nature are not pleasant. When the town siren screams, we know a tornado has been sighted, and that's not good news. But while warnings are not pleasant, they are helpful. They enable us to understand what's in the wind and to prepare for the storm.

So, how do we prepare for the coming collapse of the American economy?

The writer of Hebrews gives us both the answer and the assurance of our own well-being. "Let your conduct be without covetousness; be content with such things as you have. For He Himself has said, 'I will never leave you nor forsake you'" (13:5). In other words, if you are living the life of a Christian, you need not be anxious about the future. Just keep on doing what you're doing and trust God's promise to hold you secure in His hands.

Albert Mohler, president of the Southern Baptist Theological Seminary, made these wise observations about our Christian conduct in the present economic crisis:

> Christians should look at the economy as a test of our values. The Bible values honest labor and dedicated workers, and so should we. The Bible warns against dishonest business practices, and we must be watchful. False valuations are, in effect, lies. Dishonest accounting practices are just sophisticated forms of lying. Insider information is a form of theft. The Bible honors investment and thrift, and Christians must be wary of the impulse for short-term gains and pressure for instant profit.[60]

The important thing is not to be drawn into the thinking of the general culture and become a part of the problem. Don't get caught up in the cultural clamor for wealth and security; trust your future to God and take care to live out the gospel, reaching your loved ones, your neighbors, and your friends with the only message of real hope to a world at risk of entering eternity without Christ.

CHAPTER 2

The New World Order

Even if you were not alive on Halloween in 1938—and I was not—you probably have heard of the terror that spread across the country that night over the airwaves of the CBS radio network. Orson Welles directed and narrated the *Mercury Theatre on the Air* adaptation of H. G. Wells's novel *The War of the Worlds.*

The program began by presenting its usual fare, then suddenly a strident voice broke in, saying, "Ladies and gentlemen, we interrupt our program...to bring you a special bulletin from the Intercontinental Radio News." The rest of the program reported in realistic news bulletin format the supposed advance of aliens from Mars who had just landed near New York City.

Of course there wasn't any alien invasion. But because no radio drama had ever before been presented as if it were a special news bulletin, gullible listeners thought it was actually happening, and mass hysteria spread across the nation. It took weeks to settle it down and months for many to finally accept that the program was simply dramatic fiction.

The War of the Worlds was not H. G. Wells's only book about life-changing events on the earth. In 1940 he published a nonfiction work titled *The New World Order*, which, at the time of its writing, seemed almost as bizarre as *The War of the Worlds*. In *The New World Order*, Wells wrote of "The United States of the World" and of the need to "work out a clear conception of the world order...to dissolve or compromise upon our differences so that we may set our faces with assurance toward an attainable world peace....Human life cannot go on with the capitals of most of the civilized countries of the world within an hour's bombing range of their frontier."[1] Nothing came of Wells's urging at the time, but in recent years the call for a new world order has intensified.

The Growing Call for a New World Order

Now let's jump ahead some thirty-seven years after H. G. Wells to 1977 when space vehicles *Voyager I* and *II* were launched. A gold record was placed aboard these spaceships containing information meant for any intelligent life they might encounter. The following words of President Jimmy Carter were included on that record:

> This Voyager spacecraft was constructed by the United States of America...a community of 240 million human beings among the more than four billion who inhabit planet Earth... still divided into nation states...but rapidly becoming a single global civilization. We cast this message into the cosmos...a present from a small distant world. We hope someday, having solved the problems we face, to join a community of Galactic Civilizations.[2]

Obviously, our thirty-ninth president believed in the new world order, and he would not be our last president to do so. Fast-forward to September 11, 1990, when the forty-first president, George Herbert Walker Bush, addressed a joint session of Congress, which had been called to deal with the Persian Gulf crisis and the federal budget deficit. In this address he repeatedly referred to a new world order:

> A new partnership of nations has begun. And we stand today at a unique and extraordinary moment....A hundred generations

28

have searched for this elusive path to peace while a thousand wars raged across the span of human endeavor. And today, that new world is struggling to be born. A world quite different from the one we've known, a world where the rule of law supplants the rule of the jungle, a world in which nations recognize the shared responsibility for freedom and justice.[3]

Four months after this speech, President Bush gave another address in which he again talked about the new world order: "What is at stake is . . . a big idea—a new world order, where diverse nations are drawn together in common cause to achieve the universal aspirations of mankind: peace and security, freedom, and the rule of law. Such is a world worthy of our struggle and worthy of our children's future!"[4]

Two months after that speech, President Bush addressed Congress yet again, this time commemorating a successful conclusion to the Gulf War. And again he spoke of a new world order: "Until now, the world we've known has been a world divided—a world of barbed wire and concrete block, conflict and cold war. Now, we can see a new world coming into view. A world in which there is the very real prospect of a new world order. . . . A world in which freedom and respect for human rights find a home among all nations."[5]

Throughout his presidency, George Herbert Walker Bush was a vociferous advocate of the new world order. Now, move forward to the more recent past. In November of 2008 Henry Kissinger, Nobel Peace Prize winner, former secretary of state, and assistant to the president for national security, wrote this: "Now that the clay feet of the economic system have been exposed . . . , this requires a new dialogue between America and the rest of the world. . . . If progress is made on these enterprises, 2009 will mark the beginning of a new world order."[6]

Just a few days before the inauguration of President Barack Obama, Kissinger said this in a television interview:

The president-elect is coming into office at a moment where there are upheavals in many parts of the world simultaneously. You have India, Pakistan; you have...the jihadist movement. So, he can't really say there is one problem, that it's the most important one. But he can give a new impetus to American foreign policy partly because the reception of him is so extraordinary around the world. I think his task will be to develop an overall strategy for America in this period when, really, a new world order can be created. It's a great opportunity. It isn't just a crisis.[7]

One week after this interview, Kissinger wrote an editorial for the *New York Times* in which he warned that "the alternative to a new international order is chaos." He again pointed to Barack Obama as the key player: "The extraordinary impact of the president-elect on the imagination of humanity is an important element in shaping a new world order."[8]

In Kissinger's mind, Barack Obama is mankind's greatest hope for accomplishing the new world order. And President Obama seems determined to fulfill Kissinger's hope. As he went about Europe in April of 2009, especially at the G20 Summit in London, Mr. Obama seemed to go out of his way to paint a new picture of America's role in the international community. Sometimes it appeared to the global media as if he were running for president of the world.[9]

Heralding Obama's election, the Arabic newspaper in Tunisia said, "Today America elects 'The President of the World,'" and the *Jordan Times* called him "the American leader we need."[10] Australian foreign policy expert Michael Fullilove entitled his February 2009 Brookings Institution article, "Barack Obama: President of the World."[11] Apparently the whole world has great expectations for our president and his vision for a new world order in which "the American consensus is over."[12]

Gordon Brown, then prime minister of the United Kingdom, laid out the purpose of a new world order on a visit to Delhi in January 2008. He said, "I do not envisage a new world founded on the narrow and conventional idea of isolated states pursuing their own selfish interests. Instead, I see a world that harnesses for the common good the growing interdependence of nations, cultures, and peoples that makes a truly global society."[13]

Not only have politicians and presidents lobbied for a new world order, even Pope Benedict XVI, in his encyclical letter of July 2009, voiced his support for an international paradigm shift: "In the force of the unrelenting growth of global interdependence, there is a strongly felt need even in the midst of a global recession...of a true world political authority." He went on to say, "Furthermore, such an authority would need to be universally recognized and to be vested with the effective power to ensure security for all."[14]

What is there about a new world order that unifies the minds of scientists, presidents, politicians, and religious leaders? For many it is surely the fear of a world-ending global war. Others see the need for a new order through the lens of hunger, disease, and other social issues they believe could be addressed more effectively through centralized political power. More recently, what are termed "earth" issues, such as the possibility of global warming, overpopulation, worldwide drought, toxic pollution, and life-threatening weather crises, have been considered potential triggers for a world government. On October 27, 2009, the *Washington Times* ran an editorial entitled, "Green World Government." The editorial said:

Environmental alarmism is being exploited to chip away at national sovereignty. The latest threat to American liberties may be found in the innocuous sounding Copenhagen Climate Treaty, which will be discussed at the United Nations climate-change conference in mid-December.... The governing authority envisioned by the document reads like a bad George Orwell knockoff.[15]

Although no legally binding pact was signed, the U.N.-driven Copenhagen treaty, which would have set universal standards for emissions reductions, opened the door for an increasingly powerful global government agency to act with unprecedented authority over sovereign nations.

Today the move toward a new world order has intensified as powerful movers and shakers such as George Soros are putting their money where their mouth is. Soros is like a character in a mystery thriller. Born in Hungary in 1930, and having escaped the Holocaust with his Jewish family, he went on to become an American currency speculator, stock investor, and political activist. At last count, this multibillionaire was one of the thirty richest people on earth—and one of the most powerful and most mysterious. A shadowy figure, he exerts enormous influence behind the scenes, moving people about like a puppeteer and manipulating the global economy from highly fortified hideaways.

George Soros became known to Americans in 2003 when he declared that removing President George W. Bush from office "is the central focus of my life."[16] During the first decade of this century, he funded many liberal political movements and Web sites, donating vast portions of his fortune to advance his agenda and defeat conservative American politicians.

More recently George Soros has been in the news predicting that the global recovery is running out of steam, that the world economy will experience a devastating double-dip recession or a "Super-Bubble,"[17] and that following the collapse of the global economy a new world order will emerge. This prediction has launched Soros into the final cause of his life; he is devoting millions of dollars to fund a postcrisis think tank that will reinvent a new global order following the coming economic collapse.

A recent report by the Reuters news organization was headlined, "George Soros Unveils New Blueprint for World Financial System." Speaking via video link with students at leading universities across three continents, Soros said, "International cooperation on

32

regulatory reform is almost impossible to achieve on a piecemeal basis, but it may be attainable in a grand bargain where the entire financial order is rearranged."[18] Soros has also stated in interviews and lectures that China should step up to the plate as the leader of a new global order, and the United States should not resist the establishment of a global currency.

Whether or not you agree with Soros, there is no doubt that the attention men of his influence are giving to the world's financial future has driven that topic to the top of almost everyone's list of concerns. I was not surprised when I recently read that the *Wall Street Journal*, the nation's premier financial publication selling more than two million copies per day, claims to have surpassed *USA Today* as the most read daily newspaper in the country.[19]

In these uncertain financial times, the new economy has our attention, and almost everyone is weighing in on it—how it is affecting us and how we are to survive in it. Before we continue, let me be honest with you: I don't have any secret insider information, at least about the immediate outcome of the current global financial crisis. But what I do offer, in each chapter of this book, is information about the world's economic future from the most reliable source available—God's Word.

The Ancient Appearance of a New World Order

In spite of all the talk about the new world order, it is important to note that it is neither new nor orderly. It is built on a foundation of chaos and confusion as old as history itself. In fact, a new world order first appears in Genesis, the first book of the Bible. The civilization that arose in the world after Noah's flood possessed a unity of language and a natural nomadic tendency that caused groups of people to journey from place to place. At last, they found a plain in the land of Shinar, and they dwelt there (see Genesis 11:2).

Shinar, which was in the region now known as Iraq, was the historic location of the infamous Babylon. The Bible indicates that the mighty leader Nimrod decided to draw all peoples together to form a powerful society in this rich farmland. They decided to declare and secure their unified might by constructing a massive tower "whose top will reach into heaven" (Genesis 11:4 NASB). It would stand as a proud symbol proclaiming mankind's power and self-sufficiency and draw people into their new world order.

Craig Parshall imagines the political spin Nimrod and his advisors might have used to launch this new enterprise: "Why risk tribal warfare among differing groups? With a single unified kingdom, we can achieve universal peace! Why create differing religious viewpoints? With one unified kingdom, we will eradicate the possibility of religious disputes! With a single language, we can create a global economy and prosperity for all."[20]

This all sounds so reasonable, one might wonder just what the problem was with their plan. The answer is that it was an act of rebellion against God. The centralization of humanity violated God's purpose concerning the nations. As the apostle Paul tells us, "From one man he made every nation of men, that they should inhabit the whole earth; and he determined the times set for them and the exact places where they should live" (Acts 17:26 NIV).

God's intent for the nations was for peoples to spread across the earth, not to congregate in one place. In the beginning He had told mankind to "be fruitful and multiply, and fill the earth" (Genesis 9:1; see Genesis 1:28). He wanted the whole earth populated with His image-bearers (see Genesis 1:26–27). This command was a foreshadowing of the Great Commission in which Jesus commanded His disciples to repopulate the earth with a "new" race of spiritual people, born again in "the image of His Son" (Romans 8:29; see also Matthew 28:16–20).

As Paul explained, God scattered men and set "the exact places where they should live" so they would seek after God. Mankind, settling in smaller communities throughout the world, would not be tempted toward the self-importance and sense of power that massive centralization would foster. Centralization would tempt them to rely on their own collective wisdom and strength instead of trusting in the Lord.

Nimrod's new world order was an act of rebellion against God because it was motivated by pride. The presumption of self-sufficiency forced God out of the people's hearts and deposed Him as the rightful King of their lives and replaced Him with self. In Genesis 11:4 we discover that the two idols of the tower builders' hearts were security and significance—the security to control their circumstances and the significance of creating a city and a tower that would magnify their name.

Bible expositor C. H. Mackintosh puts his finger on the motivation that drove them and often drives us: "The human heart ever seeks a name, a portion, and a center in the earth. It knows nothing of aspirations after heaven, heaven's God, or heaven's glory. Left to itself, it will ever find its objects in this lower world; it will ever build beneath the skies."[21]

It is significant that in two verses (Genesis 11:3–4 KJV) the tower builders used the word *us* five times and the name of the Lord not once. Clearly this original new world order was driven by pride, self-sufficiency, fear, and rebellion. It was a resounding echo of Satan's unholy ambition: "I will ascend into heaven," said Satan. "I will exalt my throne above the stars of God;...I will be like the Most High" (Isaiah 14:13–14).

Like Satan, the men and women of this original new world order became heady with megalomanic pride and defied God. Violating His decreed separation of the nations, they came together, built their own world, and with their tower attempted to ascend to heaven and become their own gods.

God knew this first human attempt to build a new world order could succeed beyond the wildest dreams of its founders. Neither their plan nor their tower was a threat to Him—any more than a backyard fire ant mound is a threat to you. But He knew that they could infect all creation with their madness and, as in the days before the Flood, wipe the knowledge of God from the minds of men. Therefore, God determined to shut down the tower project before it could be completed.

Eugene Peterson describes what happened next in his paraphrase of Genesis chapter 11:

> GOD came down to look over the city and the tower those people had built. GOD took one look and said, "One people, one language; why, this is only a first step. No telling what they'll come up with next—they'll stop at nothing! Come, we'll go down and garble their speech so they won't understand each other." Then GOD scattered them from there all over the world. And they had to quit building the city. That's how it came to be called Babel, because there GOD turned their language into "babble." From there GOD scattered them all over the world.[22]

In spite of Babel's failure, the allure of uniting nations for strength and security has persisted to the present time. But it is still a fatal mistake and an affront to God. Prophecy theologian David Breese has written,

> I think we need to understand that political internationalism is not the will of God. Nationalism is God's will. God has ordained individual nations and not a complex of nations. . . . When men try in their own unregenerate power to put together a complex of nations and make them cohere without God, then you have built into the complex the seeds of its own destruction. And that's exactly what will happen to the future world order that men are working on now.[23]

Individual nations are also part of God's long-term plan to preserve cultural diversity and identity. Individual nations will still exist during the Millennium and beyond: "And the *nations* of those who are saved shall walk in its light, and the kings of the earth bring their glory and honor into it" (Revelation 21:24; emphasis added).

The Modern Attempt at a New World Order

As it was so aptly observed by C. T. Schwarze, "Wars usually have an end. But the ends of wars on earth appear to be getting more and more unsatisfactory. Each succeeding peace treaty seems to be but the [justification] for the next war."[24] To that end, the League of Nations, established in 1919 after World War I, was the first of modern man's attempts to establish world peace. It was disbanded in 1946 after World War II. But the shock of nuclear weapons and the possibility of global annihilation so frightened political leaders that once again steps were taken to move the world toward a unified global government.

In the immediate postwar world, Congressman Lyndon B. Johnson was deeply impressed by the speeches of Dr. Robert Montgomery of the University of Texas, who warned that another war in an atomic age would mean the end of humanity. Montgomery declared, "We've got to have peace. We probably have to have one world government. A United States of the world." At that time Johnson owned KTBC, the first television station in central Texas, and his news director, Paul Bolton, reported the speech, adding, "He is preaching salvation, yours and mine." Johnson had Bolton's report added to the Congressional Record. It was this kind of fear that led to the development of the United Nations in 1945 and to the first cries for a politically unified globe under a single controlling authority.[25]

The United Nations, headquartered in New York City on an eighteen-acre campus, both symbolizes and fosters the modern attempt at creating a new world order. The U.N. campus is actually international territory—the sovereign territory of the world—not the property of New York City, New York State, or the United States of America. It exists as an island in the city of New York.

One who visits the U.N. campus is confronted throughout by the many works of art and gifts from nations emphasizing the theme of peace. Many of these works contain biblical allusions, though Bible passages are often misquoted and certainly misapplied by their use in support of globalism. For example, a gift from Russia is titled, "Let Us Beat Swords into Plowshares." Within the Security Council chamber is a large stained glass "Peace Window," the creation of Jewish artist Marc Chagall. The window depicts the tree of the Garden of Eden, the serpent, and the cross of Christ. There is even a mosaic called "The Dove of Peace" given by the Vatican. My personal favorite is a bronze sculpture of a .45-caliber revolver with the barrel twisted into a knot, a gift from Luxembourg. Everywhere you look there are works of art portraying the world's desire for peace.

"A Room of Quiet," the Meditation Room of the U.N., was designed and superintended by former Secretary-General Dag Hammarskjöld to be a "spiritual" retreat within the compound. Its V-shape is intended to enable people to "withdraw into themselves," regardless of their faith, creed, or religion. In the center of the room a lone spotlight casts a beam onto the polished surface of a 6.5-ton iron ore block, which Hammarskjöld designed as an altar to "the god whom men worship under many names and in many forms."[26] The tiny room, which contains nothing else but some benches and an abstract mural, was envisioned as a place where visitors could "fill the void with what they find in their center of stillness."[27] In reality, the room is a temple for the worship of the human self.

For all its noble declarations, the United Nations has been an example of bureaucracy run amok. It is overrun with fraud, pointless debates, international mismanagement, and ludicrous behavior. For example, in 2005 then Secretary-General Kofi Annan charged the United Nations with the task of investigating human rights abuses by member nations. The Human Rights Commission members were:

Sudan, Zimbabwe, China, Russia, and Saudi Arabia. Every one of these countries has itself been accused of major human rights violations. It was a classic case of sending the fox to guard the hen house.[28]

In Rwanda U.N. peacekeepers did nothing to prevent 800,000 Tutsi deaths. In Bosnia U.N. peacekeepers failed to protect approximately 8,000 Serbs. In Darfur, some of the worst human rights abuses of recent times continue despite a U.N. peacekeeper presence.

If we look at the conflicts in the world since 1945, it is clear that the U.N. has failed to keep world peace. More than 350 international and intranational armed conflicts have occurred since the U.N.'s founding in 1945—at least five of which are major conflicts ongoing as I write (wars in Somalia, Afghanistan, Iraq, Pakistan, Yemen/ Saudi Arabia). The United Nations has been powerless to prevent these past and ongoing conflicts.[29]

But perhaps the greatest failure of the United Nations is her unfaithfulness to member nations. In 2005 Secretary-General Kofi Annan went on record with a pledge of support for Israel, saying, "A United Nations that fails to be at the forefront of the fight against anti-Semitism...denies its history and undermines its future. That obligation links us to the Jewish people and to the state of Israel, which rose, like the United Nations itself, from the ashes of the Holocaust."[30]

But Annan's words were empty; Israel continues to be forgotten by the United Nations. A case in point: the U.N. has held an International Day of Solidarity with the Palestinian people on November 29 every year since 1977. But shamefully, the U.N. took almost another three decades to finally hold its first commemoration of the Holocaust. Without question, the Holocaust is the worst human tragedy in the history of the world, and the U.N. recognizes it only reluctantly.

When tyrants such as Hugo Chavez, Mahmoud Ahmadinejad, and Muammar al-Gaddafi are invited to speak in the General Assembly, as they did in September 2009, one can hardly consider the U.N. to be a serious forum for world peace. In Ahmadinejad's famous speech before that exalted assembly one year earlier, he declared, "The American Empire in the world is reaching the end of its road." He went on to identify the U.S. as a "bullying power" that is exerting "political and economic pressures against Iran" in her pursuit of "peaceful nuclear activities."[31] Hiding nuclear plants is hardly indicative of peaceful purposes!

I am not a fan of the United Nations. It is ineffective because of the widely varying aims and interests of its members; its consensus is often blocked by special interests; its directives to rogue states are consistently ignored; its peacekeeping efforts are resounding failures; and its human rights commission borders on irrelevancy. The U.N. can no more accomplish world peace than the Tower of Babel could accomplish a new world order.

But even if the U.N. were effective in all the above areas, I still would not be a fan. In fact, its effectiveness would make its presence in the world even more alarming as an ominous portent of a coming world government in violation of God's ordained intent for mankind.

The Future Arrival of a New World Order

As Babel, the League of Nations, and the United Nations demonstrate, from antiquity to modernity mankind's attempts at world peace have failed. And they will continue to fail because as long as fallen man rules the earth, Christ told His disciples, "you will hear of wars and rumors of wars....For nation will rise against nation, and kingdom against kingdom" (Matthew 24:6–7). That does not mean, however, that we must despair of world peace ever coming to our planet. In fact, the Bible promises that it will come. God's

Word anticipates a future time when Jesus Christ will reign in perfect righteousness.

Pastor Brian Orchard writes, "After humans have exhausted every way to create peace and to govern themselves apart from God, after they have tried everything, from the Tower of Babel to the United Nations, Jesus Christ will come to this earth and set up His government over all nations and peoples. And, at last, the world will live in peace."[32]

This biblical new world order of the future is commonly referred to as the Millennium. Let me put the Millennium into its proper prophetic context. As I understand God's Word, the next event on the prophetic calendar is the Rapture, when Christ comes *for* His saints. Following the Rapture there will be seven years of unspeakable tribulation on the earth. At the end of that seven-year period, Christ will come back *with* His saints to rule and reign on this earth for one thousand years.

I have written an entire chapter in this book on the subject of the Millennium, but let me just whet your appetite. Many passages in the Old Testament describe this time as a period of peace, which will extend even to the animal kingdom. According to the prophet Isaiah, lambs will live in peace with wolves and goats with leopards. Calves will lie down with lions, and cows and bears will be friends. Little children will be able to play near poisonous snakes and not be in danger (see Isaiah 11:6–8).

This millennial reign of Jesus Christ is the finally arriving new world order that will bring an end to all war. Isaiah 2:4 says, "They shall beat their swords into plowshares, and their spears into pruning hooks; nation shall not lift up sword against nation, neither shall they learn war anymore."

The Bible tells us that the Millennium will be a time of justice and prosperity. Psalm 72, speaking of the reign of Christ, says, "He will judge Your people with righteousness, and Your poor with justice" (v. 2). "He will bring justice to the poor of the people; He will save the children of the needy" (v. 4). "In his days the righteous will flourish; prosperity will abound till the moon is no more" (v. 7, NIV).

We are told that during the Millennium King David will be resurrected from the dead (see Ezekiel 34:23–24; Jeremiah 30:9; Hosea 3:5). He will reign alongside Jesus Christ during the Millennium. Not until that time will there be a new world order with any chance to create world peace. We should put no hope or trust in any other efforts prior to the Millennium because all are doomed to failure.

This biblically affirmed futility of man-made peace is an issue that creates tension for some Christians. Does the Bible not say that we are to be people of peace? Romans 12:18 urges us to do all we reasonably can to "live peaceably with all men." So why shouldn't Christians support global efforts to secure peace among the nations?

We must remember that passages in the Bible that apply to us individually may not always apply to governments. Governments are ordained to perform certain functions that individuals must not. For example, when we as individuals are unlawfully wronged, we are forbidden to take the law into our own hands, execute judgment, and avenge ourselves (see Romans 12:19). The government, on the other hand, is charged to do that very thing (see Romans 13:1–6). The same principle applies in reverse when it comes to seeking peace. We as individuals are urged to seek peace in our relationships with other individuals. Our government, on the other hand, has a duty to protect and defend all of its citizens, which means maintaining military capacity and constant vigilance against potential international enemies. In a world plagued with sinfulness and craving for power, peace among nations can be achieved only by means of defensive strength.

Rome's *Pax Romana* is a good example of peace through strength. For about two hundred years (27 BC to AD 180), Rome ruled England, all of Europe, Asia Minor, the Middle East, and the northern coast of Africa. During this period there were rebellions and battles fought in the outlying parts of the empire, but it was Rome's strength that ensured her victory and two centuries of relative peace.

The Fallout from Inadequate Human Efforts

Christians should refrain from supporting political efforts that call for the uniting of nations to achieve world peace—not only because the consolidation of nations opposes God's intent for mankind, but also because all attempts at man-made global peace are futile. Just as every one of man's attempts to supplant God's plan has failed, so too will man's attempt to achieve peace by producing a new world order. Let's explore four potential outcomes of any such man-made plan.

A New World Order Promises Peace It Cannot Produce

After all the attempts at peace throughout the centuries, we still find nations constantly at war somewhere on the globe. In his book *Shadow Government*, prophecy scholar Grant Jeffrey writes: "Since 1945 the number of wars has increased tremendously. As dozens of new nations demanded independence and many old empires disintegrated, more than 350 wars have been fought between World War II and the current time."[33] Jeffrey goes on to expand on this sad fact and show where the world is inevitably headed with the advent of national alliances and modern technology:

> *The War Atlas*, a military study, concluded that the world has not known a single day since World War II without some nation waging war or engaging in a form of armed conflict. Despite thousands of negotiations and peace treaties, the twentieth century was truly the century of war. As a result of the obvious

dangers to national security, most nations have joined alliances to protect themselves. Far more sobering than the increasing frequency of war and terrorist acts is the fact that modern weapons research and enormous military budgets have combined to produce devastating weapons of mass destruction. In the next major war, it is virtually certain that millions of people will be destroyed.[34]

In the face of such dire predictions, national governments around the world are coming to realize that world peace is vital but will continue to elude us unless new and drastic measures are taken. That is why today we are hearing unprecedented talk about a new world order. Worldwide unity among the nations is seen as the only deterrent to the destruction of the planet we now seem capable of bringing about.

But the unity they aspire to cannot produce world peace because the heart of man remains unregenerate. Unifying under a power strong enough to enforce peace will result in a corrupted authority that will instead produce unprecedented tyranny.

A New World Order Presumes a Unity That Is Impossible

We are being led to believe that the economic and military instability in today's volatile world has brought the nations to the point where they must unite in the common cause of survival. But any such global accord would be a surface unity only. The differences in cultures, religions, goals, and economics among the nations are far too vast to be melded into a true unity. It would be a unity of mere appearance—a false unity. The difference between false unity and true unity is the difference between surface appearance and inner reality. Permanent and genuine unity must come from within. There must be a oneness of spirit and heart among peoples that serves as the basis for true unity. False unity can be imposed by external force, suppressing people's true beliefs, convictions, and aspirations, but it lacks the power to bind together their hearts. Therefore it always comes unraveled.

In 1971, megastar John Lennon wrote a song called "Imagine" that quickly achieved massive worldwide popularity. Former President Carter once remarked, "In many countries of the world... you hear John Lennon's song 'Imagine' used almost equally with national anthems."[35] Many of us probably sang the song without realizing what we were singing.

The song asked listeners to imagine a time when there was no heaven, no hell, no countries, nothing to kill or die for, no religion, no possessions, no need for greed or hunger... a time of living for today, living life in peace... a time when the world will live as one.[36]

This song captured the attention of an entire generation and expressed the utopian dream of a world unified and at peace. But like all utopian dreams, the song has no basis in reality. Contrary to what the lyrics wish for, there *is* such a thing as religion; there *is* a heaven and a hell. There *are* ideals worth dying for. Wishful thinking, no matter how lofty, will not produce a wizard's wand to sweep these realities out of existence and give us a world where differences in religion, ethics, ideals, economics, and culture don't matter.

Furthermore, people will never find true unity because the sinful nature of man will prevent our coming to a consensus on truth. The prophet Jeremiah puts it this way, "The heart is deceitful above all things, and desperately wicked; who can know it?" (Jeremiah 17:9). Humanity may unite with good intentions, but as long as hearts remain wicked, nothing good will be produced. As C. S. Lewis is credited with saying, "No clever arrangement of rotten eggs will make a good omelet."

A New World Order Paves the Way for a One-World Ruler

In the late 1970s, theologian and apologist Francis Schaeffer looked into the future and described the world in which we are now living:

History indicates that at a certain point of economic breakdown people cease being concerned with individual liberties and are ready to accept regimentation. The danger is obviously even greater when the two main values so many people have are personal peace and affluence.... In this mix the threat of war... would cause those who have only the values of personal peace and prosperity to be ready for almost any kind of authoritarian government which would be able to remove the threat of war, particularly if... it was brought in while seemingly keeping the outward forms of constitutionality.[37]

We can already see the truth of this prediction coming to pass. It seems apparent that the dominant values in today's culture are personal peace and prosperity. These values are beginning to be threatened by our nation's shaky economics and weakening defense capabilities. As those threats intensify, you can be sure that the rest of Schaeffer's prediction will also become reality. People will be willing to sell their souls to an authoritative government that will promise continuing peace and prosperity.

In fact, the Bible tells us in Daniel 7 and Revelation 13 that such an authoritative government will emerge under the control of a powerful world leader. The nations will open their arms to welcome this leader's promise of peace. But it will be a false promise extended in deception in order to manipulate humanity. In reality, this charismatic leader will be the Antichrist, and his deceptive promise of peace will lull the nations to sleep while he sets up his reign of terror and destruction. Daniel tells us, "By peace [he] shall destroy many" (Daniel 8:25 KJV).

That false peace will be in its early stages when Jesus Christ comes back for the church. It will be in full bloom at the beginning of the Tribulation period when people will believe prosperity and security are here to stay. But "when they say, 'Peace and safety!' then sudden destruction comes upon them, as labor pains upon a pregnant woman. And they shall not escape" (1 Thessalonians 5:3).

We will have more about the Antichrist later in this book where an entire chapter is devoted to this end-time personality. For now, suffice it to say that Christians should not support or place hope in a new world order because such a global union will give the Antichrist the political framework he needs to inflict his horrors on an unsuspecting world.

A New World Order Provides the Rationale for a Global Economy

"All we need is the right major crisis," said financier David Rockefeller in a 1994 speech at the United Nations, "and the nations will accept the New World Order."[38] Many believe that the 2008 financial meltdown was that crisis. Shortly after that meltdown, Yale marketing expert Bruce Judson warned:

> The potential for a severe *economic* shock to undermine the stability of a long-standing national government has been demonstrated throughout history: the French Revolution of 1789 began when the national government effectively declared that it was bankrupt; the Soviet Union fell in large part because oil revenues, which supported the bulk of the economy, declined dramatically, leading, in part, to severe inflation; the hyperinflation that accompanied the Weimar Republic opened the door to the Nazi victory and dissolution of the newly established German democracy. The extent to which an economic shock can lead to political instability depends on three things: the extent of the suffering of the people, the trust of the people in the existing government, and the degree to which the tragedy had been anticipated or expected....
>
> *In the more than 200 years since the American Revolution, we have faced existential crises three times: the Civil War, the Great Depression, and now.* The preconditions are almost all in place. We face historic levels of economic inequality. We have suffered an economic shock whose full consequences are not

yet known. Finally, our vitally important middle class is perilously weak. What would happen if a trigger were set off?[39]

Much of the current talk about a new world order is in recognition of the fact that when the U.S. economy fails, it will pull the world's economy down with it. With America's economy now teetering on the brink, people are groping for a new system that will end the concentration of wealth and power in one nation and spread it around the globe so that one sinking nation will no longer carry inordinate weight that pulls the others under.

The bottom line is that the new world order is all about the consolidation of power in the coming together of nations. That concentration of power will enable the Antichrist to rule the world during the latter part of the Tribulation. This new world order will demand a new global economy, which will be the topic of the next chapter.

Babel Revisited

What we are seeing today is almost an exact repetition of the central events depicted in the Genesis account of the Tower of Babel. It may be hard for many of us modern sophisticates to see ourselves in this ancient story, but I believe the masterful prose of Max Lucado can help us make the connection. I close this chapter by excerpting from his book *Fearless* his vivid account of the Tower of Babel.

The nations that spread out after Noah's flood decided to circle their wagons, "Come, let us build ourselves a city, and a tower whose top is in the heavens, let us make a name for ourselves lest we be scattered abroad over the face of the whole earth" (Genesis 11:4).

Do you detect fear in those words? The people feared being scattered and separated. Yet rather than turn to God, they

48

turned to stuff. They accumulated and they stacked. They collected and they built. News of their efforts would reach the heavens and keep their enemies at a distance. The city motto of Babel was this: "The more you hoard, the safer you are." So, they hoarded. They heaped stones and mortar and bricks and mutual funds and IRAs and savings accounts. They stockpiled pensions, possessions, and property. Their tower of stuff grew so tall they got neck aches looking at it.

"We are safe," they announced at the ribbon-cutting ceremony.

"No, you aren't," God said. And the Babel-builders began to babble. The city of one language became the glossolalia of the United Nations minus the interpreters. Doesn't God invoke identical correction today? We engineer stock and investment levies, we take cover behind the hedge of hedge funds. We trust annuities and pensions to the point that balance statements determine our mood levels. But then come the Katrina-level recessions and the downturns, and the confusion begins all over again.[40]

Some things never change! Given man's persistence in repeating his sordid history, the immediate future of our world does not look good. But Christians can take hope in the fact that God has given us prophetic warnings enabling us to resist the scramble for a man-made solution to today's economic and political folly. We can rest assured that His plan includes our protection until He Himself returns to set the earth right with a true new world order of peace and prosperity.

CHAPTER 3

The New Global Economy

Armageddon seemed to arrive in Manhattan on Monday, September 29, 2008, not just in New York, but in Moscow, Hong Kong, London, and Frankfurt, too.... Then, on Tuesday, plagues and locusts were loosed on the world: The U.S. stock market fell hard again. Japan was sinking into the sea. Brazil's market was down 51 percent, year to date. Central banks were cutting rates like pulpwood. Even so, unemployment was still on the rise. Consumer spending was falling. House prices were going down.[1]

You may find it strange that in the above paragraph secular financial writers William Bonner and Addison Wiggin describe current economic woes with biblical imagery. It seems that when crises loom large enough, the word *Armageddon* starts getting its time in the spotlight. Is *Armageddon* too strong a term for what has happened in the last three years? Perhaps not if its use indicates where we are headed. When we experience a worldwide crisis, we should expect it to have long-term implications.

Crises are catalysts to an organized progression of changes. And there is little doubt that the world has been driven toward greater globalization by crises. In his book *When a Nation Forgets God* my friend Erwin Lutzer details the role that Germany's economic crisis played in Hitler's seizure of power:

Let us not be quick to condemn those who were willing to give Hitler a chance, given the economic chaos that spread through Germany after World War I. He could never have come to power if the German economy would have remained strong after World War I. He rode to victory simply because he promised to rebuild the collapsing German mark and put the nation back to work. He cleverly exploited the economic crisis that postwar Germany was experiencing. Yes, it was the economy that gave rise to National Socialism.[2]

In an earlier book I described the financial fallout in Germany after World War I:

The German Treasury...was low in gold. The budget was unbalanced and inflation went out of sight. In 1919, the German mark was worth twenty-five cents. Within four years, it declined in value until four trillion marks were needed to equal the buying power of one dollar. The German middle class lost all of its savings and every pension in the nation was wiped out.[3]

In 1929 the global depression hit Germany and gave Hitler the opportunity to make his move: "When Austria's biggest bank collapsed, it forced the banks in Berlin to close temporarily. Germany was unable to make its war payments; millions were unemployed as thousands of small businesses were wiped out. Deprived of jobs and a decent living, ravaged by hunger, the Germans were willing to do anything to survive."[4]

Today's proponents of the one-world economy embrace the philosophy of Georg Wilhelm Friedrich Hegel, a German philosopher of the 1800s. Hegel theorized that by planning and actually producing crises, leaders can gain enormous power by stepping in and promising solutions. As we will see in greater detail in the next chapter, desperate people will give power to those who seem to have the answers to the crises. As a result, little by little, fewer and fewer make more and more of the decisions.[5]

Hegel's thoughts are haunting for those of us who observe the workings of our own government. Using crises and other manipulations, our leaders have now discovered ways to bypass the checks and balances that were put in place by our forefathers. They simply appoint czars to manage the crises, bypassing representational solutions and reporting only to the president.

A series of recent crises have led to increased government control. Government-imposed loan standards precipitated a banking crisis, which was solved by a government bailout and control of the banks. As a result, little by little, fewer and fewer are making more and more banking decisions. Government regulations and union concessions produced an automobile industry crisis resulting in a government takeover of a huge manufacturer. And now, little by little, fewer and fewer are making more and more corporate automobile decisions. Government "solutions" produced a healthcare crisis resulting in a government takeover of national health care. And now, little by little, fewer and fewer are making more and more healthcare decisions. Little by little we are being prepared for the coming centralized government of the final world order and its global economy.

The Birth of the Global Economy

Webster added the term *globalization* to the dictionary in 1951 with the definition, "the development of an increasingly integrated global economy marked especially by free trade, free flow of capital, and the tapping of cheaper foreign labor markets."[6]

Most historians and economists point back to 1944 as the official beginning of what we now call the global economy. As World War II was winding down, 730 of the world's leading politicians from all forty-four allied nations convened at the plush Mount Washington Hotel in Bretton Woods, New Hampshire. Their purpose was to stabilize and reorganize the world economy. The Bretton Woods conference was the culmination of two and a half years of planning for postwar monetary reconstruction. It resulted in history's first example of a fully negotiated monetary order intended to govern currency relations among sovereign states. The delegates were challenged to establish rules for global commerce, to find new ways to facilitate international trade, and to stabilize international exchange rates. In response, the Bretton Woods delegates gave birth to the International Monetary Fund (IMF), the World Bank Group, and the General Agreement on Tariffs and Trade (GATT).

The World Bank provides loans to poorer countries for capital/infrastructure programs with the goal of reducing poverty. The International Monetary Fund is more attuned to economic control in the future. It oversees the global financial policies of member nations in order to stabilize exchange rates (balancing the flow of money) between nations. It also provides loans to poorer countries. Both the World Bank and the IMF have a presence in 186 countries.

At the Bretton Woods conference, each country obligated itself to a monetary policy based on the gold standard. They agreed to maintain the integrity of their currencies within the framework of a fixed value. That value was set at plus or minus 1 percent of the price of gold regulated at U.S. $35 per ounce.

According to one expert, the delegates at Bretton Woods "wanted to create…a system that would eventually evolve into a global currency and a global monetary system. This was the beginning of the economic side of building a new world order…and it has been unfolding pretty steadily, exactly according to their plan."[7]

Bretton Woods established the U.S. dollar as the reserve currency for the post–World War II world because, at that time, America had the world's largest and most stable economy and also the most dollars, or units of currency, of any country.

Since the end of World War II, the United States dollar has continued to be the reserve currency of the world in spite of the fact that the U.S. no longer backs up its dollars with gold. In other words, just as central banks once issued their currencies as a marker for gold, under the Bretton Woods agreement foreign central banks now hold United States dollars against which they issue their own currencies. The amount of U.S. dollars in their possession determines volume and value of the currency they issue.

The term *reserve currency* means the currency that is used as the value standard for other currencies. It is the most trusted, stable currency in the world by virtue of the issuing nation's stability and trustworthiness. This means that universal commodities like oil and gold are priced in terms of the reserve currency...the U.S. dollar. That gives the United States an edge in buying commodities because we have plenty of dollars. Nations without U.S. dollars in their reserves have to pay a fee to exchange their own currency for U.S. dollars. As I write, almost two-thirds of foreign currency reserves are held in dollars. That fact has helped make the United States the world financial leader for the past sixty years.

In January of 2010, Congress raised the ceiling for our national debt to $14.2 trillion. Our growing debt is causing investors anxiety about the U.S. dollar, and this anxiety is generating apprehension among other nations. One economist put it this way: "As they watch America's debt soar, some of the passengers aboard the dollar/debt express have reached for the emergency cord in hopes they can stop the train and get off."[8]

In August 2009 the *Wall Street Journal* reported that doubts about the dollar were growing as the budget deficit grew. The *Journal* quoted global economic strategist Claire Dissaux as saying, "There has been a lot of disappointment with the way the U.S. credit crisis was handled. The dollar's loss of influence is a steady and long-term trend."[9]

Former U.S. Deputy Treasury Secretary Roger C. Altman, after describing the financial crash of 2008 as "the worst in over 75 years," went on to observe,

> Trends are shifting the world's center of gravity away from the United States. Much...of the world is turning a historic corner and heading into a period in which the role of the state will be larger and the private sector will be smaller....This historic crisis raises the question of whether a new global approach to controlling currencies and banking and financial systems is needed.[10]

A recent e-mail bulletin from Robert Kiyosaki, author of the popular *Rich Dad, Poor Dad* books, contains a little blurb called "Why the Dollar Is Toast." In it he said, "The dollar is losing its power as the reserve currency of the world. In other words, the American empire of debt is coming to an end."[11]

Here is a fact from top-ranked global economist Wilfred J. Hahn that you may not have known:

> It was recognized long, long ago—in fact at the inception of the world's current monetary regime—that the U.S. dollar was fated to lose its central reserve role....In order to provide the currency backbone of the world, the United States needed to run deficits (supplying U.S. dollars to the rest of the world). But this can be done only so long before mounting international debts would overwhelm the U.S. aid. Indeed, in part, this is what has happened.[12]

Larry Kudlow, an anchor at CNBC, presented his opinion in the form of a letter to the president of the United States. He said, "We know the dollar is slumping...we need a stable dollar...and we need to stop printing so much debt from Congress."[13]

These expert observers make it obvious that the nations of the world are well aware of America's growing financial instability.

Many nations (Russia, China, Brazil, Taiwan, Sri Lanka) have been quietly adding to their stores of gold as a defensive play against the U.S. dollar's weakness, and this trend is likely to continue. China and India continue to vie for domination in amassing supplies of gold.[14] If the value of their U.S. dollars is going to drop, they want to hold something that has innate value to offset the dollar's decline. And that something is the same as it has been throughout human history: gold.

Fearing a continuing drop in the value of the U.S. dollar, many U.S. citizens are beginning to buy gold. The price of gold rose more than 25 percent in 2009 due to investor demand. For gold to reach its former inflation-adjusted peak of $875 an ounce in 1980, it would have to rise to around $2,000 an ounce in 2009 dollars—and it's only around $1,200 an ounce at this writing. So the gold-buying train has just begun to leave the station. It will pick up momentum as the value of the dollar falls in the years ahead.

If the world's nations agree to implement a new universal currency, it will be a way of conveying that the United States is no longer the only stable, trustworthy country in the world. And that is gradually becoming true: the BRIC nations (Brazil, Russia, India, and China) are on the ascendancy even as America is suffering. If we can't manage our affairs well enough to keep our currency's value above that of others', then perhaps the dollar deserves to lose its reserve currency status.

Remember that gold was established as the international monetary standard at Bretton Woods, and its price was fixed at U.S. $35 per ounce. This agreement stabilized the major world currencies by linking them to a tangible commodity. When President Richard Nixon summarily eliminated the gold basis for our currency on August 15, 1971, the U.S. and the rest of the world were no longer bound to the Bretton gold fixed rate, and the demise of the dollar began, dropping to its current status of less than 90 percent of its 1971 valuation. Since then all the world's currencies have been free-floating fiat money—as empty of real value as Bernie Madoff's false profits.

We should not be surprised that at the April 2009 meeting of the G8 nations in London, consisting of the heads of state of the world's eight richest industrialized nations, Russia's president Dmitry Medvedev called for the creation of a new "supranational currency"—a currency that would transcend national boundaries and national authorities. This new currency would replace the U.S. dollar as the world reserve currency. At the group's subsequent meeting in July, Medvedev proudly showed off a sample coin of "a united future world currency." The coin bears the imprint, "Unity in Diversity." The other three members of the BRIC nations joined Russia in its call for a replacement to the dollar as the world's reserve currency. French president Nicolas Sarkozy added his voice, saying, "We cannot stick with just one single currency."[15]

The fact that America's economic irresponsibility is seriously weakening the dollar is no secret to the rest of the world. China and

Russia's Suggested
"UNITED FUTURE WORLD CURRENCY"

Russia recently took concrete steps to implement their demand to replace the dollar with their domestic currencies by reaching mutual agreements worth several billion dollars.[16] China wants to replace the dollar with their yuan as the regional reserve currency.[17]

One of Canada's principal newspapers, the *Globe and Mail*, ran a story in late 2009 entitled "Calls Rise for a New Global Currency." The article said, in part, "The days of one country's currency as the global benchmark are numbered. The U.S. dollar remains the currency standard, but globalization demands a new global currency that provides representation for the growing importance of a variety of major economies." The article went on to quote former IMF official Eswar Prasad as saying,

> The U.S. and China are caught in "a dangerous game of chicken that could easily spin out of control...a precipitous action by China to shift out of U.S. dollar instruments, or even an announcement of such an intention, could act as a trigger that nervous market sentiments coalesce around, leading to a plunge in bond prices and the value of the U.S. dollar." Facing deficits...over the next decade, the United States desperately needs China's cash to finance its profligate ways.[18]

In 1920 John Maynard Keynes, eminent British economist and considered by many to be the architect of our current economic system, quoted Lenin in one of his books:

> By a continuing process of inflation, governments can confiscate, secretly and unobserved, an important part of the wealth of their citizens....There is no subtler, no surer means of overturning the existing basis of society than to debauch the currency. The process engages all the hidden forces of economic law on the side of destruction, and does so in a manner which not one man in a million is able to diagnose.[19]

Let's face it: what Keynes warned us of is happening here and now. Our nation's currency is "debauched," and more and more of our wealth is winding up in the hands of the government. It appears that America's economy may be in its death throes, and as a result, a globalized economy looms, perhaps in the not-too-distant future.

Preparing for the End-Time Economy

As we look back at history through the lens of prophecy, we can begin to see the future plan unfolding. This lens shows that what we have been discussing is more than just a worldwide financial meltdown. According to prophetic scholar Mark Hitchcock, the current economic chaos is "the first domino to fall in a chain of events that is setting the stage for the economy of the end times."[20]

In an article titled "Racing Toward the New World Order," attorney Craig Parshall explains how modern proponents of a global society borrow the term *critical mass* from the world of physics, "where it means the smallest amount of fissile nuclear material required to begin an unstoppable nuclear chain reaction." According to Parshall, "In the world of social movements, it means...the minimum support needed to begin an unstoppable new, global, social order."[21]

I don't know if we are yet at a *critical mass*, but the pressure is building and support for a global economy is growing. Here are just a few of the significant global trends moving us ever closer to that reality.

Influential Global Institutions

It is significant that two global financial institutions already exist that could provide a framework for a future global economic system: the World Bank and the International Monetary Fund. As we noted earlier, these institutions were created in 1944 at the Bretton

Woods Conference. While not banks in the traditional sense, their global presence and existing infrastructure make the idea of a globally controlled economic system easier to imagine. Since the terms *World Bank* and *International Monetary Fund* have been in existence all our lives, we have become accustomed to them. Because of this familiarity, the populace as a whole will not likely be greatly shocked by or resistant to the idea of global economics.

Both the World Bank and the IMF are headquartered in Washington, D.C., and have critics and supporters alike. It is not my point here to imply judgments about them but to demonstrate that it will not require the introduction of a new idea in the end times for a real global bank to come into existence—a bank with real control of the world's economy.

A Global Regulatory Board

Another trend moving us toward a global economy is the push for international regulatory organizations. In April of 2009, a group of twenty central bank governors and finance ministers from the world's largest economies held a summit meeting to lay the framework for a new world order. The catalyst for this G20 Summit was the worldwide impact of the banking crisis and the global recession. The G20 nations are America, Argentina, Australia, Brazil, Britain, Canada, China, France, Germany, India, Indonesia, Italy, Japan, Mexico, Russia, Saudi Arabia, South Africa, South Korea, Turkey, and a representative from the twenty-seven-member European Union (EU).

According to the *New York Times*, these nineteen nations plus the EU "represent about 90 percent of the world's gross national product, 80 percent of world trade (including trade within the European Union) and two-thirds of the global population."[22] The importance of this gathering of national leaders was not lost on then British prime minister Gordon Brown. One month before the summit, he said, "Historians will look back and say this was no ordinary time but a defining moment: an unprecedented period of global change, and a time when one chapter ended and another began."[23]

The result of the G20 Summit seems to have flown under the radar for most Americans. A global plan was adopted that called for uniform regulations and bylaws that will be governed by the Financial Stability Board (FSB). This board includes representatives from all G20 countries, Spain, and the European Commission and will "comprise senior representatives of national financial authorities... international financial institutions, standard setting bodies, and committees of central bank experts."[24]

The Board of Governors of the Federal Reserve System, the U.S. Securities and Exchange Commission (SEC), and the U.S. Department of Treasury are listed as member institutions representing the United States.

A new global economic government designed to monitor potential risks to the stability of the global economy is developing right before our eyes. Whether or not they intend to keep their commitment, all the G20 members have agreed to put their important financial institutions, instruments, and markets under the authority of a single regulatory agency: the Financial Stability Board.

The World Bank, the IMF, and now the FSB are organizations-in-waiting. The leader of the one-world government of the Tribulation will need such organizations in order to control the economic lives of nations and their people. As we will learn in chapter 6, in the middle of the Tribulation period the False Prophet will demand that every citizen of the world take a special mark on his or her forehead or hand (see Revelation 13:16; 14:9). Without this mark a person will not be allowed to buy or sell or do business. The World Bank, the IMF, and the FSB may very well be at the center of this global regime, helping its demonic leaders carry out their plan.

The Growing Influence of Europe

Another factor moving us toward a global economy is a shift of power back to the European nations. Twenty-five hundred years ago, God gave His servant Daniel one of the most comprehensive biblical prophecies ever revealed to man. The message of that prophecy was conveyed to Daniel through a dream given to King Nebuchadnezzar of Babylon. Daniel interpreted the dream, which outlined a composite history of the four great empires that would rule the world from the time of Babylon until the end of days.

Much of what God revealed to Daniel has already happened. But not all of it. Three of the prophesied kingdoms have come and gone, and the fourth kingdom, the Roman Empire, has also made its appearance in history. That kingdom, however, has actually never been destroyed as Daniel foretold it would be. Rather, it gradually weakened and receded from prominence.

Today we are currently seeing a resurgence of the Roman Empire, or a reconstituted form of it. This seems to align with the prophecy of Daniel, who said there is to be a powerful reemergence of the Roman Empire in the last days. He foretells that this empire will consist of ten kingdoms or leaders, and clearly states that in this final form it will be on the earth when God sets up His earthly kingdom: "And in the days of these kings [the rulers of the ten segments of the Roman Empire] the God of heaven will set up a kingdom which shall never be destroyed; and the kingdom shall not be left to other people; it shall break in pieces and consume all these kingdoms, and it shall stand forever" (Daniel 2:44).

Gradually but steadily, the nations of Europe have come together, creating a modern replica of the ancient Roman Empire. Europe is more integrated today than at any time since the days of ancient Rome. The United States of Europe is now considered by many to be the second most powerful political and economic force in our world.[25]

As I noted in a previous book, "Currently the EU government is organized into three bodies: a Parliament, the Council of European Union, and the European Commission. The Parliament is considered 'the Voice of the People' because citizens of the EU directly elect its 785 members. The Parliament passes European laws in conjunction with the Council. Its president is elected to serve a five-year term."[26]

On almost every front, the influence of the EU is increasing. According to an article in *Forbes* magazine, it was the European leaders who called for a global summit "to establish a new world order for regulating the banking system."[27] According to United Nations data, "Today, the fifty largest financial corporations in the world represent well over one third of total world banking assets. Interestingly, as a group they are the most internationalized of the world's transnational corporations. Thirty-six of these fifty largest companies are headquartered in Europe."[28]

With America's economic decline and the rise of the EU, many are predicting that the euro will be the next universal reserve currency. In light of Daniel's prophecy, that would be an important sign pointing toward the coming reconstituted Roman Empire as the controller of the new global economy.

Instantaneous Global Money Transfer

Another financial trend that indicates coming economic globalism is the growing ease with which citizens of one nation can make purchases or conduct business internationally. And just think, it wasn't until after Congress passed the Interstate Banking bill in 1994 that banks could even operate across state borders. Now they can operate without any international barriers.

MasterCard continues to develop a global network for the transfer of funds. Today its customer financial institutions have the capability to offer MasterCard cardholders money transfers from any

MasterCard or Maestro card to any other MasterCard or Maestro card in the world.

In a 2009 press release, MasterCard executive Joshua Peirez said, "We are focused on developing convenient and secure solutions for the day-to-day financial realities of consumers around the world. As the flow of money between global workers and their families continues to grow, *MasterCard MoneySend* provides a valuable, convenient and reliable money transfer option for consumers."

In the same release, another MasterCard executive, Walt Macnee, said, "*MasterCard MoneySend* removes barriers impeding the transfer of money around the world and provides the global economy with a robust infrastructure that supports growth in international transfers as consumers continue to remit funds globally."[29] With such innovative technology, national boundaries matter little or not at all in monetary transactions. When you need local currency in London, Paris, or Bonn, just insert your card into the nearest sidewalk ATM and your card issuer makes all the exchange calculations and delivers to you the correct funds. It seems that we ordinary citizens are already sliding into economic globalism even as you read this book.

New Attitudes for a New World

Wilfred J. Hahn is correct when he writes that "the real essence behind global financial trends are essentially spiritual issues... and the affections of the human heart... that build this monstrous, world-controlling edifice of financial tentacles."[30]

Joseph Stiglitz, whom I mentioned in chapter 1 as the coauthor of *The Three Trillion Dollar War,* is the former chief economist of the World Bank. In a 2009 article for *Vanity Fair,* Stiglitz predicted that one of the legacies of the current global financial crises would be "a world-wide battle over ideas—over what kind of economic system is likely to deliver the greatest benefit to the most people."[31] Included with the article was a cartoon by Edward Sorel that was designed to cast a historically biblical pall over modern society. What kinds of ideas are likely to find their way into Stiglitz's suggested global system? By including the cartoon he seems to suggest that the new ideas will be the very ones that created the crises in the first place.

Illustration by Edward Sorel. Used by permission.

Sorel captioned his cartoon, "The Four Horsemen of the Wall St. Apocalypse." The title and imagery allude to the four horsemen that appear in the beginning of the book of Revelation—the original Apocalypse. The cartoon pictures skeletons riding four horses in a wild stampede over the ruins of the New York Stock Exchange. Each skeleton is labeled with one of the four heart attitudes that contributed to our current financial situation: mendacity, stupidity, arrogance, and greed. Because the cartoon intentionally evokes a King James feel, one of the labels is somewhat obscure to modern Americans. It is the word *mendacity*, which simply means "characterized by deception."[32] The cartoonist pictures how heart attitudes contributed to the recent Wall Street crisis and will bring about the ultimate destruction of an economy. Unfortunately, these are the heart attitudes that currently rule the world, the nations, and the people. To demonstrate the truth of this statement, let's examine these attitudes one by one.

Deception (Mendacity)

Almost every day we read or hear of identity theft, mail fraud, Internet theft, hoaxes, pyramid schemes, extortions, and rip-offs. Many of these scams are directed at the elderly, and authorities tell us that in times of economic uncertainty these crimes increase exponentially. Deceit is not a new heart attitude. In the days of Ezekiel the prophet, our Lord spoke out against it: " 'In you they take bribes to shed blood; you take usury and increase; you have made profit from your neighbors by extortion, and have forgotten Me,' says the Lord GOD. 'Behold, therefore, I beat My fists at the dishonest profit which you have made, and at the bloodshed which has been in your midst' " (Ezekiel 22:12–13). We can all identify with God's angry response to dishonesty and deception. When we hear of innocent people being robbed or extorted, we want to pound our fists on the table too.

I don't think any objective observer would deny that deception is rampant today, and not only among scammers and con men. It happens in business corporations, as when a major automobile manufacturer hides a flaw in its cars' acceleration mechanism to avoid a massive recall. Deception is rife in our own government and media as leaders and reporters spin the negative elements out of their explanations of political agendas, hiding costs and consequences in order to sell programs that increase their power. Deception is rampant among us, and it will be a major factor in bringing down our national economy.

Stupidity

The second horseman of Wall Street is stupidity. I might have preferred a somewhat kinder word, such as *foolishness* or *mindlessness* or *irrationality*. But *stupidity* is the word the artist used, so we will go with it.

Peter's exhortation in his famous sermon delivered on the day of Pentecost urges us, "Be saved from this perverse generation" (Acts 2:40). In his paraphrase, *The Message*, Eugene Peterson rendered Peter's phrase, "Get out of this sick and stupid culture!"[33]

While Jesus never used the word *stupid*, He did use the word *fool* in a parable about a rich man who thought his wealth gave him an advantage in life: "And I will say to my soul, 'Soul, you have many goods laid up for many years; take your ease; eat, drink, and be merry.' But God said to him, 'Fool! This night your soul will be required of you; then whose will those things be which you have provided?'" (Luke 12:19–20).

During the last year, I have read dozens of stories about the stupid things people do in their pursuit of wealth. One story involved a woman who fell for a TV infomercial offering reprint rights to forty-five books, which, she was assured by fake testimonials, were in great demand. She invested $3,000 into the program only to find that most of the books were easily available free government publications. After several months of advertising, she received only one response.[34]

In reading stories like this, I am reminded of the words the apostle Paul wrote to his young protégé Timothy: "But those who desire to be rich fall into temptation and a snare, and into many foolish and harmful lusts which drown men in destruction and perdition. For the love of money is a root of all kinds of evil, for which some have strayed from the faith in their greediness, and pierced themselves through with many sorrows" (1 Timothy 6:9–10).

Please note that being rich is not the problem; the problem is the inordinate desire for riches—lusting after riches. And it is not money that is the problem; it's the love of money. Now that we have that straight, look again at the descriptive terms Paul uses to describe the risk we take when we become obsessed with money and wealth. He warns that we are likely to fall into temptation, fall into a snare, drown in destruction, drown in perdition, and become pierced through with many sorrows. Given this grim picture of the outcome, you can see why it is...well...stupid to plunge headlong after wealth. Yet people continue to do it.

As part of my research for this project, I read two books and dozens of articles about Bernie Madoff. I reported some of my findings in chapter 1. Most of what has been written about the Madoff scam reports that he stole $65 billion from his investors. But in reality, the total amount of money invested with Madoff appears to have been more like $20 billion. The $65 billion includes the false profit—the phantom earnings that were reported to the investors each month, which they were led to think was their growing wealth. But Madoff never invested his clients' money in any of the reported stocks; therefore, all his victims actually lost was their initial $20 billion investment.

Here's where the story gets stupid. When these investors got their IRS 1099 Forms each year, they paid taxes on their supposed earnings—money that never existed. Some of the victims are trying to get their tax money back from the government—the only apparent beneficiary of Madoff's scam. But filing under "theft deductions," as currently allowed by the IRS, they will be fortunate to recover a dime for every dollar they paid in taxes.

These investors did not know that they were being cheated, but surely they must have been smart enough to know that their reported earnings were impossible. Most of Madoff's investors were financially sophisticated people who knew better than to believe you could make a steady return of 12 to 20 percent when the stock market had been flat for months. In their desire to be rich, in their love of money, they made unwise decisions that caused them to pay taxes on money that never existed.

Arrogance

Cartoonist Sorel's third Wall Street horseman is labeled *Arrogance*. Once again the Word of God addresses our propensity to harbor this heart attitude: "Command those who are rich in this present age not to be haughty, nor to trust in uncertain riches but in the living God, who gives us richly all things to enjoy" (1 Timothy 6:17).

I love this verse because it is so balanced. The part we all like is "God gives us richly all things to enjoy." With a Scripture like that staring me in the face, I'm not about to put a guilt trip on you for having lots of nice stuff. God bless you. Enjoy it. But don't let those riches be your life. Don't let your possessions be what you live for. Particularly, as this verse pointedly says, don't allow your riches to make you haughty and arrogant, as if your wealth makes you superior to those who do not have it.

Money can give a person a certain amount of power and control over others—his employees, his vendors, his debtors, his renters, or even his community or church. And, as we know, power tends to corrupt. It can go to one's head and lead him to assume a sense of superiority that leads to arrogant disregard for the rights, wants, and needs of others. This, of course, is an all-too-common response to wealth, and the one against which Paul warns.

But, as he goes on to tell us, there is a proper way to respond to wealth: "Let them do good, that they be rich in good works, ready to give, willing to share, storing up for themselves a good foundation for the time to come" (1 Timothy 6:18–19). Our riches are given to us so that God can bless others through us. We are merely conduits of His blessings. As Paul says, by using wealth in this way, we are preparing ourselves for "the time to come." A new global economy will not prevail against the person who is rich in good works and uses his or her wealth to bless others.

Greed

If you were asked to vote on which of the four heart attitudes Sorel illustrates was most responsible for our current economic situation, which would you choose? I am certain that most of us would select greed as the underlying cause of our economic woes.

In his book *The Screwtape Letters*, C. S. Lewis writes that unhealthy and inordinate desires create "an ever increasing craving for an ever diminishing pleasure."[35] This serves as an excellent definition of greed and describes the heart attitude behind the current financial crisis. As people become dissatisfied with their houses, cars, and other possessions, their craving grows beyond their means until their personal economy both reflects the nature of the national economy and contributes to it. Thus they become a part of the collapsing financial system. Our Lord's counsel concerning greed is simple and to the point: "Take heed and beware of covetousness, for one's life does not consist in the abundance of the things he possesses" (Luke 12:15).

It is all too easy to find appalling examples of greed in our current economic condition. While foreclosed homeowners have few options and are increasingly turning to shelters to get out of the elements, banks and companies that received government bailout money are paying extravagant executive bonuses at prebailout levels.[36] Kenneth Feinberg, the Obama administration compensation czar and watchdog over the seven companies that received TARP funds, said, "It doesn't seem right that the people who caused this tragedy should be so richly rewarded."[37]

But these bonuses must be paid because many are contractually mandated when executives are hired. They are an unfortunate cost of doing business on Wall Street because if the seven banks that received bailout funds did not pay bonuses, the very executives with the talent to lead the companies back into profitability would have left for jobs where bonuses would be paid. All of which demonstrates that greed in the top tier of our financial leaders is at the core of our current economic trouble.

The Bible has a lot to say about greed, and it's not good. Here are just two proverbs from the Old Testament: "So are the ways of everyone who is greedy for gain; it takes away the life of its owners"; and "He who is greedy for gain troubles his own house" (Proverbs 1:19; 15:27).

Perhaps you've read of the astonishing acquisitiveness of Nicolas Cage. This popular actor has made millions and used it to snatch up European castles, a fleet of cars (including nine Rolls-Royces), a virtual museum of art treasures, four yachts, fifteen houses around the world, an island in the Bahamas, and a Gulfstream jet. Among his houses were two historic French Quarter homes in New Orleans, valued at more than $4 million. Now Cage is in financial crisis. He owes the government $6.6 million, and his homes are being sold in foreclosure auctions.

According to the *New York Post*, Cage's former business manager warned him he would need an annual income of $30 million just to maintain the things he had bought. The manager said, "[Cage] knows that his losses are entirely and solely the result of his own compulsive, self-destructive spending."[38]

In one of his most bizarre purchases, "Cage outbid fellow actor Leo DiCaprio at a 2007 auction by offering over a quarter-million dollars for a dinosaur skull." Cage admitted, "I find ways of spending money that mystify everybody around me." As Cage's runaway spending shows, greed can take over any life and lead to financial ruin. Incidentally, his outlandishly decorated Bel Air mansion failed to receive even one bid in a recent foreclosure auction.[39]

The apostle Paul knew that greed could also be a destructive force in the life of a believer. After outlining to Timothy the deadly nature of greed, he told the young man how to deal with it: "But you, O man of God, flee these things and pursue righteousness, godliness, faith, love, patience, gentleness" (1 Timothy 6:11). The way to deal with greed is simply to run from it and fill your heart instead with godly attributes that will replace the need to validate your worth by the accumulation of wealth.

Greed is one of four things from which Paul tells followers of Christ to run. In other letters he tells us to flee idolatry, fornication, and adultery (see 1 Corinthians 10:14; 2 Timothy 2:22; 1 Corinthians 6:18). Greed, like these other temptations, destroys lives of believers and unbelievers alike. Greed is one of the four horsemen that will reduce both individual lives and our economy to a heap of rubble.

As we have seen, several signs—from history, current events, and biblical prophecy—indicate that a new global economic order is on the horizon that may be a signpost of the end times. We, as individual citizens, can do little or nothing to stop or even slow its approach. What we can do, however, is maintain vigilance in our opposition to the spiritual causes of America's decline and not get caught up in the prevalent but destructive heart attitudes that are bringing it about. If we stand against deception, stupidity, arrogance, and greed and, following Paul's admonition, pursue righteousness, faith, love, patience, and gentleness, great blessings will follow. Not only will we retain peace in the midst of turmoil, we will stand as beacons to others who by our example may be drawn out of the current economic frenzy and into the peace of Christ.

I will close this chapter by repeating a story that my friend John Ortberg tells about himself in his wonderful book with an even more wonderful title: *When the Game Is Over, It All Goes Back in the Box.* In his book, he tells about how he travels around the country helping people deal with materialism. In his words:

> Materialism is for most of us God's rival. And it is possible to get increasingly free of it. Sometimes when I am speaking, I try a little exercise in dethroning the idol. I ask the people to take out their wallets.... Hold it for a moment. Caress it if they want. Look inside to see if anybody's home.
>
> It looks like a piece of leather. But it's really the temple of the twenty-first century. Most people in our day believe that their ability to experience happiness is directly associated with the contents of this little container. This is where the god Mammon lives. We give this little piece of leather the power to make us feel secure, successful, and valuable.
>
> It is very hard to surrender control of this little piece of leather.... So, as a little baby step of surrender, I ask the people to hand their wallet to the person next to them. At this point, the attention level in the room goes way up. And then I announce that we are going to take an offering. And I encourage people to give with the extravagant generosity they have always wanted to exhibit.
>
> Wallets fly back to their owners real fast at that point. I then invite people to declare today "Enough Day." What I have now—my home, my possessions, my lifestyle—is enough. I will seek another and better kind of wealth than terminal acquisition. Circle the day on your calendar. From this day on, your race with the Joneses is over. *The Joneses win!*[40]

John Ortberg's advice may not stop the headlong plunge toward America's financial ruin and an ensuing global economy, but it will certainly give you a foothold in your own struggle to avoid both economic and spiritual ruin. If the four horsemen of Wall Street demolish our economy and diminish our wealth, we must remember that our possessions are not our lives. Our lives are invested in God, and in His hands they remain secure and unshakable regardless of the economic chaos around us.

In the new global economy it doesn't matter whether a new currency usurps the U.S. dollar or a new global conglomeration is formed that excludes the dollar. Whatever happens, we have this promise: "Let your conduct be without covetousness; be content with such things as you have. For He Himself has said, 'I will never leave you nor forsake you'" (Hebrews 13:5).

CHAPTER 4

From Crisis to Consolidation

The announcement in early May 2010 that the European Union and the International Monetary Fund had agreed to a $140 billion bailout plan for Greece was good news for that debt-ridden nation. So why did that news lead to public employee strikes, days of riots, and the deaths of three people? There were at least two possible reasons. The first was the fear that the rescue would only delay Greece's inevitable bankruptcy by a few months. In other words, the bailout was seen as insufficient.

The second was the Greek people's objection to the harsh austerity measures imposed by Germany and other EU countries as a condition for receiving the bailout money. These measures included higher consumer taxes and significant cuts in pensions and civil servants' pay. In reality, this meant the citizens were being asked to contribute more than $38 billion to save their government from collapse. Beyond the burning barricades and firebombed buildings was "widespread anger... that the entire country would have to bear the burden of accumulated decades of corruption and mismanagement by the political elite."[1]

Greek prime minister George Papandreou told his parliament, "There was only one other solution—for the country to default, taking the citizenry with it. And that would not have affected the rich; it would have affected workers and pensioners. That was a real possibility, however nightmarish."[2] The lower and middle classes in Greece will be disproportionately affected by the grave financial measures. They were the ones—the publicly employed teachers, doctors, nurses, port workers, airport and government employees—who took to the streets and shut down the nation for days.

Greece may be the first of many nations that seem headed toward a similar crisis. For example, with its budget deficit of 11.6 percent of GDP, Great Britain's government "promised more than it could afford to deliver" and it cost Gordon Brown his position as prime minister. The U.S. is also facing double-digit budget deficits, and "the federal government will borrow fully 40 percent of the $3.6 trillion it is on course to spend this fiscal year."[3]

In spite of such massive spending—or perhaps because of it—the American economy seems only to worsen. In the same week of the Greek riots, the U.S. Bureau of Labor Statistics reported that 290,000 new jobs were added during the month of April, continuing an upward trend for a fourth consecutive month.[4] But this seemingly good news turned out to be not so good. Many of those new jobs were only temporary census positions. Factoring in the large number of discouraged unemployed people who ventured back into the job search process that month and who were competing for those new jobs, the unemployment rate actually rose from 9.7 percent to 9.9 percent. Far from confirming that the recession was over, the newly created jobs were simply not enough, and 15.3 million Americans remained unemployed.

If you have ever been dependent on an unemployment check, you know that it is barely adequate to pay even the most basic bills. The *New York Times* reported the plight of a woman from Queens who has been unemployed since 2008, when her company downsized in the financial crisis. She went from earning $65,000 annually to receiving $430 monthly in unemployment benefits. Those benefits finally ran out in April 2010, and she had not been able to find new employment even though she sought it diligently. With no income or health insurance, she was barely getting by. The paper quoted her as saying, "I would rather be out working and I can't find anything. It is not for lack of trying. The economy is broke."[5]

This growing financial pressure on the average people of the world brings to mind the famous first sentence of a Charles Dickens novel: "It was the best of times, it was the worst of times, it was the age of wisdom, it was the age of foolishness...in short, the period was so far like the present period...for good or for evil."[6] So begins *A Tale of Two Cities*, the classic tale of the political and economic turmoil of 1775 in the two dominant cities in the world of Dickens's day—London and Paris.

If he were writing that story today, Dickens would likely have to expand its geographical scope to include all of Europe and the country that was still struggling to be born in that fateful year—the United States of America. If he found those inclusions too broad to give him the needed focus for a manageable plot, he could limit his story to a few representative cities. London, Athens, and Washington, D.C., would serve very well—three national capitals teetering on the brink of financial destruction and carrying the potential for popular uprisings and street violence even more dangerous than the chaos of the French Revolution.

In each of the political crises noted above, the problem was created largely by growing dependence on government to take responsibility for its citizens' well-being. This dependence, in turn, leads to greater government control and a consolidation of power in the hands of a few. Like the frog in the kettle, the citizens, focused on their own comfort, tend not to notice the increase in control. Nor do they seem to care as long as their needs are met and their comfort level maintained. But as we will see in this chapter, this casual acceptance of government dependence is leading us into severe results that loom just beyond the horizon.

Causes and Evidences of Power Consolidation

It is as true today as it was in the French Revolution: "With their way of life at risk, desperate people will sometimes do desperate things."[7] A scarcity of money, jobs, or food will often lead people to accept extreme measures in order to survive.

In his book *When a Nation Forgets God*, Erwin Lutzer writes:

After the fall of the Berlin wall a cartoon appeared in a Russian newspaper picturing a fork in the road. One path was labeled *freedom*; the other path was labeled *sausage*. As we might guess, the path to freedom had few takers; the path to sausage was crowded with footprints. When given a choice, most people probably will choose bread and sausage above the free market and individual liberties. It was Lenin's promise of bread in every kitchen that ignited the communist revolution. Bread with political slavery was better than freedom and starvation. Bread fills the stomach, freedom does not.[8]

In times of despair, people often move to accept a strong centralized government to provide for them. A centralized government is one in which all authority in a country is vested in one person or a very limited group and to whom all other governments, state and local, are subjugated. The founders of the United States knew personally the oppressive implications of such a form of government. Thus they purposed that the colonies would be under a federated system of decentralized government in which each state holds home rule sovereignty under the limits of the Constitution. It is this type of government that allows a free market economy regulated by just laws rather than restrictive dictatorial control.

I don't think there is any doubt that our nation has for years been experiencing a shift away from the intent of the founding fathers and toward a heavily centralized government. There are several strong indicators of this shift, which we will consider one by one.

The Federal Budget

One of the clearest indicators of our move toward a consolidated government is the way the government spends our money. Beginning slowly but with exponentially accelerating speed, government spending has both ballooned and shifted in emphasis from necessities to entitlements, with a corresponding shift in priorities. David M. Walker waves a red flag of warning with this observation:

> In fiscal 2008, you could trace less than 40 percent of our federal government spending back to the bedrock responsibilities envisioned by the founders. In budget language, all of those original programs and the others that relate to the responsibilities reserved for the federal government under the Constitution, including national defense, foreign relations, and the federal judicial system, are now considered discretionary.[9]

Big government is now an established fact in the United States, and it's about to get much bigger. In the aftermath of our recent financial crisis, the cost of our government has mushroomed into an even larger percentage of the GDP. If the workforce necessary to manage the new tax initiatives and healthcare programs is anywhere near what has been projected, we will soon be a full-fledged socialist state.

The Banking Institutions

Another indicator of consolidation can be found in our banking institutions. In 1940 there were 14,399 banks in the United States. Today there are about half that many, and the number continues to drop precipitously.[10]

Long gone are the days when a banker actually knew his depositors and took care to ascertain their credit worthiness for loans or mortgages. Such scrutinizing tactics are deemed too expensive these days. The increased risk and expense of loan default is passed on to the customer in the form of higher-priced financial services, fewer personal loans, higher credit card finance charges, and lowered credit card limits.

One of the worldwide results of the recent global financial crisis has been the consolidation, concentration, and control of the world's money by a dwindling number of banks. The primary fallout from consolidation is that it leads to greater government control through intervention and regulation.

One such consolidation took place on October 30, 2009, here in my corner of the world. The once-proud San Diego National Bank became a failure statistic. It is now one of the 140 banks in the United States that failed and was taken over by the Federal Deposit Insurance Corporation (FDIC) in 2009. All twenty-eight of the branch offices operating under the name of San Diego National Bank closed at the end of one business day and opened the next day under a new name: U.S. Bank of Minneapolis.

Without a word of warning, customers of eight other banking institutions from Arizona to Illinois to Texas faced the same surprise that day. With no action or approval on their part, the customers now had a new bank with a new name and a new owner. The switchover was seamless. Their old bank ATM cards worked flawlessly at the new bank's machines, and their direct deposits and automatic withdrawals were simply transferred to the new bank.[11]

According to the FDIC, in the first 117 days of 2010, seventy-two more banks were added to the list of failed financial institutions.[12] The total 2009 payout from FDIC funds topped out at $36 billion, twice the payout rate of 2008.[13] These closures meant the loss of thousands of jobs in the financial sector. As this trend continues, small bankers may soon become an endangered species.

While small banks are becoming extinct, big, consolidated, financial institutions that have been rescued by government bailouts are managing to pull off some unbelievable feats. Bank of America, JP Morgan, Citibank, and Goldman Sachs managed to pay back their billions of dollars in bailout funds early. Then, amazingly, in the first quarter of 2010, not one of these banking giants posted a loss—a virtually impossible feat equivalent to four different major-league pitchers each pitching a perfect game on the same day. As one *New*

York Times financial writer put it, "In 2009, the banks posted losses on less than 20 percent of the trading days; during the turmoil of 2008, losses occurred as much as 40 percent of the time."[14]

How was such an astounding turnaround even possible? Was some kind of manipulation going on here? Some suspect it was a preplanned event designed to show the effectiveness of governmental intervention, thus furthering the argument for more regulation. That brings us to the next evidence that shows the trend toward a major concentration of power in big government.

Financial Regulation

Plans for more regulation sent President Obama into the heart of Wall Street in April 2010 to drum up support for a bill that would end the "too-big-to-fail" phenomenon by increasing governmental regulation over the financial sector.[15] In his speech Obama insisted that reform of financial institutions is necessary "to make certain that taxpayers are never again on the hook because a firm is deemed 'too big to fail.' . . . A vote for reform is a vote to put a stop to taxpayer-funded bailouts. . . . Not only [will it] safeguard our system against crises, this will also make our system stronger and more competitive by installing confidence here at home and across the globe."[16]

Treasury Secretary Timothy Geithner also weighed in on the matter, saying, "Financial reform is not the war of choice; it is a war of necessity."[17] Beneath the rhetoric of necessity and public protection, there can be little doubt that financial regulation is another way in which big government intends to become even bigger.

The Stock Market

And then there is the strange case of the stock market "flash crash" miracle of early May 2010. If you are a market watcher, you may have experienced simultaneous apoplexy and angina as the stock market took a frightening bungee ride that Thursday. Call it panic buying, a plunge, a market correction, or some other euphemism; the Dow Jones Industrial Average posted its greatest intraday loss since the crash of 1987. The hour-by-hour graph of that day's trading showed a gradual decline until shortly after 2:30 p.m. EDT when the bottom dropped out. In just five minutes, the Dow was down "400 to 800 points."[18] It went on to lose nearly one thousand points in that precipitous dive. At 2:40 p.m. the descent stopped with a curious and startling upward jerk as if the bungee cord had reached its nadir and its rider was sent vaulting back up to the apex. By 3:40 p.m. the Dow had recovered 383.17 points—an almost "miraculous" recovery in the space of less than an hour![19] At the 4:00 closing bell the ride was over and the Dow had leveled off to a loss of 348 points for the day.[20] A financial miracle?

Maybe not.

Surely there must be a logical explanation for such a dramatic turnaround. Some were offered: it was technical glitches, not a sell-off; fears of euro contagion had abated with Germany's vote to aid in Greece's recovery; consumer spending was up and, oh yes, in advance of its official release the following morning, the April unemployment data was leaked, indicating another month of job creation. Still, there was hardly enough good news in those explanations to produce such an amazing result. It would appear more likely that there might have been intervention by a behind-the-scenes committee.

Back in 1988, by executive order, President Ronald Reagan created what has been referred to as "The Plunge Protection Team," or sometimes "The Four Dictators." The group includes the heads of the Federal Reserve, the U.S. Treasury, the U.S. Securities and Exchange Commission, and the U.S. Commodity Futures Trading Commission. In order, the current members are: Ben Bernanke, Timothy Geithner, Mary Schapiro, and Gary Gensler. Under executive order #12631, the committee functions to intercede when the stock market appears headed for a plunge. Please note that the people do not elect these officials; they are all selected by the president of the United States. The Plunge Protection Team (PPT) has been called in to execute a rescue on three occasions since September 11, 2001: January 2008, October 2008, and most recently, May 6, 2010.

American investment expert Robert Kiyosaki is straightforward in his opinion of the limits of this team's future effectiveness: "I believe the end is near. I believe The Four Dictators will be unable to prevent many more plunges. When they can't stop the plunge, the poor and middle class will be wiped out."[21]

The PPT acts only upon the directive of the president of the United States and, we assume, in the best interests of the American people. There is, however, a good deal of suspicion directed toward the PPT. Credible sources charge that "the Federal Reserve and the Treasury (in league with top Wall Street firms) is rigging the stock market on a daily basis" and the stock market is not really a free market.[22]

For example, in January 2010 stock analyst Charles Biderman said, "The massive stock market rally in the past nine months is mostly due to secret government buying of stock-index futures."[23] As of early May that nine-month stretch of growth had increased to fourteen months. If it is true that market manipulation is taking place, we must remember that such buying of stocks by the Federal Reserve, no matter how the end might appear to justify the means, is illegal.

The PPT is simply more power and wealth consolidated in the hands of a few. Since the president selects these four people, it is essentially power consolidated in one man.

As the examples above have shown, this process of ever-increasing consolidation of power in the hands of fewer and fewer people is well under way. Next we will explore a historical, biblical example that shows what can happen when power is consolidated in the hands of a single individual.

The Famine Forecast

In the first book of the Bible we find an early record of crisis and consolidation. This dramatic story tells how God used one man to save his nation from the death ravages of famine.

The story begins with the birth of a boy named Joseph. The second-to-last of twelve brothers born to Jacob, Joseph was the first son of Rachel, Jacob's favorite wife. This is likely why Joseph became Jacob's favorite son.

As a young boy, Joseph had dreams about his future in which his father and brothers would bow down to him. The combination of the dreams and his father's favoritism incited the hatred of Joseph's brothers. It did not help that Jacob violated the protocol of birth order and selected Joseph as the family heir, giving him a richly colored coat to signify his choice.

When Joseph was about seventeen, Jacob sent him on a mission to check up on his brothers, who were away from the family homestead tending their flocks. When the brothers saw Joseph approaching, their hate and jealousy boiled over, and they determined to kill him. Only the intervention of Reuben, the oldest of the brothers, saved Joseph's life. Instead of killing him they sold him to a band of Midianite slave traders. Joseph was taken to Egypt where he was sold to Potiphar, the chief of police in Egypt.

Joseph rose by his integrity to become the administrator of Potiphar's household affairs. Potiphar's wife tried to seduce Joseph into adultery, and when he refused, her false accusation of attempted rape landed him in the royal prison.

Again Joseph's integrity and industry caught the attention of prison officials, and he rose to become a prison trustee. He became acquainted with two men who had been imprisoned by Pharaoh, king of Egypt. One night these men had dreams that they could not understand. Joseph interpreted their dreams, telling the first prisoner that his dream revealed his imminent restoration to his former position as the king's butler. Joseph asked the butler to remember him before Pharaoh "and get me out of this house" (Genesis 40:14). As Joseph had predicted, the butler was released and returned to his position. But he forgot all about Joseph, and two long years went by before Joseph learned in a spectacular way that God had not forgotten him.

It happened like this: Pharaoh had a dream that he could not understand. When all the brain trust of Egypt failed to uncover its meaning, the butler finally remembered Joseph and recommended him to Pharaoh as the possible interpreter. Joseph was duly summoned before Pharaoh of Egypt, at that time the most powerful monarch of the known world.

Giving God full credit for his interpretation, Joseph explained to Pharaoh the meaning of his dream. It was a prophecy that his nation was about to experience seven years of unprecedented harvest and great plenty. But those seven years would be followed by another seven of famine that would devastate the entire nation and the lands around it.

Joseph went on to make a recommendation to the king, giving him a way to save his nation from the coming famine:

> Now therefore, let Pharaoh select a discerning and wise man, and set him over the land of Egypt. Let Pharaoh do this, and let him appoint officers over the land, to collect one-fifth of the produce of the land of Egypt in the seven plentiful years. And let them gather all the food of those good years that are coming, and store up grain under the authority of Pharaoh, and let them keep food in the cities. Then that food shall be as a reserve for the land for the seven years of famine which shall be in the land of Egypt, that the land may not perish during the famine. (Genesis 41:33–36)

Pharaoh knew a good idea when he heard it. Joseph had declared that God was the source of his wisdom, and Pharaoh seemed to acknowledge the fact, saying, "Can we find such a one as this, a man in whom is the Spirit of God?" (Genesis 41:38). This pagan king may not have understood just who that God was, yet he had the sense to recognize good leadership when he saw it, even in a thirty-year-old foreigner. Pharaoh took the bold step of assigning to Joseph the task of implementing his plan, giving him final authority over everything in Egypt except his throne and the lands of the pagan priests.

That must have been a heady experience for Joseph. He now possessed the primary symbol of the king's power—his signet ring—along with a designer wardrobe, royal jewelry, the second chariot (ancient Egypt's equivalent of Air Force Two), public obeisance from the Egyptians, a new name, and a new wife.

Joseph's Plan for Centralized Government

Joseph's crisis management plan was to centralize the government around Pharaoh. He toured the land to assess the production potential and set up a system to gather and store the bounty in the cities nearest to the fields. At some point he apparently stopped counting the collected influx of grain because it was as immeasurable "as the sand of the sea" (Genesis 41:49).

We find no record of Joseph's paying the people for that 20 percent of their seven years of produce. Wilfred J. Hahn suggests that if Joseph were paying for the grain from the royal treasury, he would not have stopped accounting for how it was spent.[24]

After the seven years of plenty,

the seven years of famine began to come, as Joseph had said. The famine was in all lands, but in all the land of Egypt there was bread. So when all the land of Egypt was famished, the people cried to Pharaoh for bread. Then Pharaoh said to all the Egyptians, "Go to Joseph; whatever he says to you, do." The famine was over all the face of the earth, and Joseph opened all the store-houses and sold to the Egyptians. And the famine became severe in the land of Egypt. (Genesis 41:54–56)

Despite this widespread shortage in crop production, the people of Egypt had bread, thanks to Joseph's planning. He opened the storehouses for them, but this wasn't exactly a compassionate government dole. Joseph sold them grain and collected their money. Other nations, hearing that there was grain in Egypt, went to Egypt to buy grain as well.

At this point there is a parenthetical interruption in the biblical account. Six chapters are inserted into Joseph's story recording details of his family and their ultimate move from Canaan to Egypt (see Genesis 42:1–47:12). While Joseph was administrating a government in crisis, he was also orchestrating the reconciliation of his family.

Joseph's Plan for Survival

In Genesis 47:13, the focus returns to Joseph and how he dealt with the worldwide food shortage. When the famine was at its height, the Egyptians realized that there was no hope apart from Joseph. They were willing to submit to him at all costs and on any terms. Egypt was bankrupt, and its survival would have been hopeless without the solution Joseph offered: to consolidate everything under his control as the vice-regent of Pharaoh. This consolidation took several forms.

The Consolidation of the Egyptians' Livelihood

"And Joseph gathered up all the money that was found in the land of Egypt and in the land of Canaan, for the grain which they bought; and Joseph brought the money into Pharaoh's house" (Genesis 47:14).

The Egyptians could no longer trust in money simply because

they no longer had any. They had used every cent to buy bread. All men, rich and poor, were reduced to the same level. The formerly personal and private economy of every household was now under the control of the throne.

The Consolidation of the Egyptians' Livestock

So when the money failed in the land of Egypt and in the land of Canaan, all the Egyptians came to Joseph and said, "Give us bread, for why should we die in your presence? For the money has failed." Then Joseph said, "Give your livestock, and I will give you bread for your livestock, if the money is gone." So they brought their livestock to Joseph, and Joseph gave them bread in exchange for the horses, the flocks, the cattle of the herds, and for the donkeys. Thus he fed them with bread in exchange for all their livestock that year. (Genesis 47:15–17)

With all money gone and the famine continuing, Joseph accepted the herds of sheep and cattle as payment for more grain. The wealthy might have been able to hold out longer, but eventually everyone gave in. As a result, the throne again saved the people and, in the process, gained control not only of their purses but also of their possessions.

Most of us are city folk, and livestock has little meaning to us other than creatures we may see at the annual county fair. Economist Wilfred J. Hahn notes that in the economy of Joseph's day, livestock was the equivalent of today's factories. They were the source of products such as milk, meat, and hides—as well as transportation. In giving up their livestock, the people became both poorer and more dependent on the central government while Pharaoh's treasury burgeoned.[25]

The Consolidation of the Egyptians' Land

> When that year had ended, they came to [Joseph] the next year and said to him, "We will not hide from my lord that our money is gone; my lord also has our herds of livestock. There is nothing left in the sight of my lord but our bodies and our lands. Why should we die before your eyes, both we and our land? Buy us and our land for bread, and we and our land will be servants of Pharaoh; give us seed, that we may live and not die, that the land may not be desolate." Then Joseph bought all the land of Egypt for Pharaoh; for every man of the Egyptians sold his field, because the famine was severe upon them. So the land became Pharaoh's. (Genesis 47:18–20)

The people now came to Joseph with empty pockets and paddocks. All they had left with which to barter was their persons and their land. They offered themselves and their now-desolate fields in exchange for grain from which to make bread.

The Consolidation of the Egyptians' Location

Next, Joseph relocated the people from their relinquished lands into the cities "from one end of the borders of Egypt to the other end" (Genesis 47:21).

We learned in Genesis chapter 41 that during the booming years, Joseph had stored Egypt's grain harvest in the cities. "He laid up in every city the food of the fields which surrounded them" (Genesis 41:48). Since the fields were barren and useless during the years of famine, Joseph eliminated transportation and distribution problems by moving the people to locations where the food was stored.

The Consolidation of the Egyptians' Labor

"Then Joseph said to the people, 'Indeed I have bought you and your land this day for Pharaoh. Look, here is seed for you, and you shall sow the land. And it shall come to pass in the harvest that you shall give one-fifth to Pharaoh. Four-fifths shall be your own, as seed for the field and for your food, for those of your households and as food for your little ones'" (Genesis 47:23–24).

As the famine was ending, Joseph put the people back to work planting seed in anticipation of the return of the land's fertility. Now, however, they were working by the government's direction on government-owned land and distributing their harvest according to government directives. All control of every aspect of the people's economic lives had been consolidated under the power of Pharaoh.

Was Joseph a Hero or a Tyrant?

You may have experienced conflicting reactions as you read the story of Joseph. On the one hand, you may have reacted positively to his ingenious plan for saving Egypt. On the other hand, you may have reacted negatively to his consolidation of power and wealth in the hands of the government while reducing the people to the status of serfs. Making our reactions even more complex is the positive way in which the Bible presents Joseph. Stephen, in his address before the high priest (which led to his martyrdom), strongly affirms that Joseph was a man of God (see Acts 7:9–10), and Joseph is among the heroes of faith listed in Hebrews 11 (see v. 22). Yet his use of Egypt's famine crisis to consolidate governmental power over the citizens seems to fly in the face of the personal independence and freedom we believe to be a healthy alternative to tyranny.

How are we to resolve this conflict? Before we rush to judgment, we must consider three factors: Joseph's time, the circumstances, and God's ultimate intention. In exploring these factors, we have help from several informed sources.

According to Hebrew scholar Nahum Sarna, "Joseph's actions cannot be measured by the moral standards that the Hebrew Bible, especially the prophetic tradition, has inculcated in Western civilization. Rather they must be judged in the context of the ancient Near Eastern world, by whose norms Joseph emerges here as a highly admirable model of a shrewd and successful administrator."[26]

In other words, the historical era in which Joseph lived was a factor. Democracy had not yet arisen in the ancient world. In those precarious times, people often needed, wanted, and respected a strong leader who could protect them from the crises of famine, wars, plagues, or other recurrent disasters.

Dr. Henry Morris shows that even after Joseph's takeover, the people of Egypt had a much lower tax burden and retained much more of their income than their ancient neighbors. Addressing Joseph's requirement that the Egyptians pay 20 percent of their produce to the king, Morris writes:

> In effect, this amounted to a permanent annual income tax of 20 percent of gross income. This is not excessive in terms of present-day standards, especially since the farmers had no rent to pay, no cost of investment or upkeep, in fact nothing except their own personal expenses. Pharaoh and the governmental bureaucracy administered by Joseph financed all government functions on the 20 percent.... It is noteworthy that there was little, if any, complaining about these terms. To the contrary, the citizens were grateful to Joseph for saving their lives, recognizing that they were being treated fairly and generously and there could really be no other plan which would work as well under the circumstances. They only desired to "find grace," or favor, in the eyes of Joseph, so that arrangement would remain in operation. As a matter of fact, it seemed to work so well that it continued to remain in force "unto this day"—that is, until at least the time of Moses.[27]

Best-selling author Kent Hughes notes that the 20 percent tax Joseph imposed on the Egyptians was actually very low for its day: "Forty percent was not uncommon in Mesopotamia. And there are examples as high as 60 percent.... As the famine worsened, everyone in Egypt was equitably fed. And the 20 percent? No one complained about it. Joseph was Egypt's national hero. They all would have been dead without him."[28]

Hughes also points out that in the cultural and historical context of ancient Egypt, there was little concept of welfare systems and property rights that made the later nation of Israel unique to that time:

> We must remember that there was no welfare system and no concept of entitlements. Moreover, this was not Israel but Egypt. In later Israel, family members would help destitute relations by buying their land and employing them as servants or slaves (cf. Leviticus 25:13–55). And those who were thus indentured received their land back in the year of Jubilee, which was supposed to occur every fifty years. Egypt was not as enlightened or humane as Israel. And later Pharaohs were not as magnanimous as the present Pharaoh. Finally, by the standards of all the people of Egypt, Joseph was hailed for what he did as their earthly savior—the man who saved Egypt (cf. v. 25). The Egyptians loved him![29]

As we can see, governmental consolidation in this ancient context was not viewed as the evil thing it would have been in a more humane land such as Israel or a nation based on freedom and democracy such as ours today. The people were grateful for the humaneness and care Joseph provided for them.

Dr. Henry Morris amplifies this idea, explaining how Joseph's actions must have appeared in the eyes of the Egyptians:

Some people have felt that this was a scheme of Joseph not only to get wealth but also to enslave the people. However, it was their proposal, not Joseph's, and . . . the alternative—that of placing everyone on a dole system—would have destroyed personal and national morale, would have bankrupted the government, and probably would have culminated in social anarchy. The stores of food would soon have been depleted and mass starvation would have followed.

The people had learned to trust Joseph. He had always charged them a fair price and, even though they had used up all their money and marketable possessions, they still had their self-respect.[30]

Another factor in evaluating Joseph's actions in Egypt is how it advanced God's overall plan. As we look at what God was doing in Egypt through Joseph, what can easily slip beneath the radar is how the result meshed with what God was also doing for His own people, Israel. In fact, many biblical scholars believe that the entire famine narrative is all about Israel— how God was using the pagan nation of Egypt to ensure the survival and numerical increase of His chosen people. Two verses strongly support this conclusion: "So Israel dwelt in the land of Egypt, in the country of Goshen; and they had possessions there and grew and multiplied exceedingly" (Genesis 47:27). Earlier in this same chapter we are told that Joseph's family was settled in "the best of the land" (Genesis 47:11).

This gives evidence that Joseph's "takeover" of Egypt was not done to provide a long-term benefit for the Egyptians, but rather to advance God's plan for Israel. Joseph clearly understood this. He told his brothers, "God sent me before you to preserve a posterity for you in the earth, and to save your lives by a great deliverance. . . . God meant it for good, in order to bring it about as it is this day, to save many people alive" (Genesis 45:7; 50:20).

Joseph's plan brought about God's good for Israel; subsequent events show that it did not bring long-term good to the Egyptians. God may have used Joseph's power consolidation to set up that pagan nation for the spectacular demonstration of His power that was to come in the future. Pharaohs that succeeded the one of Joseph's time took advantage of the consolidated governmental system they inherited and used it as a means of cruel tyranny. That tyranny led to Egypt's utter decimation 430 years later by the famous series of plagues under the rod of Moses.

Joseph's method of dealing with Egypt was a positive thing in its time and place, and while it advanced God's long-range plans for Egypt and Israel, clearly Joseph was not providing a positive model of government for all times and all circumstances. Far from it.

The Long-Term Result of Power Consolidation

I have spent considerable space recounting Joseph's administration in Egypt because it gives us a vivid picture of what could easily happen today, given the current financial situation in the world and in our own country.

Just as the long-term result of Joseph's actions turned out to be disastrous for Egypt, the consolidation of power is certain to be disastrous for the people of any nation. As Hahn observes, "Wealth cannot be heaped and concentrated without there being a depravation of someone else's wealth."[31] Let's look at some of the factors that show us why this is true.

Sacrificing Tomorrow on the Altar of Today

What Joseph did in Egypt was part of the divine providential care of Israel. This fact does not negate the long-term negative effects of his consolidation policy. In almost every situation where consolidation is employed to deal with a crisis, the result is immediate gain and long-term loss. Watch how this plays out in the years after Joseph's death.

Anglican scholar Griffith Thomas writes: "We must not forget that this policy led eventually to the affliction of Israel under a new Pharaoh. With all the power in the hands of the King it was at once easy for the Pharaoh of Joseph's time to protect Israel, and for the new Pharaoh to afflict Israel when Joseph and his work were forgotten."[32]

The book of Exodus begins with these sobering words: "Now there arose a new king over Egypt, who did not know Joseph" (Exodus 1:8). The chapter goes on to describe the slavery that the people of Israel were subjected to by the new Egyptian pharaoh.

Joseph's policies of consolidation may have solved a short-term problem, but the end of the story is not encouraging. This is truly the lesson of history, whether it be Roman history, German history, or the history of many other nations. When crisis comes, people are prone to accept a solution that sacrifices the future on the altar of the immediate. I believe this is what we now see happening in our nation. Bailouts, buyouts, underwrites, and consolidations may seem to be the quickest fixes when crises hit us, but what will these solutions do to us in the future? The steps toward increasing government control that have characterized the U.S. in the past year or so will change our nation forever! And not for the better.

Submitting the Good of the Many to the Control of One

In recent decades we have seen what happens when a one-person government assumes ultimate power over people. The twentieth century, one of the bloodiest centuries ever, was marked by a series of evil leaders such as Joseph Stalin, Mao Tse-tung, and Pol Pot—all of whom were committed to the same economic theory: communism. Their regimes share characteristics with that of the coming Antichrist.

Communism under Stalin overran other nations in a move to establish the Union of Soviet Socialist Republics. He usurped control over key areas of the economy, destroying the livelihoods of untold numbers of factory workers and producing the man-made famine of 1932–33.

One of Stalin's favored tactics was the purge—the massive massacre of millions of the Soviet Union's own population. According to author Jay W. Richards, "In 1937 and 1938, there were *on average* one thousand political executions per day."[33]

Mao's "Great Leap Forward" was his plan to create more than just a new world order; it was a plan to create God's new heaven and new earth—but without God. Implementing his plan cost the lives of more than 20 million Chinese, and his labor camps claimed the lives of another 20 million.

It has been asserted that in the last four years of the 1970s, "no other regime ever worked so hard to create an egalitarian society" than Pol Pot of the Khmer Rouge in Cambodia. But neither does any other regime have his record of terror. Under his "Year Zero" plan he redistributed wealth in one stroke: he abolished money. He relocated 2.5 million people from the city to the country. In the words of Jay Richards, "In forty-four short months, the regime pruned the Cambodian population by about 2 million—more than a quarter of the total population."[34] That is proportionally equivalent to 75 million Americans being slaughtered by our own government in three and one-half years!

The estimated total of human lives snuffed out by these tyrants is about 90 million—in the last century alone.[35]

The U.S. has not reached the point where consolidation gives one man the power to perform such atrocities. But during the past three-quarters of a century small steps have been taken that have led to an alarming increase in governmental power in the hands of fewer and fewer people. When Roosevelt first proposed the idea of Social Security in 1935, I doubt he envisioned the current situation in which "nearly 35 percent of Americans rely on Social Security for 90 percent or more of their retirement income."[36] This program, designed to assist those in need, is now an expensive, budget-wrecking entitlement that has caused millions to become government dependent.

The more that people look to the government as the provider of their retirement subsistence, the less they save for their future and the more they live for present pleasures. A study released in March 2010 by the Employee Benefit Research Institute says that "43 percent of Americans have less than $10k saved for retirement...27 percent said they had less than $1,000."[37]

This statistic reflects the third consecutive year in which retirement savings did not grow. We as a nation are relying increasingly on the government for our income, financial security, rescue from imprudent business decisions, and now to provide health care. With each of these dependencies we are giving up basic freedoms and risk selling ourselves to unscrupulous pharaohs.

That was exactly the point Niccolò Machiavelli made in his book *The Prince*. Written in Italian in 1513 and translated in 1908 by W. K. Marriott, Machiavelli gives advice to would-be leaders. Not least among his counsel is this: learn to use the expediency of deception. Machiavelli wrote that, historically, the most successful leaders have been those who had little use for honesty. They learned to speak in ways that deceive "those who have relied on their word." A wise leader should not even consider keeping his promises when doing so would not be in his own best interests. Why? "If men were entirely good this precept would not hold, but because they are bad, and will not keep faith with you, you too are not bound to observe it with them."

In other words, since the people are dishonest, their leader might as well be dishonest too. As evidence he referred to the number of treaties subsequently voided by leaders who changed their minds. He observed that a leader could always find plausible excuses to justify his duplicity.

Machiavelli went on to warn: "But it is necessary to know well how to disguise this characteristic, and to be a great pretender and dissembler; and men are so simple, and so subject to present necessities, that he who seeks to deceive will always find someone who will allow himself to be deceived."

Therefore, according to Machiavelli, it is not necessary for a leader to actually be good; he "must only give the impression to his people that he is merciful, faithful, humane, religious, upright," in such a way that provides the front for him to act in just the opposite way.

> Inasmuch as men judge generally more by the eye than by the hand, because it belongs to everybody to see you, to few to come in touch with you. Every one sees what you appear to be, few really know what you are, and those few dare not oppose themselves to the opinion of the many, who have the majesty of the state to defend them; and in the actions of all men, and especially of princes, which it is not prudent to challenge, one judges by the result.[38]

Then, Machiavelli adds, such a leader will be praised because the common people "are always taken by what a thing seems to be and by what becomes of it."

C. S. Lewis, who would never have endorsed Machiavelli's model of leadership, agreed with him concerning the nature of men: "Mankind is so fallen that no man can be trusted with unchecked power over his fellows. Aristotle said that some people were only fit to be slaves. I do not contradict him. But I reject slavery because I see no men fit to be masters."[39]

Are we really in danger of being controlled by such power-hungry leaders today? The evidence strongly suggests it. Perhaps you heard news reports about a speech by Donald Berwick, President Obama's nominee to head the Centers for Medicare and Medicaid Services. He said, "Any health care funding plan that is just, equitable, civilized and humane must, *must* redistribute wealth from the richer among us to the poorer and the less fortunate. Excellent health care is by definition redistributional."[40] As we learn from the story of Joseph in Egypt, government control of personal wealth is one of the major steps toward the consolidation of power over the people.

In addition to wealth redistribution, one of the favorite arenas of leaders with statist aspirations is the limitation of religious expression. The state determines which forms of religious expression are to be tolerated and which are to be prohibited. An example is the recent furor over a simple prayer of thanks offered before lunch at the Ed Young Senior Citizen Center in Port Wentworth, Georgia. Since the seniors' six-dollar meals were subsidized by federal money, the company operating the center declared that "saying a communal prayer...is a violation of federal regulations."[41] Such redefining of First Amendment rights is a powerful means of extending government influence and power.

Honest and upright leadership is possible. Joseph was true to his promise to provide for the Egyptians' needs and preserve their lives. Unlike a leader in the Machiavellian model, he had dealt with them in an honest and forthright manner, and they were willing to trust him, even to the point of becoming slaves. But such leaders are extremely rare, and I doubt that they ever occur except through dependency on God.

Virtually all leaders who consolidate power turn out to be tyrants, first gaining power by addressing crises and hiding their true intent behind a Machiavellian mask of deceit. Hitler was the poster boy for the Machiavellian philosophy of deceit to gain control.

Hitler had lowered wages; state governments and economies were consolidated under the totalitarian regime.... Virtually every area of German life was under the control of the Nazi regime, yet most citizens did not seem to care. Fed a steady dosage of propaganda by the press and entertained with massive rallies, parades, and "gifts" from "The Fuhrer," the German people swelled with pride at their nation's apparent comeback.[42]

Hitler and other tyrants give us a chilling warning of what can happen when a nation in crisis puts too much power in the hands of a single leader. It is a danger that stares us starkly in the face today. As Erwin Lutzer explains,

> We can learn from history that politicians often use an economic crisis to make their subjects more government dependent, and with that dependency comes more control...no government in history has had a great record in providing expanded benefits without eventually also expecting more control of its citizens.[43]

One of Aesop's fables tells of a shepherd who was alarmed by the sound of an approaching enemy. He urged the grazing animal to flee with him to avoid capture. The animal replied, "Is it likely the conqueror will place on me two sets of saddlebags?" "No," replied the shepherd. "Then why should I flee?" replied the donkey. "As long as I carry the saddlebags, what difference does it make to me whom I serve?" The moral to Aesop's story is that with a radical change in the governing system, the people often change nothing more than the name of their master.[44]

It appears more and more today that our "present necessities" are moving us in the direction of carelessly accepting a change in government, either willingly or by default, assuming that nothing will change radically. Yet both history and the nature of power show clearly how wrong this is. The consolidation of political and economic power will set the stage for the ultimate in evil governance, the reign of the Satan-empowered Antichrist. In the next two chapters we discover what will happen in the future when this one man—the personification of evil—gains control over the nations of the world.

CHAPTER 5

Satan's CEO

What exactly is a CEO? According to the dictionary, the acronym stands for *chief executive officer*.[1] It refers to the person in a company whose primary role is to make decisions and to carry the authority of leadership. The CEO has the highest management role in an organization and is ultimately responsible for the success and failure of it. The CEO sets the direction for implementing the vision of the firm and is usually its public voice.

I recently came across a list of the twenty best and twenty worst CEOs of all time. The best included familiar names such as Warren Buffett of Berkshire Hathaway, Sam Walton of Wal-Mart, and Bill Gates of Microsoft. Among the worst CEOs were infamous leaders such as Dick Fuld of Lehman Brothers and Jimmy Cayne of Bear Stearns—both major players in today's market collapse. Many of these CEOs have faced legal problems, including conviction, for activities similar to what the Antichrist will do during his seven-year reign of terror—lies, fraud, deceit, theft, abuse of power, duplicity, self-interest, self-aggrandizement, and so on.

As we are about to discover, the Antichrist is indeed the CEO of Satan's evil enterprise. As CEO, he carries out every wish of Satan and is empowered to do whatever Satan bids him to do. The Antichrist is described in 2 Thessalonians as "the man of sin" and "the son of perdition" (2:3). He is also identified with "the first beast" of Revelation 13, as "the little horn" of Daniel 7:8, and with offering the "abomination of desolation" of Matthew 24:15.

God gave to Daniel the prophet a revelation concerning the coming of the Antichrist at the end of days. The revelation was delivered in the form of a dream, and it was so important that God dispatched the angel Gabriel to interpret it. When Daniel finally understood the meaning of the dream, we are told that he "fainted and was sick for days" (Daniel 8:27). Gabriel's terrifying words were:

> And in the latter time of their kingdom, when the transgressors have reached their fullness, a king shall arise, having fierce features, who understands sinister schemes. His power shall be mighty, but not by his own power; he shall destroy fearfully, and shall prosper and thrive; he shall destroy the mighty, and also the holy people. Through his cunning he shall cause deceit to prosper under his rule; and he shall exalt himself in his heart. He shall destroy many in their prosperity. He shall even rise against the Prince of princes; but he shall be broken without human means. And the vision of the evenings and mornings which was told is true; therefore seal up the vision, for it refers to many days in the future. (Daniel 8:23–26)

Daniel's dream foretold the coming of the Antichrist. The word *antichrist* refers, of course, to one who is against Christ. But the prefix *anti*, which we know to mean "against," can also mean "instead of." In the Tribulation, the Antichrist will seek to be a substitute for Christ. Since Christ is the "Anointed One," or "the Messiah," the Antichrist will claim to be the Messiah...a pseudo-Christ, if you will. He will be both in opposition to Christ and in imitation of Him.

The English word *antichrist* is found in only four biblical verses. All four are from the writings of the apostle John (1 John 2:18, 22; 4:3; 2 John 7). When John writes of the Antichrist, he seems to be addressing the contemporary spirit of the Antichrist more than the actual evil person who will appear in the last days. Paul seems to be addressing the same principle when he writes, "For the mystery of lawlessness is already at work" (2 Thessalonians 2:7). According to

John and Paul, the spirit of the Antichrist is at work even before the person of the Antichrist is revealed.

There are more than twenty-five different titles given to the Antichrist, all of which help to paint a picture of the most despicable man ever to walk on the earth. Some people think he is Satan incarnate. We know for certain that Satan gives him his power, his throne, and his authority.

John Phillips describes the Antichrist in these graphic terms:

The Antichrist will be an attractive and charismatic figure, a genius, a demon-controlled, devil-taught charmer of men. He will have answers to the horrendous problems of mankind. He will be all things to all men: a political statesman, a social lion, a financial wizard, an intellectual giant, a religious deceiver, a masterful orator, a gifted organizer. He will be Satan's masterpiece of deception, the world's false messiah. With boundless enthusiasm the masses will follow him and readily enthrone him in their hearts as this world's savior and god.[2]

The Coming of the Antichrist

The Antichrist will make his debut in history at the beginning of the Tribulation (see Daniel 9:24–27). Some of the same words used to describe his appearing on the earth are also used to describe the appearing of the Lord Jesus. According to 2 Thessalonians 2:3, the Antichrist is going to be *revealed*. "Revealed" is translated from the Greek word *apokalupto*, which means "to make visible to the eye." That word is also used in reference to Jesus Christ's appearing in 2 Thessalonians 1:7, where we are told that "the Lord Jesus is *revealed* from heaven with His mighty angels" (emphasis added). Just as there will be a time when the Lord Jesus will be revealed, so there will be a time when the Antichrist will be revealed.

When the subject of the Antichrist is mentioned, people inevitably have a myriad of questions, such as: Who is he? Is he alive on the earth today? When will he be revealed?

In his second letter to the Thessalonians, Paul answers some of these questions. He provides a context for the coming of the Antichrist by listing certain things that must happen on earth before he can be revealed. Notice that I did not say before he will be *born*. There are no signs pointing to the birth of the Antichrist. For all we know he may already have been born. But before he can be revealed—before he can be identified as the Antichrist—certain events must take place. Let's look at those events one by one.

The Rapture of the Church

The Rapture of the church will precede the revelation of the Antichrist. The apostle Paul wrote a letter to the church in Thessalonica to straighten out certain misunderstandings the Thessalonians had about the future. First, since the believers in that city were going through some difficult experiences, Paul issues encouraging words of commendation. He applauds the Thessalonians for "patience and faith in all your persecutions and tribulations that you endure" (2 Thessalonians 1:4).

It is apparent that false teachers had planted the idea that the Thessalonians' current persecution was evidence that they were already living in the Tribulation. According to 2 Thessalonians 2:2, these believers thought this teaching was valid because it had come to them by one of three methods: by the Spirit, by the Word, or by a letter from Paul. So along with his word of commendation, the apostle now adds a word of correction. He denies that God is the source of any teaching that tells them they are experiencing the Tribulation judgment. He denies that God has sent to them any word to this effect orally. He also assures them that he has not written this spurious message to them in any letter.

106

Apparently a false teacher purporting to be Paul had sent a letter to the Thessalonian believers suggesting that in light of their present trials, either there was no such thing as the Rapture of the church or it had already occurred and they had been left behind. This totally contradicted everything Paul had taught them in his earlier letter. In that letter the apostle had written about the sudden character of Christ's coming and the importance of being prepared for it (see 1 Thessalonians 5:1–11).

It seems that the false teacher had changed "sudden coming" to "immediate coming," so Paul begins this second letter by reminding the Thessalonians about the Rapture and arguing that since that event had not yet occurred, there was no way they could be living in the Tribulation period. Paul's first sentence in chapter 2 confirms the coming Rapture: "Now, brethren, concerning the coming of our Lord Jesus Christ and our gathering together to Him" (2 Thessalonians 2:1). You will notice that Paul does not use the actual word *rapture*, but he leaves no doubt that this is what he intends to convey.

This verse gives us two separate phrases that refer to a combined event: "the coming of our Lord Jesus Christ" and "our gathering together to Him." The *New Living Translation* (second edition) is helpful in connecting the two parts: "Now, dear brothers and sisters, let us clarify some things about the coming of our Lord Jesus Christ and how we will be gathered to meet him." Eugene Peterson's *The Message* is even clearer: "Now, friends, read these next words carefully. Slow down and don't go jumping to conclusions regarding the day when our Master, Jesus Christ, will come back and we assemble to welcome him."

Thus Paul corrects the Thessalonian Christians with sound reasoning: since the Rapture has not occurred, they could not be living in the Tribulation.

From commendation and correction Paul now moves on to comfort. He urges his readers "not to be soon shaken in mind or troubled, either by spirit or by word or by letter" (2 Thessalonians

2:2). False teaching can cause people to be troubled and shaken in mind, and the letter from the false teacher had troubled the Thessalonians deeply. Paul assures them that they need not fear that they have missed the Rapture and are now suffering the judgment of the Tribulation. The Rapture must occur before the Tribulation begins, which tells us that the Rapture is a necessary prerequisite to the revealing of the Antichrist.

The Rejection of the Truth

In 2 Thessalonians 2:3, Paul assures us that the Antichrist will not be revealed until after the world sees a widespread rejection of God's truth: "Let no one deceive you by any means; for that Day will not come unless the falling away comes first."

The key to understanding this verse is found in Paul's use of "that Day." This is a shortened version of "the day of the Lord," which the apostle uses three times in his letters (see 1 Corinthians 5:5; 2 Corinthians 1:14; 1 Thessalonians 5:2). Dr. John F. Walvoord explains the "day of the Lord" in easy-to-understand language:

> It is the period of time predicted in the Scripture when God will deal directly with human sin. It includes the tribulation time preceding the second advent of Christ as well as the whole millennial reign of Christ. It will culminate in the judgment of the great white throne. The Day of the Lord is therefore an extended period of time lasting over one thousand years.... Our present day is a day of grace....The purpose of God in this day is to proclaim His grace, that souls may be saved by trusting in Christ and receiving God's gift of grace....The Scripture clearly presents the fact that the Day of the Lord is a day of divine judgment upon the world.[3]

According to Dr. Walvoord, "that day" includes the moment the Lord returns, the Rapture, the Tribulation, and Christ's thousand-year reign. As Paul tells the Thessalonian believers, "that day" will not come until there is first a "falling away." The Greek word for "falling away" is the word *apostasia*, which appears only one other time in the New Testament. There it is translated "forsake" (Acts 21:21). Paul is telling us that before the Tribulation comes, before the Antichrist can be revealed, there will be a falling away, a forsaking on the part of professing believers. Because the article "the" precedes "falling away," we are to understand that this is a specific apostasy. It is probable that some of the persecution and suffering of the Tribulation period will have begun to escalate in the days before the Rapture. When those who merely profess to be Christians experience this time of testing, they will "fall away" from the faith.

Spiritual apostasy is not an ignorance of truth; it is a departure from truth. It occurs when a person forsakes truths that he formerly believed. In other words, it is premeditated and deliberate.

In the Olivet Discourse, Jesus predicted such a time: "And then many will be offended, will betray one another, and will hate one another. Then many false prophets will rise up and deceive many. And because lawlessness will abound, the love of many will grow cold" (Matthew 24:10–12). Jesus' multiple use of the word *many* in this passage shows us clearly that this apostasy will be widespread.

Paul wrote about this coming apostasy in his second letter to Timothy: "For the time will come when they will not endure sound doctrine, but according to their own desires, because they have itching ears, they will heap up for themselves teachers; and they will turn their ears away from the truth, and be turned aside to fables" (2 Timothy 4:3–4).

Such an apostasy occurred before the first coming of Christ, instigated by the infamous Seleucid king Antiochus Epiphanes (175–164 BC). We will have more to say about Antiochus later in this chapter, but for now suffice it to say that he forced upon Israel idol worship and many departures from Jewish law. Many Jews simply went with the flow and fell into apostasy. This is recorded in the First Book of

Maccabees, a nonbiblical but historically important intertestamental book:

> At that time, lawless men arose in Israel and seduced many with their plea, "Come, let us make a covenant with the gentiles around us"...and underwent operations to disguise their circumcision, rebelling against the sacred covenant. They joined themselves to the gentiles and became willing slaves to evildoing....The King wrote to all his kingdom, for all to become one people and for each to abandon his own customs. All the gentiles agreed to the terms of the king's proclamation. Many Israelites, too, accepted his religion and sacrificed to idols and violated the Sabbath....The King wrote to all his kingdom, for all to become one people and for each to abandon his own customs. All the gentiles agreed to the terms of the king's proclamation....The king's officials *in charge of enforcing apostasy* came to the town of Modeïn to make them sacrifice. (1 Maccabees 1:11, 15, 41–43; 2:15, emphasis added)[4]

Just as these Jewish people fell away from their faith before the first coming of Christ, many "Christians" will fall away before His second coming. Paul alerts his young friend Timothy to a future "falling away" with a warning similar to that which he gave the Thessalonians: "Now the Spirit expressly says that in latter times some will depart from the faith" (1 Timothy 4:1).

The apostle Peter adds that many people will see the warnings of the Second Coming as alarmist scare tactics: "Scoffers will come in the last days, walking according to their own lusts, and saying, 'Where is the promise of His coming? For since the fathers fell asleep, all things continue as they were from the beginning of creation'" (2 Peter 3:3–4).

If we had no other prophetic sign than this one warning of a massive apostasy, it would likely be sufficient to persuade us that we are indeed approaching the Lord's return. In so much of organized religion today there is a growing resistance to biblical truth. Most of us are familiar with the faith compromises that many mainstream American churches have made in recent years. Though the following list is far from exhaustive, it identifies some of the most common deceptions that have crept into these churches:

- Denial of the revealed nature of the Triune God—Father, Son, Holy Spirit (including the use of "Parent" or "Father/Mother" in reference to deity)
- Denial of the deity of Jesus Christ
- Denial of the inspiration, inerrancy, and absolute authority of the Bible
- Denial of salvation by grace, through faith alone, based on the blood of Jesus Christ
- Denial of biblical creation, the historicity of Adam and Eve, and a historical Fall
- Denial of Jesus Christ as the only means of salvation
- Denial of the supernatural and historical miracles of Scripture
- Denial of Israel's status as God's chosen people through His covenant with Abraham
- Denial of the virgin birth, substitutionary death, and the bodily resurrection of Jesus
- Denial of Christ's return, His righteous judgment, and eternal rewards and punishment

I recently read of an astonishing example of apostasy in Marilyn Sewell's interview of Christopher Hitchens in the *Portland Monthly* magazine. Hitchens is a prolific journalist and renowned atheist who wrote the number one *New York Times* best-seller *God Is Not Great: How Religion Poisons Everything*. Needless to say, he is not a big fan of Christianity. Sewell, on the other hand, is a self-described liberal

Christian, who, before her retirement, grew Portland's First Unitarian Church into one of the largest congregations of that denomination in the United States.

In an introduction to one of her questions, Sewell states, "I am a liberal Christian, and I don't take the stories from the scripture literally. I don't believe in the doctrine of atonement (that Jesus died for our sins, for example)."

Hitchens's blunt response to Sewell is remarkable: "I would say that if you don't believe that Jesus of Nazareth was the Christ and Messiah, and that he rose again from the dead and by his sacrifice our sins are forgiven, you're really not in any meaningful sense a Christian."[5]

The atheist appears to have a better knowledge of Jesus Christ than the apostate Christian. I am not sure that I have read a more ironic example or a clearer definition of spiritual apostasy.

While we may not yet be experiencing the full-blown *apostasy* that Paul speaks of in 2 Thessalonians and 1 Timothy, we are surely on the leading edge of it. "Evil men and seducers shall wax worse and worse, deceiving, and being deceived" (2 Timothy 3:13 KJV). In my more than forty years as a pastor, there has never been a time when biblical truths, historical facts, and moral absolutes have been so increasingly up for grabs.

There are seven letters addressed to seven different churches that are recorded in the second and third chapters of Revelation. The seventh and last of those letters was written to the church of Laodicea. Most prophetic scholars believe this church represents the church that Jesus will find on earth when He returns. It will be a church of lukewarmness, complacency, and rejection of Christ. What does the Spirit of God have to say to the Laodicean church? Just this: "I know your works, that you are neither cold nor hot. I could wish you were cold or hot. So then, because you are lukewarm, and neither cold nor hot, I will vomit you out of My mouth. Because you say, 'I am rich, have become wealthy, and have need of nothing'—and do not

know that you are wretched, miserable, poor, blind, and naked..."
(Revelation 3:15–17).

John Phillips writes: "Some think we can look for a worldwide
spiritual awakening before the Rapture, but the passage in 2 Thessalonians indicates the opposite; a worldwide departure from the
faith can be expected. God might indeed send a revival before the
Rapture but the Scriptures do not prophesy one."[6]

This age will close in a great falling away. This is a prophetic
fact of Scripture that nothing can alter, for it is indelibly set in the
councils of God. The Antichrist cannot be revealed before either the
Rapture or the great apostasy occurs.

The Removal of the Holy Spirit

The Bible tells us that before the Antichrist can be revealed, the
Holy Spirit must be removed. "And now you know what is restraining, that he may be revealed in his own time. For the mystery of
lawlessness is already at work; only He who now restrains will do so
until He is taken out of the way" (2 Thessalonians 2:6–7).

"He who restrains" is a reference to the Holy Spirit. The Holy Spirit,
acting through the church, is currently engaged in a strong effort to
hold back evil and to delay the appearance of the Antichrist.

The Holy Spirit also exercises a distinctive work with respect to
the lost world. Jesus announced this work as He prepared His disciples for His own return to heaven and the subsequent coming of the
Holy Spirit: "Nevertheless I tell you the truth. It is to your advantage
that I go away; for if I do not go away, the Helper will not come to
you; but if I depart, I will send Him to you. And when He has come,
He will convict the world of sin, and of righteousness, and of judgment: of sin, because they do not believe in Me" (John 16:7–9).

Paul also teaches that a time is coming when the Holy Spirit will
be taken out of the way. Actually, this is more of a rescinding of
the Holy Spirit than a removal. When the Rapture occurs and every

believer is taken to heaven, the Holy Spirit, who indwells every believer, will by default "be taken out of the way."

After the Rapture, when the church and the Holy Spirit are removed, Satan will be released to dominate completely without any hindrance or restraint. While it is true that the "mystery of iniquity" is already at work in the earth (2 Thessalonians 2:7 KJV), it is being restrained or held back by the ministry of the Holy Spirit, the influence of believers, and the salt and light of the church. During the Tribulation, however, the restraint will have been removed and iniquity will go unchallenged.

Will the Holy Spirit be present during the Tribulation? Certainly! He may very well *fall upon* people as He did in the Old Testament instead of indwelling them as He does Christians. He will bring conviction from without, but not from within as He does now. John Phillips helps us to understand this more clearly:

> The church age is a parenthesis in God's dealing with the world. The church, injected supernaturally into history at Pentecost and supernaturally maintained throughout the age by the baptizing, indwelling, and filling works of the Holy Spirit, will be supernaturally removed when this age is over. What is to be removed then is the Holy Spirit's mighty working through the church. Until that happens, Satan cannot bring his plans to a head.... After the rapture of the church, the Holy Spirit will continue His work in bringing people to salvation, but He will no longer baptize them into the mystical body of Christ, the church, nor will He actively hinder Satan from bringing His schemes to fruition. Once Satan has achieved his centuries-long goal, Christ will return and demolish the whole thing![7]

After the Rapture of the church, after the rejection of the truth, after the removal of the Holy Spirit, then, and not until then, will the Antichrist, the man of sin, the son of perdition, be revealed (see 2 Thessalonians 2:3).

The Characteristics of the Antichrist

In my book *What in the World Is Going On?* I reminded readers that since no one could know the identity of the Antichrist until after the Rapture, if they thought they knew who he was, they must have been left behind. The Bible is silent about the identity of the Antichrist. We cannot now know *who* he is, but we can know *what* he is. Both the Old and the New Testaments contain more than one hundred passages that describe the Antichrist, which means that God obviously wants us to know something about this coming prince of darkness. Let's review some of his more prominent attributes.

He Will Be a Dynamic Leader

In Daniel 7:8 we are told that the Antichrist has "a mouth speaking pompous words." Not only pompous words, but "pompous words against the Most High" (Daniel 7:25). The NIV translates "pompous" as "boastful." John, writing in Revelation says, "And he was given a mouth speaking great things and blasphemies" (Revelation 13:5). John uses two Greek words, *megas* and *blasphemia*, neither of which needs explanation. The Antichrist knows the power of the spoken word!

As Satan's CEO, the Antichrist will also be his public voice. He will be able to sway crowds with his eloquence. He will, no doubt, be a superb television communicator. People will naturally want to follow him. Orators like Abraham Lincoln, Winston Churchill, John F. Kennedy, Martin Luther King Jr., and yes, even Adolf Hitler, were masters at captivating and moving large audiences. But even their best and most passionate speeches would be dull compared to the rhetoric of the Antichrist. One author has observed:

So it will be with this daring counterfeiter: he will have a mouth speaking very great things. He will have perfect command and flow of language. His oratory will not only gain attention, but command respect. Rev. 13:2 declares that his mouth is "as the mouth of a lion," which is a symbolic expression telling of the majesty and awe-producing effects of his voice. The voice of a lion excels that of any other beast, so the Antichrist will out-rival orators both ancient and modern.[8]

He Will Be a Defiant Leader

The Antichrist will be the most defiant, arrogant, proud, and self-impressed person who has ever walked on this earth. He will reject all traditional views of diety. "He shall exalt and magnify him-self above every god, shall speak blasphemies against the God of gods.... He shall regard neither the God of his fathers nor the desire of women, nor regard any god; for he shall exalt himself above them all" (Daniel 11:36–37). Paul describes him as: "the son of perdition, who opposes and exalts himself above all that is called God or that is worshiped, so that he sits as God in the temple of God, showing himself that he is God" (2 Thessalonians 2:3–4).

Satan will put his CEO on display in the temple of God, show-ing himself to be god. By this time, the Jews will have rebuilt the temple in Jerusalem. As a condition of his covenant with Israel, the Antichrist will allow the Jewish sacrificial system to be restored. But once the Jews have served his purpose, he will push them aside. He will surround Jerusalem with his troops and seize their temple. And then, as one last mockery of God, Satan will install his man of sin as god in the temple.

The Antichrist will also place his debased image in the temple, bringing ultimate fulfillment to Daniel's prophecy of the abomina-tion of desolation: " 'So when you see the "abomination of desola-tion," spoken of by Daniel the prophet, standing where it ought not' (let the reader understand), 'then let those who are in Judea flee to the mountains' " (Mark 13:14).

When the Antichrist sits in the temple as god, "all who dwell on the earth will worship him, whose names have not been written in the Book of Life of the Lamb slain from the foundation of the world" (Revelation 13:8).

He Will Be a Deceitful Leader

"The coming of the lawless one is according to the working of Satan, with all power, signs, and lying wonders" (2 Thessalonians 2:9).

Power, signs, and *wonders* are all words that describe the genuine miracles of Christ. However, those same three words in this passage are modified to describe the false miracles of the Antichrist—"power, signs, and lying wonders." The difference is that the word *lying* discredits the Antichrist's so-called miracles. Satan will empower him to perform certain signs and lying wonders, and the whole world will marvel and say, "Who is like the beast?" (Revelation 13:4).

The Antichrist will deceive many into believing his lie. Those who have heard the gospel and rejected it will be sent a deception so strong that they will not be able to believe the truth even if they want to. As Paul explains it, the work of Satan through the Antichrist will bring about "all unrighteous deception among those who perish, because they did not receive the love of the truth, that they might be saved. And for this reason God will send them strong delusion, that they should believe the lie, that they all may be condemned who did not believe the truth but had pleasure in unrighteousness" (2 Thessalonians 2:10–12).

I am often asked whether I believe there will be a chance for people to be saved after the Rapture. The answer, of course, is yes. Many will be saved during the Tribulation period. Some believe a revival will occur during the Tribulation that will be like a second Pentecost. But usually, when I answer in this way, I discover that I have missed the point of the question. What the questioner really wants to know is, "Will those who have heard and rejected the gospel in today's age of grace be given a second chance during the Tribulation period?" John Phillips gives us the answer:

> Millions of people will be saved and swept into the kingdom after the Rapture (Rev. 7), but those who have heard and rejected the gospel in this age will be excluded from their number. All such will believe the lie and be damned....A threefold repudiation of truth is expressed in the solemn verses just quoted. The *heart* is involved because it is said that the unrighteous "received not the love of the truth"; the *mind* is involved because they believed not the truth; and the *will* is involved because they "had pleasure in unrighteousness." Paul was describing not a casual, accidental missing of the way, but a deliberate rejection of the truth as it is in Christ Jesus. At the Rapture, all those who have thus slighted the gospel of God's grace will be handed over to Satan. Since they would not have the truth, let them have the lie. They spurned His Holy Spirit, so let them become a prey to evil spirits. They wanted no part in Christ, so let them have their part in Antichrist. Could anything be more just or more terrible?[9]

A question as important as this one deserves an appeal to another scholar. John F. Walvoord, with some moderating insights, agrees in principle with John Phillips:

> Some understand from [2 Thessalonians, chapter 2] verse 11 that if a person in this present age of grace hears the gospel and does not receive Christ as Savior, then when Christ comes and takes His church home to glory these will find it impossible to be saved after the church is translated. It is unlikely that a person who rejects Christ in this day of grace will turn to Him in that awful period of tribulation. But the usual principle of Scripture is that while there is life there is hope. It is

possible, though very improbable, that a person who has heard the gospel in this present age of grace will come to Christ after the rapture. The Scriptures definitely teach that God will send strong delusion to those who do not believe after the church is gone. God will judge their hearts, and if they deliberately turn away from the truth He will permit them to believe a lie. They will honor the man of sin as their god and as their king, instead of acknowledging the Lord Jesus Christ. The result will be "That they all might be damned who believed not the truth, but had pleasure in unrighteousness" (v. 12).[10]

As we can see, the deceptive power of the Antichrist will be pervasive and possibly spiritually fatal to those who fall under his spell for lack of a real and solid commitment to Jesus Christ.

He Will Be a Diabolical Leader

In the early stages of his career, the Antichrist will be admired and loved. But as soon as he has gained the confidence of the people and total control of the world, he will spring his trap and initiate his murderous deeds. The Bible says he will persecute the saints (see Daniel 7:21–25), kill the two witnesses (see Revelation 11:7), and be used to lead all the nations against Jerusalem (see Zechariah 14:1–3). His heart will be filled with a murderous hatred for the Jewish people and the believing Gentiles.

The Antichrist will ultimately be revealed for who he is when he breaks the covenant with Israel that we mentioned above. After the long history of conflict in the Middle East many will see this covenant as a welcome step toward real security in a world overwhelmingly hostile to Israel. For the people of Israel, this treaty will seem long overdue. With the passage of the U.N. Security Council resolution condemning Israel's defense of its land and its people against more than 12,000 rocket attacks from Gaza came the realization that "out of 192 countries in the world today, Israel has only eighteen true friends," and even that is a shaky number.[11]

Since its rebirth, Israel's very existence has generated the hostility of many nations, primarily in the Arab world. This final CEO of the revived Roman Empire will say to the leaders of Israel, "We are now in control, and we would like to take you under our wing and defend you from your Arab neighbors who want to destroy you. If you will sign this covenant with us for seven years, we will promise peace, and we will allow you to continue to practice your religion in your new temple, and all will be well."

Israel, fatigued by its decades of continual conflict and vigilance, will sign the covenant with the Antichrist. Immediately the Jews will turn their attention and their economy away from defense and concentrate on building the financial wealth of their nation.

"But in the middle of the week [after three and one-half years] he shall bring an end to sacrifice and offering. And on the wing of abominations shall be one who makes desolate, even until the consummation, which is determined, is poured out on the desolate" (Daniel 9:27).

Suddenly the Antichrist will turn on the unsuspecting and now unprepared Jews. He will shut down their worship, and defy and humiliate them by desecrating the holy temple.

He Will Be a Dramatic Leader

The book of Revelation records a prophecy that demonstrates the lengths to which Satan will be allowed to go in his final attempt to seduce the world. Speaking of the Antichrist, John writes: "And I saw one of his heads as if it had been mortally wounded, and his deadly wound was healed. And all the world marveled and followed the beast" (Revelation 13:3).

As we have noted above, Satan's strategy is to imitate God. As these passages show, that imitation will apparently even go so far as to imitate the Resurrection. It is not hard to imagine that when the Antichrist's apparent death stroke is healed, the entire world will be so astounded that they will willingly follow him.

Several years ago, my friend Carole Carlson and I wrote a book titled *Escape the Coming Night*. We created the following dramatic description of what we thought this "resurrection" of the Antichrist might be like and how people would respond to it in the Tribulation world. Please note that our naming of the Antichrist was not an actual attempt to identify him. We named him simply to provide realism to the drama.

The world will go into shock. Men and women will freeze in unbelief as the global media shout the incredible news.

"Headlines: President Shot

"Assassin Kills Judas Christopher

"U.S. of Europe Mourns Loss of Leader

"Christopher was pronounced dead on arrival at the International Hospital of Rome this morning. The motorcade of U.S.E. officials was traveling along Via Veneto when the president was hit in the temple by a single bullet. He slumped in his seat in full view of his cabinet officials and millions watching on interglobal satellite.

"Christopher has been hailed by leaders of every country as the greatest figure in history. He was widely acclaimed as the most brilliant politician of the Second Millennium.

"The loss in world leadership cannot be measured. No other man has done more to solve the problems of the world and to unify the nations."

For three days, there will be no other story in the news. The countries of the world will be in chaos, wondering how they can find another man to guide them through these perilous times.

As his body lies in state in the Capitol Rotunda of the United States of Europe, the television networks will preempt every program to cover this one event. Surrounding the coffin will be governors of the European states. The president, and all members of Congress from the United States of America, and the leading officials of every other country. Most of them will stand frozen with grief, and many will be openly weeping.

Suddenly, the body of Judas Christopher stirs. He sits up. Slowly, he rises from his casket and walks to the nearest microphone. A gasp of disbelief is heard in the room. And then, he speaks, his resonant voice reassuring everyone that he has truly been resurrected.

"Do not fear, my friends. I am alive. Look at me. Three days ago, I had a bullet in my head. As you can see, I am completely whole. My greatest wish now is to continue with the unification of the nations and religions to bring together people of all colors and faith into peaceful coexistence. I shall have one world based upon love and mutual respect."

And the headlines will scream:

"He is alive!

"A stunned world watches as Christopher is resurrected!

"Pledges to work for world peace"[12]

Up until this moment in his career, the Antichrist will have ruled the world politically. But from this moment on, he will demand to be worshiped. And, as John tells us, this demand will be met: "And all the world marveled and followed the beast. So they worshiped the dragon who gave authority to the beast; and they worshiped the beast, saying, 'Who is like the beast? Who is able to make war with him?'" (Revelation 13:3–4).

He Will Be a Demanding Leader

During the Tribulation period, there will be many who are saved through the testimony of God's two witnesses and the 144,000 Jewish preachers. All will be subjected to the vile Tribulation regulations instituted by the evil trinity—Satan, the Antichrist, and the False Prophet, who "causes all, both small and great, rich and poor, free and slave, to receive a mark on their right hand or on their foreheads, and that no one may buy or sell except one who has the mark or the name of the beast, or the number of his name" (Revelation 13:16–17).

Mark Hitchcock writes:

> Only by worshiping the Antichrist will people be able to receive the mark that allows them to buy and sell anything. He will exercise iron-fisted control over the basic fundamentals of supply (no one will be able to sell) and demand (no one will be able to buy). No one will be able to go to the mall, eat at a restaurant, fill a gas tank, pay a utility bill, buy groceries, pay to get the lawn mowed, or make a mortgage payment without the mark of the beast—the Tribulation trademark.[13]

The Antichrist will rule ruthlessly, tyrannically, and with an iron hand.

He Will Be a Defeated Leader

No power will be able to stop the Antichrist until the Lord returns with His saints at the end of the Tribulation period. Then we are told that the Lord will destroy him with the breath of His mouth. "And then the lawless one will be revealed, whom the Lord will consume with the breath of His mouth and destroy with the brightness of His coming" (2 Thessalonians 2:8). "He shall strike the earth with the rod of His mouth, and with the breath of His lips He shall slay the wicked" (Isaiah 11:4).

The same Lord who breathed this world into existence will breathe the Antichrist into extinction. That may have been what Martin Luther had in mind in one verse of his great hymn "A Mighty Fortress Is Our God." In the third verse he wrote,

The Prince of Darkness grim,
we tremble not for him;
his rage we can endure,
for lo, his doom is sure;
one little word shall fell him.

That's all it will take: one little word! When Christ comes in His glory, this man who seems so powerful will be rendered as powerless as a flickering candle flame that can be extinguished by a little puff of breath.

When we are told that the Antichrist will be destroyed, that does not mean that he will be annihilated. He will continue to exist throughout eternity, but he will be defeated and rendered inoperative. His power and his purposes will be destroyed. As Daniel puts it, "He shall be broken without human means" (Daniel 8:25).

He Will Be a Doomed Leader

The prophet Daniel describes the final doom of the Antichrist: "I watched till the beast was slain, and its body destroyed and given to the burning flame" (Daniel 7:11).

John's description parallels that of Daniel: "Then the beast was captured, and with him the false prophet who worked signs in his presence, by which he deceived those who received the mark of the beast and those who worshiped his image. These two were cast alive into the lake of fire burning with brimstone" (Revelation 19:20).

Not only do these passages paint a clear picture of the doom of the Antichrist and the False Prophet, they add the interesting fact that these two henchmen of Satan arrive in hell long before he does. If we fast-forward one thousand years to the end of the Millennium, we read: "The devil, who deceived them, was cast into the lake of fire and brimstone where the beast and the false prophet are. And they will be tormented day and night forever and ever" (Revelation 20:10). The Beast and the False Prophet will have been in hell for a thousand years before Satan joins them at the end of the Millennium.

A Graphic Glimpse of the Antichrist's Reign

In the first thirty-five verses of Daniel 11, Daniel prophesies the future of a king whose rule was yet two to four hundred years in the future. The exact detail with which this prophecy was fulfilled has caused many liberal scholars to argue that the book of Daniel was written after these events transpired—that this chapter is a writing of history and not prophecy. There is not a shred of evidence for this explanation. In all the years it has been promoted, no one has been able to disprove the miracle of Daniel's prophetic words.

The king to which Daniel's prophecy refers is the Syrian ruler Antiochus IV, an Old Testament type of the Antichrist. Antiochus was a Syrian king who ruled Palestine, including Judea, from 175 to 165 BC. In his ascendancy to power, Antiochus had such an inflated view of himself that he adopted the title *Theos Epiphanes*, which means "manifest god." In other words, he claimed to be a god. But his apparent insanity led his enemies to twist *Epiphanes* into *Epimanes*, meaning "madman" or "insane one." Antiochus, the manifest god, became Antiochus, the madman.

Something of Antiochus's madness is revealed in his vicious attack against the Jewish people. In 168 BC, Antiochus had failed to accomplish a military mission in Egypt and was fuming with anger and disappointment as he returned to Syria. It was necessary for him to pass through Israel, and he decided to vent his frustration on the Jewish people. Daniel prophetically tells of his frustrated mission and his mistreatment of the Jews: "At the appointed time he shall return and go toward the south; but it shall not be like the former or the latter. For ships from Cyprus shall come against him; therefore he shall be grieved, and return in rage against the holy covenant, and do damage. So he shall return and show regard for those who forsake the holy covenant" (Daniel 11:29–30).

What Antiochus did next had never before occurred. As Jewish historian Solomon Zeitlin says, Antiochus became "the first person in history to persecute a people exclusively for their religious faith. Religious persecution was previously unknown in the history of civilization."[14]

As Antiochus and his enraged followers entered the city of Jerusalem, some forty thousand Jews were slaughtered, young and old, men, women, and children. Another forty thousand were taken captive and sold into slavery. Then followed a religious persecution of monstrous proportions. The first book of Maccabees tells the story:

> The king sent letters by messengers to Jerusalem and the towns of Judah containing orders to follow customs foreign to the land, to put a stop to burnt offerings and meal offerings and libations in the temple, to violate Sabbaths and festivals, to defile temple and holy things, to build illicit altars and illicit temples and idolatrous shrines, to sacrifice swine and ritually unfit animals, to leave their sons uncircumcised, and to draw abomination upon themselves by means of all kinds of uncleanness and profanation. Whoever disobeyed the word of the king was put to death.... On the fifteenth day of Kislev in the year 145 the king had an abomination of desolation built upon the altar, and in the outlying towns of Judah they built illicit altars.... Whatever scrolls of the Torah they found, they tore up and burned; and whoever was found with a scroll of the Covenant in his

possession or showed his love for the Torah, the king's decree put him to death. Through their strength they acted against the Israelites who were found in the towns each month, as on the twenty-fifth day of the month they would offer sacrifices on the altar which was upon the temple altar. The women who had their sons circumcised they put to death according to the decree, hanging the babes from their mother's necks and executing also their husbands and the men who had performed the circumcisions. Many Israelites strongly and steadfastly refused to eat forbidden food. They chose death in order to escape defilement by foods and in order to keep from violating the Holy Covenant, and they were put to death. (1 Maccabees 1:44–50, 54, 56–63)[15]

Antiochus not only forbade the Jews to follow their religious customs and worship their God, he demanded that they worship the Greek god Zeus. He forced them to build altars to Zeus and to offer swine upon them. Josephus writes: "He also compelled them to forsake the worship which they paid their own God, and to adore those whom he took to be gods, and made them build temples and raise idol altars, in every city and village and offer swine upon them every day."[16]

In the eyes of the Jews, the most abominable act of Antiochus was his deliberately blasphemous desecration of their holy temple. Josephus describes the outrage: "And when the king had built an idol altar upon God's altar, he slew swine upon it, and so offered a sacrifice neither according to the law, nor the Jewish religious worship in that country."[17]

This unholy sacrifice of an unclean animal on the sacred temple altar is the "abomination of desolation" prophesied first by Daniel and later by Jesus (Daniel 11:31; 12:11; Mark 13:14). That sacrifice was the initial fulfillment of the Daniel prophecy, which is a type of the ultimate fulfillment to which Jesus points. This final fulfillment will occur when the Antichrist breaks his covenant with Israel, enthrones himself in the temple, erects a profane image in the temple, and quite likely desecrates the temple altar with an unclean sacrifice.

Through Antiochus Epiphanes and his campaign against the Jews, God gives us a graphic and prophetic glimpse of the coming reign of the Antichrist. It will be a time of terrible persecution for the people who turn to God in the period of the Tribulation. The terror of Antiochus provides additional motivation to us as believers today. As we see in the news and in our culture signs and shadows of coming events clearly predicted in prophecy to signal the approach of the end times, graphic pictures such as those of Antiochus's reign can spur us to even greater diligence to live a life of commitment and evangelism as we see the time approaching when these prophetic events will become a present reality.

The Bright Light of Hope

I have given you the dark side of the story of Antiochus and the Jews, but that story did not end in darkness. I want to complete this chapter by giving you the rest of that story.

Jewish resistance to Antiochus's brutal reign began in the village of Modëin, located between Jerusalem and Joppa, the home of an aged priest named Mattathias. When the commissioner of Antiochus commanded Mattathias to take the lead in offering a pagan sacrifice, Mattathias killed the commissioner, overturned the altar, and fled with his sons to the hills. They became known as the *Maccabees*, a term believed to come from the Aramaic word that means "the hammer," a symbol of the ferocity of Mattathias's sons. Many other Jews joined the Maccabees and engaged in guerrilla warfare against Antiochus.

Out of this dark time in the history of God's people, the bright light of hope was kindled and still shines brightly today. Through the faith and courage of the Maccabean warriors, the temple was finally recaptured and cleansed. The Jews established Hanukkah, a perpetual feast to commemorate the cleansing and deliverance of the temple from the abomination of desolation. The word *Hanukkah* means "dedication." The celebration is sometimes referred to as the Feast of Dedication or the Festival of Lights. Jesus celebrated this feast in Jerusalem (see John 10:22–23).

When the temple was recaptured, the Maccabees wanted to light the menorah. They looked everywhere for the special oil required for use in the temple menorah and found a small flask that contained only enough to light the menorah for one day. According to tradition, miraculously, the oil lasted for eight days. That gave them enough time to obtain new supplies of the purified oil to keep the menorah lit.

Today the Jews celebrate Hanukkah beginning on the twenty-fifth day of Kislev (November–December on our calendar) by placing the menorah in a window or doorway where it will be visible from the outside. Each day during the eight-day celebration, in late afternoon, one candle is lit, with another being lit on each successive night until the eighth night when all eight candles are lit.[18]

From the darkest days of suffering and persecution to the celebration of the Festival of Lights! Only God writes such a story! In spite of the horrors coming in the period of the Tribulation, God will never forsake those who turn to Him.

CHAPTER 6

"The Mark of the Beast"

If you happened to access the search engine Google on October 7, 2009, you may have noticed that the usual Google logo had been replaced with a *Google doodle*—a simple bar code. If you rolled your mouse over the doodle, you would have seen the caption "Invention of the Bar Code."

That doodle marked the fifty-seventh anniversary of the first patent granted for what is now the ubiquitous Universal Product Code (UPC). The patent was granted to two American graduate students, and the first use of the scanning technology occurred at the checkout of the Marsh Supermarket in Troy, Ohio, in 1974. Today that code is found on virtually every commercial product, from newspapers to pet food.

In 1974 we bar-coded products; today we bar-code people. In his best-selling book *Shadow Government*, prophecy scholar Grant Jeffrey writes:

> Many military intelligence agencies, government agencies, and large corporations have introduced sophisticated security systems requiring employees to wear a badge containing a radio frequency identification microchip. This RFID chip enables companies, agencies, and organizations to monitor the location and activity of every worker during every moment that he or she is on the premises. When an employee enters the office, a computer records the exact time and begins monitoring his or her every move throughout the day. Security sensors at strategic

locations throughout the office complex record the location and the duration of the activities of the badge wearer.[1]

RFID scanners can be imbedded in the ceilings, floors, and doorways of buildings in order to monitor the movements of people inside. RFID chips can also be sewn into the seams of clothing so the wearer doesn't even know he is being subjected to monitoring. Since 2006, RFID tags have become standard in every new U.S. Passport and many credit cards. If you never leave home without your American Express Blue card, you are carrying an RFID tag in your billfold this very minute. Soon, anywhere you go, you will be tracked.

Many of us are familiar with external electronic badge systems and even the RFID chips in credit cards. But a less familiar new technology is now making it feasible for RFID microchips to be painlessly implanted beneath the skin. The chip consists of miniature integrated circuitry that holds and processes information, as well as an antenna that can receive or transmit a signal.

Kevin Warwick, a professor of cybernetics at England's University of Reading, claims to be the first person in the world to be voluntarily implanted with a chip. Warwick experimented on himself by implanting a sophisticated computer chip that enabled him to transmit signals to the university's communication system. The implanted device was three millimeters wide and twenty-three millimeters long, and it emitted unique signals you could hear only if you had transmitters working in what they call an "intelligent building."[2]

Some of my indelible memories of 9/11 are the pictures of New York City policemen and firemen who died trying to save victims of that terrorist attack. Many of these men wrote their badge numbers on their bodies to assure their own identification should they become victims. After reading of that practice, an enterprising American company saw the need for positive identification in such emergencies and went to work on what is now called the VeriChip. In 2004 the FDA approved this rice grain–sized microchip for implantation under the skin of humans to provide personal information in emergency situations.[3]

Before we go further, let me point out that an RFID or VeriChip is neither good nor evil. It is just a collection of silicone and data bits and has no moral persuasion of its own. Like money, guns, or a thousand other amoral tools, these chips are wholly dependent on the ethics, purposes, and priorities of those who use them. The chips will perform just as effectively to track a lost Alzheimer's patient as to monitor an individual for the purpose of blackmail.

Why am I spending so much time telling you about these new technologies? Because their possible uses have frightening implications. If the trends of our government continue at their current pace, it will not take long for the privacy of Americans to be added to the memories of the good old days.

More to the point, these technologies are of special concern to students of biblical prophecy. They show us that technological systems are now available to fulfill a prediction made nineteen hundred years ago. "He [the False Prophet] causes all, both small and great, rich and poor, free and slave, to receive a mark on their right hand or on their foreheads, and that no one may buy or sell except one who has the mark or the name of the beast, or the number of his name" (Revelation 13:16–17). It's easy to see how the Antichrist could use these monitoring chips as a means of applying this mark and controlling the population.

"But," you may ask, "what does this have to do with me? I'm a Christian. If these events take place during the Tribulation period, and I have already been raptured to heaven, why should I be concerned about something that happens on earth after I'm gone?"

The answer is that these events may involve you more than you think. Please don't misunderstand; I'm not suggesting that the Rapture may leave you behind. But I have found that many misunderstand the biblical end-time sequence of events. Scripture shows that the events described in Revelation 13 take place at the midpoint of the seven-year Tribulation period. The Rapture of the church will signal the beginning of the Tribulation. If you believe, as I do, that the Rapture could take place at any time, then we could easily be within three to four years of the events we are discussing in this chapter.

Future events cast their shadows before them. The events of the Tribulation will not just suddenly begin happening the day after the Rapture; they will be building momentum during the days before it. Events occurring right now show that our world is being prepared for the reign of the Antichrist and the mark of the Beast. Today's grim headlines allow us to understand prophecy as never before.

Even those who have never read the Bible are usually familiar with the term *mark of the Beast*. It has been popularized through movies like the 1976 release *The Omen*. I have been told that in the 2006 remake of *The Omen*, the mark of the Beast, represented by the number 666, was a prominent motif throughout the movie. The wallpaper pattern in the bedroom of the devil-child Damien was a floral vine swirled to form a wall of sixes. It was the child's 666 birthmark that identified him as the Antichrist. The movie's marketers pointedly released the film on 06/06/06. This secular film may not present a correct application of biblical events, but it demonstrates that almost everyone has some knowledge of a sinister mark that will come into play in the end times.

Later in this chapter I will explain more fully the connection between RFID technology and the mark of the Beast. But first I must give you some background that will reveal the full implications of the mark, as well as how it relates to the subject of this book—the coming disintegration of the world economy.

Satan Originates the Mark

In the first few words of Revelation 13 we discover that the mark of the Beast and its applications are not, as many people believe, originated by the Antichrist. After describing the coming of the Antichrist as a beast "rising up out of the sea" (v. 1), John writes this: "The dragon [Satan] gave him his power, his throne, and great authority" (v. 2). Satan is the originator of all the Tribulation evil, and the Antichrist, along with his False Prophet, are the conduits of his power. The key to this fact is found in the word *given* or *granted*. The evil power of the Antichrist and the False Prophet is *given* to them by Satan. Several verses in Revelation 13 reveal Satan's role as the source of the activity of the Antichrist and the False Prophet:

- "He was given a mouth . . . he was given authority" (v. 5).
- "It was granted to him . . . and authority was given him" (v. 7).
- "He was granted to do . . ." (v. 14).
- "He was granted power" (v. 15).

Why did Satan devise the mark of the Beast? What is its ultimate purpose? To answer those questions thoroughly, we must go back to when Satan is introduced into this earthly scene in the twelfth chapter of Revelation:

And war broke out in heaven: Michael and his angels fought with the dragon; and the dragon and his angels fought, but they did not prevail, nor was a place found for them in heaven any longer. So the great dragon was cast out, that serpent of old, called the Devil and Satan, who deceives the whole world; he was cast to the earth, and his angels were cast out with him. (Revelation 12:7–9)

Why was Satan cast out of heaven? Isaiah the prophet explains, unmasking Satan's shocking motivation using his own words:

How you are fallen from heaven,
O Lucifer, son of the morning!

How you are cut down to the ground,
you who weakened the nations!
For you have said in your heart:
"I will ascend into heaven,
I will exalt my throne above the stars of God;
I will also sit on the mount of the congregation
On the farthest sides of the north;
I will ascend above the heights of the clouds,
I will be like the Most High." (Isaiah 14:12–14, emphasis added)

As you can see by this passage, Satan has an "I" problem. Five times he uses the first person singular pronoun. Each time he makes a more audacious claim, until finally he lays out his primary goal: "I will be like the Most High." Satan is driven by a compulsion to rival the Most High God and receive the worship that belongs to God alone.

Satan's bloated pride continued to swell to the point that he even wanted God to worship him. When Satan tempted Jesus in the wilderness, we read, "the devil took Him up on an exceedingly high mountain, and showed Him all the kingdoms of the world and their glory. And he said to Him, 'All these things I will give You if You will fall down and worship me'" (Matthew 4:8–9). The devil's audacious egotism seems to have no limit.

Satan has come to realize, however, that few if any are going to voluntarily worship him. Therefore, he resorts to both deceit and compulsion. In terms of deceit, his strategy has always been to make himself appear as God, and Satan is the world's most cunning counterfeiter. He cannot defeat God, and he cannot be God, so he has devised ways to duplicate certain attributes of God. For example, he "transforms himself into an angel of light" (2 Corinthians 11:14). In Revelation 13 we read that he will actually set up his own trinity to mirror the Holy Trinity of Almighty God. Just as God has revealed Himself as one God in three persons—God the Father, God the Son, and God the Holy Spirit—so Satan has chosen to reveal himself as the three entities of the unholy trinity: Satan, the Antichrist, and the False Prophet.

When Jesus walked upon this earth, He consistently asserted that His power came solely from the Father. "For I have not spoken on My own authority; but the Father who sent Me gave Me a command, what I should say and what I should speak. And I know that His command is everlasting life. Therefore, whatever I speak, just as the Father has told Me, so I speak" (John 12:49–50). John's Gospel makes it abundantly clear that Jesus lived His earthly life in total submission to the Father (see John 4:34; 5:19, 30; 6:38; 8:28, 42; 12:49; 14:10).

In a perversely similar way, when the Antichrist walks upon the earth he will be filled with the power and authority of Satan. According to the apostle John, both Satan (the Dragon) and the Beast (the Antichrist) will receive worship: "So they worshiped the dragon who gave authority to the beast; and they worshiped the beast, saying, 'Who is like the beast? Who is able to make war with him?'" (Revelation 13:4). When Satan gains his power over the people of the world, he will demand to be worshiped in each of his three manifestations. And as we will see, he will compel compliance to his demand through the technology of the mark of the Beast.

To summarize, the mark of the Beast is Satan's brainchild. But the mark will be applied and administered by two of Satan's embodied manifestations, the Antichrist and the False Prophet, to whom he gives power and authority. Let's examine these two satanic beings to see how they fit into the overall picture.

The Antichrist Orders the Mark

We have established that Satan originates the mark of the Beast, but it is the Antichrist who orders that the mark be applied. In John's vision, the Antichrist is presented as a beast rising from the sea:

Then I stood on the sand of the sea. And I saw a beast rising up out of the sea, having seven heads and ten horns, and on his horns ten crowns, and on his heads a blasphemous name. Now the beast which I saw was like a leopard, his feet were like the feet of a bear, and his mouth like the mouth of a lion.... And I saw one of his heads as if it had been mortally wounded, and his deadly wound was healed. And all the world marveled and followed the beast. (Revelation 13:1–3)

John graphically describes the Beast as a grotesque composite of the same four animals that Daniel saw in his prophecy (see Daniel 7). In that prophecy, the four beasts represented four kingdoms that would arise consecutively: Babylon, Medo-Persia, Greece, and finally, Rome. The Beast of John's vision has seven heads and ten horns, and on each head is a blasphemous name. Some believe this beast represents the revival of the Roman Empire. Of that we cannot be sure, but it certainly portrays the ruler of that revived empire, the Antichrist himself.

John tells us that the body of the Beast is like a leopard. Some Bible scholars have noted that the leopard is the one beast with colors representing the three major races of mankind. Its coat is brown like an Asiatic; its stomach is white like the European or Caucasian; and its spots are black, the color of African peoples. Just as the leopard is a multinational, multiracial representation, the Antichrist will be an international figure. He will bring all peoples of the world together under his dynamic leadership.

That is, he will bring together all people except one group—Christians. The Antichrist will make war with those who turn to Christ during the Tribulation, but all others on earth will worship Him. As John explains, "It was granted to him to make war with the saints and to overcome them. And authority was given him over every tribe, tongue, and nation. All who dwell on the earth will worship him, whose names have not been written in the Book of Life of the Lamb slain from the foundation of the world" (Revelation 13:7–8).

How appalling it is to realize that the final form of evil will be a world in which people no longer worship the God of heaven but the Satan of hell! In our lifetime the raw evil of Satan has been truly manifested in only a few horrific instances. This is because the restraining work of the Holy Spirit puts limits on his power. But during the Tribulation, the Holy Spirit will be "taken out of the way" (2 Thessalonians 2:7). Satan will be unleashed, and the world will be exposed to the full force of evil through Satan's empowering of the Antichrist and the False Prophet. It will be a time of utter horror, almost too dreadful to imagine.

The False Prophet Orchestrates the Mark

Now we turn to Satan's other end-time manifestation on the earth: the False Prophet. We have shown that Satan is the originator of the mark of the Beast and that his puppet the Antichrist will put the mark in place. The third member of this counterfeit trinity, the False Prophet, will actually orchestrate the entire system.

The Description of the False Prophet (Revelation 13:11–12)

Here is how the apostle John introduces the False Prophet: "Then I saw another beast coming up out of the earth, and he had two horns like a lamb and he spoke like a dragon. And he exercises all the authority of the first beast in his presence, and causes the earth and those who dwell in it to worship the first beast, whose deadly wound was healed" (Revelation 13:11–12).

Whereas John describes the Antichrist as a beast rising from the sea, he sees the False Prophet as a beast coming up out of the earth—a creature that looks like a lamb but has the voice of a dragon.

In other words, the False Prophet appears to be a gentle, benevolent being, but his voice—the content and meaning of what he says—is anything but benign. The False Prophet, as the term implies, will be a religious figure, but his religion will be demonic. He is actually a Satan-possessed man who exercises authority and power in the name of the Antichrist and who causes the whole world to bow down and worship the Antichrist and his image.

Bible expositor John Phillips describes the False Prophet's deceptive strategy:

> The role of the false prophet will be to make the new religion appealing and palatable to men.... His arguments will be subtle, convincing, and appealing. His oratory will be hypnotic, for he will be able to move the masses to tears or whip them into a frenzy. He will control the communication media of the world and will skillfully organize mass publicity to promote his ends. He will be the master of every promotional device and public relations gimmick. He will manage the truth with guile beyond words, bending it, twisting it, and distorting it.... His deadly appeal will lie in the fact that what he says will sound so right, so sensible, so exactly what unregenerate men have always wanted to hear.[4]

The False Prophet of Revelation 13 is the epitome of every false prophet who has ever gone before him. Jesus warned His followers of such deceivers: "Beware of false prophets, who come to you in sheep's clothing, but inwardly they are ravenous wolves" (Matthew 7:15).

When Satan controls the world's population through the Antichrist; when everyone is forced to accept the mark of the Beast on the forehead or hand; when all who take the mark bow down and worship Satan and the Antichrist; it will be the False Prophet, the world's religious leader, who is orchestrating the entire scheme.

This often comes as a shock to most students of the Bible who have assumed that the mark of the Beast will belong exclusively to the Antichrist. Not so. It is the final religious leader of the world who orchestrates the entire scenario. This fact tells us something else about the False Prophet. Not only will he be a world-renowned religious figure, he will also be an expert in economics. Wilfred J. Hahn finds this fact more than significant:

> I have always thought it a telling alert that it will be a religious figure that ends up being the world's last "economic guru." A strange coincidence? No. Seen together, macroeconomics and globalization today are the world's largest religion. The beliefs imbedded in these bosom ideologies are the prevailing hope of humanity today. As such it is only fitting that a deceiving religious figure would preach such a final Prosperity Gospel to the entire world.[5]

Blaise Pascal said it well: "Men never do evil so completely and cheerfully as when they do it from religious conviction."[6]

The Deceptive Deeds of the False Prophet (Revelation 13:13)

The False Prophet will have the power to counterfeit the miracles of God. "He performs great signs, so that he even makes fire come down from heaven on the earth in the sight of men" (Revelation 13:13).

By calling down fire from heaven, the False Prophet will be making two connections with his followers. First, he is trying to pass himself off as the end-time Elijah promised by the prophet Malachi: "Behold, I will send you Elijah the prophet before the coming of the great and dreadful day of the LORD" (Malachi 4:5).

Elijah is the only Old Testament prophet who ever called down fire from heaven. In his contest with the prophets of Baal on Mount Carmel, Elijah challenged the false prophets of his day to ask their gods to send fire down and consume the sacrifice they had prepared. From morning till evening the prophets of Baal called upon their gods and got no response. Then it was Elijah's turn. After saturating his sacrifice with water until it puddled about the altar, Elijah called upon his God, Jehovah. "Then the fire of the LORD fell and consumed the burnt sacrifice, and the wood and the stones and the dust, and it licked up the water that was in the trench. Now when all the people saw it, they fell on their faces; and they said, 'The LORD, He is God! The LORD, He is God!'" (1 Kings 18:38–39).

By duplicating the miracle of Elijah, the False Prophet of Revelation will be saying: "I am the Elijah foretold by your own prophet, Malachi. To prove my claim, here is the fire."

By the miracle of fire, the False Prophet will deceive his followers in a second way: he will be imitating the miracle of the two witnesses who will destroy their enemies by fire. "Fire proceeds from their mouth and devours their enemies. And if anyone wants to harm them, he must be killed in this manner" (Revelation 11:5).

This miracle and others will easily deceive the people in the Tribulation period because most will assume they are truly from God. This is why Jesus warned people not to be deceived simply on the basis of a miracle: "For false christs and false prophets will rise and show great signs and wonders to deceive, if possible, even the elect" (Matthew 24:24). Ray Stedman explains:

The prophets of old did miracles to establish their credentials, their God-given authority. Moses and Elijah did great miracles, and, as the two witnesses of Revelation chapter 11, they call down fire from heaven. So this man must call down fire from heaven. Paul tells us that the devil has the power to do miracles too. Thus we must not trust every miracle as though it were done by God. It may be the work of the enemy, the Evil One. This prophet calls down fire out of heaven, and deceives the world by such means.[7]

From the very beginning, deception has been a primary tool of Satan. It started in Eden when he tempted Eve. "And the LORD

God said to the woman, 'What is this you have done?' The woman said, 'The serpent *deceived* me, and I ate'" (Genesis 3:13, emphasis added). Deception was still Satan's method when Paul wrote to the Corinthian believers, "But I fear, lest somehow, as the serpent *deceived* Eve by his craftiness, so your minds may be corrupted from the simplicity that is in Christ" (2 Corinthians 11:3, emphasis added). Satan still works by deception, which is why the Bible gives us so many warnings against it:

- "Take heed to yourselves, lest your heart be deceived" (Deuteronomy 11:16).
- "Take heed that you not be deceived" (Luke 21:8).
- "Do not be deceived" (1 Corinthians 6:9).
- "Do not be deceived" (1 Corinthians 15:33).
- "Do not be deceived" (Galatians 6:7).
- "Do not be deceived, my beloved brethren" (James 1:16).

The need to observe these repeated warnings will never be more acute than in the Tribulation period when the ultimate deception of Satan through his False Prophet enslaves the entire world.

The Ultimate Deception of the False Prophet (Revelation 13:14–15)

The deceptions of the False Prophet we've noted so far are only preludes to the one outrageously deceptive act by which he will gain ultimate control of the people. The Scripture we have been exploring, Revelation 13, describes this deed:

And he [the False Prophet] deceives those who dwell on the earth by those signs which he was granted to do in the sight of the beast, telling those who dwell on the earth to make an image to the beast who was wounded by the sword and lived. He was granted power to give breath to the image of the beast,

143

that the image of the beast should both speak and cause as many as would not worship the image of the beast to be killed. (vv. 14–15)

As this passage shows, the False Prophet will dupe the people into building an image to be used as a means of worshiping the Antichrist. I believe the False Prophet will set up this image in the most sacred area of the newly constructed Jewish temple.

At this point Satan, the Antichrist, and the False Prophet have fulfilled their own delusions by assuming the godhead and receiving worship. The False Prophet will cause the image to speak. Some think this will be done through some form of ventriloquism; others by electronic voice reproduction. Or it could be that he does it by his delegated satanic power. For we know that, like the Antichrist, he performs "according to the working of Satan, with all power, signs, and lying wonders" (2 Thessalonians 2:9).

With the people of the earth deceived, Satan, through the workings of the False Prophet, will make the move toward his ultimate tyranny.

The Demand of the False Prophet (Revelation 13:16–18)

Now we come to the heart of Satan's end-time population control system. Revelation 13:16–17 tells us that "he [the False Prophet] causes all, both small and great, rich and poor, free and slave, to receive a mark on their right hand or on their foreheads, and that no one may buy or sell except one who has the mark or the name of the beast, or the number of his name."

Prophecy scholar Arnold Fruchtenbaum has written this about the mark: "It will be given to all who submit themselves to the authority of the Antichrist and accept him as god. The mark will serve as a passport for business (v. 17a). They will be able to neither buy nor sell anything unless they have the mark.... Only those who have this number will be permitted to work, to buy, to sell, or simply to make a living."[8]

By means of this mark, Satan and his puppets will attempt once again to counterfeit God's program. God has a mark; Satan must have a mark. In the seventh chapter of Revelation, God's mark is described as a seal:

Then I saw another angel ascending from the east, having the seal of the living God. And he cried with a loud voice to the four angels to whom it was granted to harm the earth and the sea, saying, "Do not harm the earth, the sea, or the trees till we have sealed the servants of our God on their foreheads." And I heard the number of those who were sealed. One hundred and forty-four thousand of all the tribes of the children of Israel were sealed. (vv. 2–4)

Just as God seals His servants on the forehead, the Antichrist will mark his followers on the forehead. Whatever God does, Satan will try to imitate. The mark of God seals His Jewish witnesses to Him, so by the mark of the Beast the Antichrist will attempt to seal his people to him.

But there are significant differences between God's mark and Satan's. One is that the counterfeit mark of Satan will have no power over those who bear the authentic mark of God. God's seal will protect His witnesses from harm, whereas Satan's seal will subject his people to harm. Another difference is that the seal of God will be given only to a select few—the 144,000 Jewish witnesses. But the seal of the Antichrist will be required of everyone: "He causes all, both small and great, rich and poor, free and slave, to receive a mark on their right hand or on their foreheads" (Revelation 13:16).

The word for "mark" in the Greek is *charagma*, which means "stamp" or "brand." In antiquity a *charagma* could take several forms: It could be a hard-baked clay plate worn by a slave and etched with information authenticating his authorization to make purchases for his master. The *charagma* could also be a die for stamping official documents or impressing its image into a wax seal. In the Roman

145

Empire the word was always connected with the emperor and often carried his name and effigy. The *charagma* was on his coins, his seals, his slaves, and its use was authorized for his officials. The *charagma* was necessary for buying and selling, and it was required to be affixed to documents to attest their validity.

Like the emperor's seal, the satanic seal will be given so that "no one may buy or sell except one who has the mark or the name of the beast, or the number of his name" (Revelation 13:17). Now it becomes clear why the False Prophet is both an economic and a religious leader. The mark he enforces applies to both realms and ties them together. The mark will allow the Antichrist's followers to buy and sell because it identifies them as religiously orthodox—submissive followers of the Beast and worshipers of his image. Those without the mark are forbidden to buy because they are identified as traitors, perhaps similar to the way those in Muslim nations who refuse Islam are identified as infidels. The law of the Beast in that day will be, "Worship me or starve!"

What Is the Mark of the Beast?

Ruling powers have typically had identifying marks or symbols. The ancient Roman Republic was represented by a *fasces*, a bundle of rods, symbolizing unity, with a protruding axe, symbolizing authority. Nazi Germany had its swastika. Modern Israel has its Star of David, Canada its maple leaf, and the United States its eagle. Marks are also used for other reasons, as when God marked the murderer Cain in Genesis 4:15: "And the LORD said to him, 'Therefore, whoever kills Cain, vengeance shall be taken on him sevenfold.' And the LORD set a mark on Cain, lest anyone finding him should kill him."

As Revelation 13:18 tells us, the mark of the Beast is associated with the number 666: "Here is wisdom. Let him who has understanding calculate the number of the beast, for it is the number of a man: His number is 666."

Because of the evil association of that number, people today are often apprehensive about using it. When Ronald Reagan left the presidency, he and his wife moved into the wealthy Bel Air section of Los Angeles. The address of their house was 666 St. Cloud Road. Nancy Reagan promptly had the street number officially changed to 668 to avoid the sinister number 666. Superstition and astrology may have had more to do with her decision than biblical conviction, yet her action shows the sensitivity people have to that number.[9] We don't want it in our addresses; we don't want it in our phone numbers; and we don't want it on our license plates.

Yet in spite of the widespread discomfort with the number 666, few know what it really means. Many suggestions have been offered. Some can be taken seriously; others definitely not. Here are three ideas we can discard: Dr. Henry Morris points out that if you take the integers between 1 and 36, add them one to the other (1+2+3+4, etc.), and when you get to thirty-six you hit your calculator's total button, the sum that will pop up is 666.[10] That may be intriguing, but it's not meaningful. Some have suggested that in order to give everyone in the world his or her own unique number, it will take eighteen digits, or three sets of six digits each. Interesting and, for all I know, possibly true. But it's not the symbolic meaning of the biblical number. In Revelation 13, the number 666 is found in verse 18. Eighteen is the sum of six plus six plus six. Isn't that revealing? Well, whatever it reveals, it is not the meaning of 666.

Verse 18, however, does give us a clue to the number's meaning when it tells us that 666 is "the number of a man." To realize the implication of that, let's first consider another number—the number seven. Seven is considered the number of completeness. The Bible often uses the number seven in reference to God or God-related things. God rested on the seventh day. The temple candlestick held seven candles. Christ addressed seven churches in Revelation.

Revelation speaks of seven spirits before God's throne, seven golden candlesticks, seven seals, seven thunders, seven angels, seven trumpets, and seven vials.

The number six, on the other hand, being one short of seven, is a number of incompleteness. Thus man, being in the image of God but not God, is associated with the number six. Man was created on the sixth day. He is enjoined to work six of seven days. Even the largest man described in the Bible, the giant Goliath, was not a seven; he was just a combination of sixes. He measured six cubits in height, carried a spearhead weighing six shekels, and wore six pieces of armor. No matter how big man is or thinks he is, he is still not God; he is merely a man.

The number 666 designates man to the triple. Here is the best man can be without God—the ultimate in human ingenuity and competence elevated to the point where he thinks he's a god. But he is not God. He is still incomplete, imperfect. No matter how high the pedestal, the best he can be is a string of sixes; he is not and can never be a seven. Can you see how that number characterizes the Antichrist?

The Mark in Operation

Now we are at the point where we can explain how the False Prophet may employ modern technology to enforce the use of the mark. Grant Jeffrey helps us understand how this will play out in actual practice:

> Using existing technology, the mark or number 666 can be implanted under the skin of every person using an RFID microchip. A powerful electronic scanner could detect the chip from a distance and reveal all your personal information, far more than your name, address, age, and marital status. While the implanted microchip and its information would be readable

by a radio frequency scanner, a person would not know when or where his private information was being accessed—or who was accessing the information.[11]

Today when you present your credit or debit card to pay for a purchase and the card is declined, you have no option but to leave your goods behind unless you have another way to pay. During the Tribulation the scanners will be able to read people's data from the implanted RFID as they enter the checkout line. An "approved" or "declined" message on the scanner will indicate whether the purchaser has the mark. If not, no sale.

One can imagine scenarios during the Tribulation like those reported in the books of Corrie ten Boom. As she passed through the inspection line in the Nazi concentration camp, she prayed that the guards would not find the Bible she was carrying. And they did not. Or like Brother Andrew, who smuggled Bibles into communist countries and prayed that the border guards would not see the Bibles stashed in plain sight in his car. And they did not. Will there be Tribulation Christians who go through checkout lines without the mark of the Beast, praying they will be miraculously approved to purchase food even though they don't have the mark?

We cannot know just how God will protect those who turn to Him during the Tribulation, but I think we can be sure He will protect His own in some wonderful way. Especially when Christians are sure to be a defenseless minority in a time of extreme persecution and unprecedented evil.

The Doom of the False Prophet

When I read a suspense-filled novel, I don't want to know the end before I get there. I have addressed the doom of the Beast in the preceding chapter, but I think a quick review may be helpful here.

In one of the final chapters of Revelation we read of the final battle against Satan in which Christ Himself will lead the charge. Here we see the result of that battle:

And I saw the beast, the kings of the earth, and their armies, gathered together to make war against Him who sat on the horse and against His army. Then the beast was captured, and with him the false prophet who worked signs in his presence, by which he deceived those who received the mark of the beast and those who worshiped his image. These two were cast alive into the lake of fire burning with brimstone. (Revelation 19:19–20)

At the end of it all, the Beast (the Antichrist) and the False Prophet land themselves in hell. But what happens to their followers—to those who took the mark and worshiped the image? Their decisions have likewise determined their destiny. Their judgment is described in two passages:

Then a third angel followed them, saying with a loud voice, "If anyone worships the beast and his image, and receives his mark on his forehead or on his hand, he himself shall also drink of the wine of the wrath of God, which is poured out full strength into the cup of His indignation. He shall be tormented with fire and brimstone in the presence of the holy angels and in the presence of the Lamb. And the smoke of their torment ascends forever and ever; and they have no rest day or night, who worship the beast and his image, and whoever receives the mark of his name." (Revelation 14:9–11)

Then I heard a loud voice from the temple saying to the seven angels, "Go and pour out the bowls of the wrath of God on the earth." So the first went and poured out his bowl upon the earth, and a foul and loathsome sore came upon the men who had the mark of the beast and those who worshiped his image. (Revelation 16:1–2)

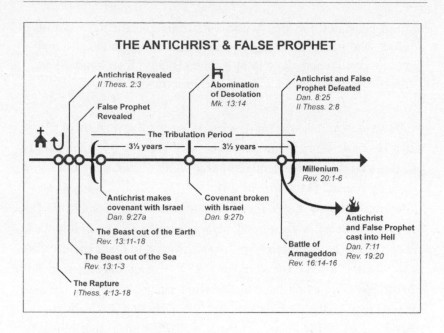

THE ANTICHRIST & FALSE PROPHET

Antichrist Revealed
II Thess. 2:3

Abomination
of Desolation
Mk. 13:14

Antichrist and False
Prophet Defeated
Dan. 8:25
II Thess. 2:8

False Prophet
Revealed

——————— The Tribulation Period ———————

— 3½ years — | — 3½ years —

Millenium
Rev. 20:1-6

Antichrist makes
covenant with Israel
Dan. 9:27a

Covenant broken
with Israel
Dan. 9:27b

Antichrist
and False Prophet
cast into Hell
Dan. 7:11
Rev. 19:20

The Beast out of the Earth
Rev. 13:11-18

Battle of
Armageddon
Rev. 16:14-16

The Beast out of the Sea
Rev. 13:1-3

The Rapture
I Thess. 4:13-18

While the Tribulation is in progress, the wicked, by virtue of the mark, appear to be getting safety and protection while the saints who refuse the mark are being persecuted and killed. But the passages above show that in the end, the mark-bearers will be punished along with the Beast and the False Prophet. And those who refused the mark will be vindicated.

The Vindication of the "Unmarked" Saints

We have just seen the end of those who accept the mark of the Beast. They prosper as long as the Beast is in control, but ultimately they face the judgment of God. What happens to the followers of Christ who refuse to take the mark? We find the answer in Revelation 20:4:

And I saw thrones, and they sat on them, and judgment was committed to them. Then I saw the souls of those who had been beheaded for their witness to Jesus and for the word of God, who had not worshiped the beast or his image, and had not received his mark on their foreheads or on their hands. And they lived and reigned with Christ for a thousand years.

Those who refused the mark were following the wisdom of Christ when He said, "And do not fear those who kill the body but cannot kill the soul. But rather fear Him who is able to destroy both soul and body in hell" (Matthew 10:28).

Again, you may think these admonitions do not apply to you because Christ will return to take His church to heaven before these events take place, exempting you from the need to make the decision as to whether to take the mark or suffer persecution. It's true that Christians today won't have to face that particular choice because we won't be in the Tribulation. But what about the "birth pangs" Paul speaks of in Romans 8:22 that will lead up to that climactic period when governments make it increasingly harder for Christians to function faithfully without paying a price?

We are already beginning to feel those pangs. Increasingly our government is passing laws that undercut the truth of God and threaten the freedom of Christians. We have already been forced to contribute to the federal funding of abortions through our tax dollars. The sanctity of marriage is up for grabs in almost every state in the union. In some venues you can be prosecuted for speaking out against homosexuality. Religious liberty is being assaulted in schools, in courts, in the media, and in churches. I believe these trends will increase prior to Christ's return.

In a very real sense, when fear keeps us from defending biblical principles, our failure to stand for Christ is, in reality, a decision to stand with Satan. When we do that, we are, in a very real sense, receiving Satan's mark. We are going along with his program out of our fear of the consequences of doing what is right. That is why the temptation to "go along to get along" rather than risk persecution is fatal.

As I end this chapter, let me pose to you one final question. And it's a tough one. What would you do if you were forced to decide between honoring God by refusing the mark or accepting it for the safety, security, and well-being of you and your family? We have a superb biblical example that shows us the right answer—a story of three young Jewish men who had to make such a decision. Daniel tells us the story:

> Nebuchadnezzar the king made an image of gold, whose height was sixty cubits and its width six cubits. He set it up in the plain of Dura, in the province of Babylon.... Then a herald cried aloud: "To you it is commanded, O peoples, nations, and languages, that at the time you hear the sound of the horn, flute, harp, lyre, and psaltery, in symphony with all kinds of music, you shall fall down and worship the gold image that King Nebuchadnezzar has set up; and whoever does not fall down and worship shall be cast immediately into the midst of a burning fiery furnace." (Daniel 3:1, 4–6)

More than one scholar has noted that Nebuchadnezzar's image was sixty cubits high, six cubits wide, and there were six musical expressions that summoned its worshipers. Sound familiar? That statue was obviously a prototype of the one of the Antichrist in Revelation 13.

Next we meet three young Hebrew men who refused to be bullied into the idolatry of their day. We know them by their strange Babylonian names: Shadrach, Meshach, and Abednego. The entire population of the great city of Babylon, hearing the musical signal to worship the statue, immediately went to their knees. But right in the middle of the crowd were these three young men, standing tall and confident. Nebuchadnezzar was furious at their refusal to obey his decree and even more by their insistence that, given the chance, they would refuse again. He decreed that they should be thrown into the fiery furnace.

From the very first time I read their words of response, I have loved these three guys and prayed that if I were ever tested as they were, I would follow their courageous example. Here is their reply to the king:

> O Nebuchadnezzar, we have no need to answer you in this matter. If that is the case, our God whom we serve is able to deliver us from the burning fiery furnace, and He will deliver us from your hand, O king. But if not, let it be known to you, O king, that we do not serve your gods, nor will we worship the gold image which you have set up. (Daniel 3:16–18)

In essence, these brave young men refused to wear the mark of the Beast. And by their example they show us how we can avoid it as well. Decisions sometimes seem complex because we want to weigh all the factors and follow all the nuances and ramifications of the probable outcome. But when it comes down to the essence of almost any moral decision, it is usually quite simple: either we follow God or we follow Satan. The mitigating factors may be inconvenient or even painful, but they are ultimately not valid considerations in making the decision. The nuances are mere distractions. All it takes is the clarity to know whose side you're on and the courage to follow His commands.

Yes, the result may be a fiery furnace. It may mean denial of rights or freedoms. But we have God's promise that if we stand true to Him in the midst of trials and persecution, we will ultimately reign with Him.

CHAPTER 7

Financial Signs of the End Times

Best-selling author Robert Kiyosaki made a frighteningly accurate statement that characterizes the financial world: "When people are struggling financially, they are more willing to have a government save them, unwittingly exchanging their personal freedom for financial salvation."[1]

His words bring to mind the lyrics of a pop song from the 1970s: "You lay your bets and then you pay the price, the things we do for love, the things we do for love."[2] Today people have bet their lives on financial security, and now they are willing to pay the price to back up that bet—financial salvation at any cost. The willingness to sell our freedom for our financial security is an obvious sign that the love of money is truly the hallmark of our age. When that love is wed to the capabilities of modern technology to access and control every area of our lives, we face an increasing potential for a confrontation between our faith and the forces of evil.

Love of money is far from new in the human experience. It is as old as man. From cover to cover the Bible often addresses the issue of material wealth in all its facets, from inordinate love of it to utter disdain; from overabundance to total lack; from good uses to bad; from prudence in its use to outlandish carelessness. From the beginning of time, money and material wealth have dictated the actions of people and nations.

Abraham and Lot parted company because the land would not support the abundant livestock both possessed. Esau sold his

155

birthright for a mere bowl of stew, effectively reducing his inheritance—his future wealth—by half. Joseph's brothers abandoned their plan to kill him when they found they could gain a little profit by selling him into slavery. Moses disavowed the wealth of Egypt to do what God called him to do. The Israelites used the wealth plundered from their Egyptian masters to fashion a false god. God promised His people the wealth of the land of Canaan, but then allowed them to suffer defeat when one greedy warrior kept plunder against His command. Ruth and Naomi were reduced to abject poverty until they found God's favor through the wealthy man Boaz. David went from rags to riches, while Solomon went from riches to despair. The Pharisees craved wealth, while the Son of Man had nowhere to lay His head. Ananias and Sapphira lied and died for claiming a false church contribution, while the Macedonians gave until it hurt. And a day is coming when God promises that we will walk with solid gold under our feet.

Considering the historical influence of wealth for good or ill, it should not surprise us to discover that many signs of the end times have financial overtones. In the previous chapter we learned that we are heading toward a time when almost every person on planet Earth will be controlled through one diabolical economic system. If this time is imminent, as I believe it is, what are the signs that it is approaching? What should we be looking for?

I will address that question in this chapter. In the following pages we will identify and explore four distinct financial signs that signal the end times and the coming of Christ to take His church to heaven.

The Proliferation of Technology

In the closing verses of his prophecy, Daniel is instructed to "shut up the words, and seal the book until the time of the end" (Daniel 12:4).

"The time of the end" is described as an era when "many shall run to and fro, and knowledge shall increase" (Daniel 12:4). Both parts of this prophecy have certainly come to pass. Knowledge has increased and spread via technological communications to the point that the present time has been aptly called the "Information Age." It's no less true that in our time people are "running to and fro." Along with dependable cars, and a network of good roads and interstate highways, global air travel has given us unprecedented and relatively safe mobility.

In early 2010 the *Jerusalem Post* reported that Ben Gurion Airport in Tel Aviv had implemented a first-of-its-kind biometric security system to make air travel safer and security screening more efficient than ever before. The Unipass Airport Management System was developed by the Israel Airports Authority, adding to Israel's reputation for having the most advanced airport security of any in the world. The new system, currently in the test phase, is expected to be in widespread use by 2012. It creates a personal smart card for each participating international traveler by scanning the person's passport, fingerprints, and facial image in a one-time registration process.

The machine at the first airport security checkpoint scans both the passport and the Unipass smart card to verify the person's identity. Once cleared, the passenger moves to another machine with a touch screen to answer security questions. Once the passenger is cleared through these two stations, the Unipass card is again scanned at luggage, check-in, and carry-on checkpoints.

While the rationale most often given for the implementation of this new system is to "significantly reduce waiting time for various security checks,"[3] there can be no doubt that it is a secure and equally applied means of identifying potentially dangerous airline passengers.

And it has an even more sinister potential: it is a perfect weapon in the arsenal of a tyrant bent on world control. As we know from a previous chapter, a despotic ruler will govern the entire world during the last half of the Tribulation period, and he will likely use technology to accomplish his purposes (Revelation 13:16–17).

New technology for the Internet is also tailor-made for the Antichrist. According to a *WORLD* magazine article titled, "The Tower of Google," the Internet is "society's brain, continually patrolled by cyber bots that make connections."[4] The already seemingly omnipresent search engine—whether Google, Bing, or some other—is now extending its reach through "search engine optimization." With this enhancement, Google can target marketing specifically to our interests by following us around the Internet noting where we stop, shop, and search.

Not only can they figure out what we like and want; they go beyond that by creating those very needs and wants for us. Sergey Brin, cofounder of Google, has expressed a somewhat frightening desire to see "the development of a wireless chip to be implanted directly into the human brain."[5] That is the kind of control the Antichrist is all about.

In 1965, Intel cofounder Gordon Moore formulated a rule of thumb that has become known as "Moore's Law." This law quantifies technology's exponential growth by stating that the number of transistors that can be placed on an integrated circuit doubles approximately every eighteen months. This rule explains the ever-increasing power in ever-decreasing space we have witnessed in all electronic applications from supercomputers to cell phones.

Robert Samuelson, political, economic, and social issues columnist for the *Washington Post*, draws a straight line between our technological advances and the financial world:

It's one of those vast social upheavals that everyone understands but that hardly anyone notices, because it seems too ordinary: The long-predicted "cashless society" has quietly arrived, or nearly so. Electronic money [is] cheaper than cash or checks...[and] it's more convenient....We have crossed a cultural as well as an economic threshold when plastic and money are synonymous.[6]

Add to this the voice of Peter Ayliffe, chief executive of Visa in Europe: "Paying for goods with notes and coins could be consigned to history within five years...and some retailers could soon start surcharging customers if they choose to buy products with cash."[7] If you have flown on any of our national airlines recently, you've already encountered the cashless cabin where food, drink, and even $2 earphone purchases can be made only with a credit card.

For a number of years, the banking systems of this country have been inundated with a mass of paper, from both checks and credit card expenditures. Do you remember those old credit receipts that were made in triplicate—one page for the customer, one for the seller, and one for the bank? And how about that archaic, knuckle-grinding machine that was used to imprint your name and account number through those two lightweight paper sheets and one tagboard sheet, each separated by carbon paper? In those early days of credit cards, a phone call to the card issuer was necessary to obtain authorization for the charge.

Some readers may even remember when you had to completely fill out your personal check at the checkout stand and then wait while the clerk wrote down both your driver's license and home phone numbers. Today at many checkouts, the check is written by the same machine that totals your bill, and all that's required of you is a signature.

Samuelson tells us, "In 1996, checks and cash represented almost 80 percent of consumer payments—now, they're less than half."[8] He went on to project that in the near future credit or debit cards will account for 70 percent or more of all payments. This trend tells us it is likely that in the near future, no actual money will exchange hands at all. Even your paycheck will be electronically credited to your

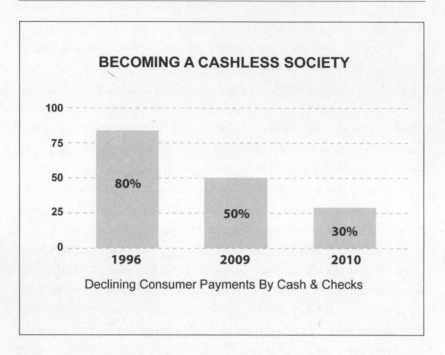

bank account like that of 83 percent of all Social Security recipients—if it isn't already.

Paperlessness has the obvious benefit of saving time and trees, but there is another motivation for a cashless society. The 2009 pandemic of the H1N1 flu may prove to be one of those crises that lead us another step closer to cashlessness. Money is dirty. I'm not referring to the filthy lucre spoken of in 1 Timothy 3, but to the simple fact that "banknotes may be reservoirs" for flu viruses. *Scientific American* noted in their "60-Second Science" feature of January 5, 2009, that "influenza viruses can survive on banknotes for as long as seventeen days."[9]

"Okay," you say, "then if I am using my credit card, couldn't germs survive on the plastic, too?" Probably a little less so because paper is more porous. But have you noticed the proliferation of point-of-sale card swiping terminals where nobody touches the card but you?

The number of those terminals tripled in six years. Today there are reportedly well in excess of seven million of these devices in use throughout the world, but like all technology, even they are increasingly becoming obsolete.[10]

Today many of us carry our own personal point-of-sale terminals around in the form of our cellular telephones.[11] Because of the enormous boom in the use of these devices, most financial futurists foresee a global economy that is operated largely from cell phones. This widespread and growing technological phenomenon deserves a closer look because it has ominous implications relating to end-times prophecy.

Cell phones are tiny, convenient, easy to use, and offer an increasingly wide range of applications. In the thirty-seven years since their inception, portable phones have gone from the bulky, thirty-ounce, brick-like prototypes to pocket-sized modules weighing as little as three ounces. An iPhone 3G weighs less than five ounces and enables its user to access the Internet and watch TV and movies in widescreen by use of digital videos, in addition to e-mailing, texting, and—oh, yes—voice conversations.

Not only are cell phones convenient; they are becoming ubiquitous. Almost everyone has a cell phone these days, even "more than half of all twelve-year-olds."[12] Pew Research reports that 85 percent of Americans have cell phones and 56 percent of them have accessed the Internet wirelessly.[13]

The more than 229 million wireless subscribers in the United States used 2.2 trillion minutes, sent 1 trillion text messages, and brought in total wireless revenue of $148.1 billion in 2008.[14] Third-quarter 2009 statements for Apple's proprietary provider, AT&T, report a one-year increase of 2 million subscribers and 8 percent in revenues to $13.65 billion. Verizon was up 24.4 percent at $15.8 billion with a million new subscribers.[15]

This growth is true not only in the United States. The rapidly developing economy of India reported 391.76 million wireless subscribers, 109.7 million in the rural areas of the country alone. That figure was up 50 percent during the same period just one year before.[16] Even tightly controlled North Korea had 20,000 cell phone users at the end of the first quarter of 2009 and announced the planned expansion of their 3G network to the whole nation by 2012.[17]

To sum up these figures, by 2009 the number of cell phone users had reached 4.4 billion globally. According to the iTWire network, this worldwide usage of cell phones makes it "technologically feasible to connect the world to the benefits of information and communication technology."[18]

Couple this widespread usage of cell phones with their growing range of applications, and you begin to see their enormous potential for either good or evil. In the modern era of personal computers, two operating systems dominate: Microsoft Windows and Apple OS X. With cell phones, a third "platform" is now in existence: smartphones, characterized by Apple's wildly popular iPhone. Just as the personal computer has platform-specific applications to handle tasks (such as financial management), so smartphones now have their own suites of applications. In November 2009 the iPhone had 100,000 separate applications, about twenty of which dealt with some aspect of finances.[19]

While only .02 percent of all applications were once banking related, recently banks have been actively expanding them and many more are coming.[20] Bank of America began the trend in late 2007, making mobile banking apps available to their customers with iPhone technology. Now Chase, PNC, and Wells Fargo also provide similar apps. Along with banking, other financial apps allow users to trade stocks with a free E*Trade app, send funds via a PayPal app, and manage finances with a Quicken app.[21] Innovative USAA bank even updated their apps to allow customers to deposit checks wirelessly by sending a photo image of both sides of the check—with their cell phone, of course—to the bank for verification and depositing.[22]

Jim Bruene, writing on NetBanker.com, speculates that there may well be upward of 10,000 financial apps developed, especially once other mobile players enter the Apple-dominated arena. He forecasts that "more than half of the U.S. online banking population will be using mobile banking" by the middle of this decade. Given the meteoric three-year rise from zero mobile banking users in 2007 to an estimated 40 million by 2015, it appears that mobile banking is the rising star of convenience banking.[23]

Financial technology can now be incorporated into a phone, making it possible to use it for purchases as you would a credit or debit card. In 2009, Filipino SMART Money cardholders were encouraged to use its "electronic wallet service" to "perform safe and secure online purchases with the help of their cell phones."[24] The U.S. is behind other countries in "smart wallet" implementation. People in Japan, for example, pay for goods and services by swiping their cell phones, not a plastic card.

These cell phone wallets are also taking the place of the desktop personal computer as they become another option for Internet connection. According to Facebook, 65 million, or 25 percent, of their 250 million current users access their service through a cell phone.[25]

A debated downside of the wireless financial revolution is the possible risk of brain cancer from cell phone radiation, although to date no corroborating data confirm any link.[26] The risk is minimized, however, because talking is not required for most wireless financial transactions via cell phone.

Very likely, your banking institution provides you with a myriad of electronic services that are available with just a few keyboard strokes. One example is an "Internet branch," where you can do all your banking at home—transfer your funds, pay your bills, or just about everything except make cash withdrawals. And if you're away from home? No problem. Just use your cell phone. For some of you that is not future; it may be how you purchased this book.

At our radio and television ministry Turning Point, we believe that the last wave of preaching the gospel worldwide may not necessarily be on television or radio, but through cell phone apps. Cell phones function almost like radios. At a recent National Religious Broadcasters convention, I saw several new applications that make the teaching of the Word of God available through the cell phone.

I bring to you this elaborate summary of new technology and what it can do in order to restate one reality: prophetic events cast their shadows before them. As these technological innovations show, we are on the cutting edge of having all the technology that the Antichrist and False Prophet would need to wire this world together for their evil purposes. Right now it is well within the range of possibility for a centralized power to gain worldwide control of all banking and purchasing. As we see things that are prophesied for the Tribulation period beginning to take shape right now, we are made aware of the fact that surely the Lord's return is not far off.

If you wonder what financial technology has to do with the mark of the Beast, I urge you to remember that prophecy was written with the words and from the context of human authors in their day. Therefore, when the apostle John wrote of a *mark*, he naturally thought of the slave or criminal branding of his day, which would inflict a literal and permanent mark on the hand or forehead. While that happens to fit closely to the RFID chip scenario discussed in the previous chapter, we cannot be sure that the mark will conform that specifically to John's conception of it. The mark may well be an electronic identification signature via cell phone or other device that will control one's ability to make purchases if the world has gone totally cashless by the time of the Antichrist.

The Polarization of Wealth

In the sixth chapter of Revelation, the apostle John describes a future scene in heaven. The Lord Jesus Christ is unrolling the scroll that records the sequence of events that will transpire on the earth for the next seven years. As the scroll unrolls, successive seals are removed from it disclosing a series of judgments, each a more frightening horror than the one before. Ultimately, three series of seven judgments are revealed: the seven seals, the seven trumpets, and the seven bowls.

When the first seal is opened, John sees one of the infamous four horsemen of the Apocalypse—a rider on a white horse. This rider symbolizes the Antichrist in the early days of the Tribulation. The second seal is opened to reveal the rider on the red horse of bloodshed and war. Once again the scroll is unrolled, and the third seal is removed to reveal the third horseman of the Apocalypse. As this rider charges forth, John describes what he sees:

When He opened the third seal, I heard the third living creature say, "Come and see." So I looked, and behold, a black horse, and he who sat on it had a pair of scales in his hand. And I heard a voice in the midst of the four living creatures saying, "A quart of wheat for a denarius, and three quarts of barley for a denarius; and do not harm the oil and the wine." (Revelation 6:5–6)

The black horse is famine, and it follows the red horse because famine naturally follows war. This is the famine that Jesus predicted as part of the "beginning of sorrows" in Matthew 24:7–8: "For nation will rise against nation, and kingdom against kingdom. And there will be famines, pestilences, and earthquakes in various places. All these are the beginning of sorrows."

The "quart of wheat" John mentions in his vision was the least amount of food necessary to sustain one person on a daily basis. The denarius was a Roman coin that was equal to a worker's wage for one day. Before the famine of the Tribulation, it would have been possible to buy five or six quarts of wheat for a denarius. This passage tells us that in the early days of the Tribulation period, a man will have to work all day just to get enough food to feed himself. Obviously, one quart of wheat would not have filled the hungry stomachs of a man's family in John's time. The man would be forced to buy barley, a cheaper grain usually reserved for cattle. For one denarius he could buy three quarts of barley, but there would be no money left for oil or salt, much less for meat or milk. The application is clear: in the early Tribulation, people will have only the bare minimum required for subsistence living.

But notice, not all the world population will be touched by this famine. The text says that oil and wine will be exempted from this judgment. Oil and wine were considered rich man's fare in John's world. This suggests that although the poor man's food will be severely restricted, the luxuries of the wealthy will remain untouched. In other words, the affluent will escape major hardship while the masses will encounter a severe struggle to get by. One must wonder what will become of the aged, the incapacitated, and the children.

Addressing the growing division between the rich and the poor of the world, global nutritional expert Arnold Schaefer wrote, "An empty stomach is the worst political advisor in the world. But an empty stomach is acting as Secretary of State for nearly half the population of the globe."[27]

As Schaefer noted forty years ago, the polarization between wealth and poverty had begun, and it is getting much greater. The trend will grow even more until it reaches desperate levels in the end times. Mark Hitchcock writes:

During the coming Tribulation, the gulf between rich and poor will grow wider than ever before. Food will be so expensive that only the very wealthy will have enough. Famine will relentlessly hammer the middle class until the middle class disappears. The vast majority of people will wallow in misery, but the rich will continue to bask in the comfort of their luxurious lifestyle. The world will be radically divided among the elite "haves" and the mass of the "have-nots." ... This will make the suffering of the have-nots even more unbearable as they watch the privileged few indulge themselves in the lap of luxury.[28]

Economic chaos always hits the poor and middle classes harder than the rich. Indeed, the superrich are rarely touched by it at all. If a billionaire's net worth falls by 50 percent, he is still worth $500 million. Even the wealthiest people can spend only so many dollars in a day. But if a poor or middle-class person who lives day-to-day or month-to-month is hit by economic recession, he is plunged immediately into a lower standard of living.

We have recently observed this phenomenon in America. Since Americans tend to live at or beyond their means and maintain little or no savings, a downturn in economic conditions impacts their lifestyle immediately and drastically.

During our most recent recession, I noticed a profusion of books and seminars being promoted to help people take advantage of the bad economy. These offerings are built around a common theme: predation. During times of economic chaos, those with money can get richer by stepping in and buying at bargain rates what the lower classes must abandon, such as real estate and stocks. Thus with each economic upheaval, the gap between rich and poor widens and will continue to do so until it reaches crisis proportions at the time of the Tribulation.

In late October 2009, the Pew Research Center reported that the leading story in the "news hole," or topics covered on television news, was the economy. More airtime was spent on economic news than on the rapidly spreading H1N1 flu and the panic over vaccine shortages. The ratio of time distribution between the economy and the swine flu was about 4 to 1. More airtime was spent on the economy than on the wars in Iraq and Afghanistan or anything else.

The story driving the economic coverage was the public furor over the perceived unfair distribution of wealth in the current financial crisis. In particular, as summed up by CBS's Chip Reid, "For the titans of Wall Street, it's like the recession never happened. Less than a year after the big banks helped cause the financial meltdown, they're on track to pay out a record of $140 billion in bonuses this year."[29]

In 2006, the United Nations published the results of the first comprehensive study of the distribution of wealth among the households of the world. They defined wealth as the measure of income, assets, debts, land, and other tangible assets. Data was gathered from more than thirty-eight countries.[30]

The report showed the following: More than 33 percent of the world's wealthy live in North America; 27 percent live in Japan; 6 percent in the UK; 5 percent in France; and half the world's adult population own barely 1 percent of global wealth.[31]

The United States of America, Canada, and Mexico possess 33 percent of the world's wealth. By far most of this wealth is concentrated in the United States, though the U.S. is far from the world's most populous nation.

"According to the Worldwide Distribution of Household Wealth, issued in December 2006 (the first wealth survey in history), the rich have become richer. The top 2% and 1% of the world's population is estimated to own 51% and 40% of world household wealth, respectively. Very likely, the world today has a much more imbalanced wealth skew—the rich being richer, and the non-rich relatively poorer—than ever before in history."[32]

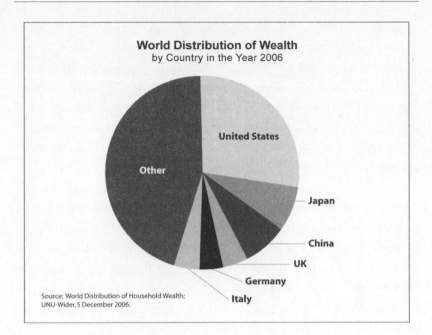

World Distribution of Wealth
by Country in the Year 2006

United States

Other

Japan

China

UK

Germany

Italy

Source: World Distribution of Household Wealth;
UNU-Wider, 5 December 2006.

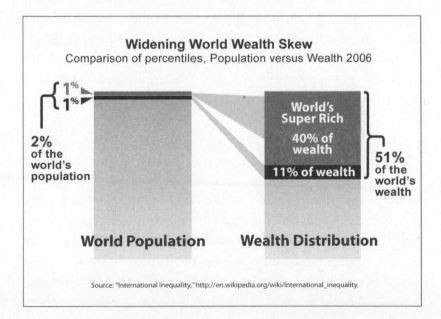

Widening World Wealth Skew
Comparison of percentiles, Population versus Wealth 2006

1%
1%

2%
of the
world's
population

World's
Super Rich

40% of
wealth

11% of wealth

51%
of the
world's
wealth

World Population   **Wealth Distribution**

Source: "International Inequality," http://en.wikipedia.org/wiki/International_inequality.

When the rich get richer and the poor get poorer, the result is what is called the "middle-class squeeze." The major cause of this squeeze is wages not keeping pace with inflation, causing income to decrease in buying power and thus forcing middle-class earners down into poorer categories. The world economy is setting itself up for years of increased inflation due to the massive amounts of newly printed dollars created primarily by the U.S. stimulus efforts.

As billions of printed dollars are injected into the economy, the result is a decrease in the value of each dollar, which is the same as an increase in prices. Increased prices reduce the buying power of earned dollars, forcing people to lower their living standards or even do without vital necessities. We have seen this growing phenomenon in the number of families who no longer have health care, in the emergence of tent cities in major metro areas, and in formerly middle-class families now depending on food banks.

These developments may be the result of a temporary economic crisis and not necessarily a permanent condition. But if inflation moves to hyperinflation, the ability of formerly middle-class people to regain their position will be seriously hindered. By the time of the Tribulation, the gap between the rich and the poor will widen into a chasm, and the middle class will disappear altogether.

The Priority of Oil

Although I devoted an entire chapter to the topic of oil and to the related Battle of Gog and Magog by the new axis of evil in an earlier book, I must revisit this subject here because it is one of the major financial signs pointing us toward the Tribulation. To show how this subject relates to the coming end times, we will turn to the words of the prophet Ezekiel:

Thus says the Lord GOD: "On that day it shall come to pass that thoughts will arise in your mind, and you will make an evil plan: You will say, 'I will go up against a land of unwalled villages; I will go to a peaceful people, who dwell safely, all of them dwelling without walls, and having neither bars nor gates'—to take plunder and to take booty, to stretch out your hand against the waste places that are again inhabited, and against a people gathered from the nations, who have acquired livestock and goods, who dwell in the midst of the land." (Ezekiel 38:10–12)

We know from the earlier part of Ezekiel 38 that this prophecy concerns the war of Gog and Magog against Israel. Some think this war might take place before the Rapture. I believe it will take place right after the Rapture, in the early days of the Tribulation. Either way, we should give some primacy to understanding this war, for if we believe that Jesus could come in our lifetime, that means the war could well take place within the next five years.

Ezekiel tells us that the Gog-Magog assault against Israel is the result of an evil thought that is put into the mind of the leader of a coalition army made up of many nations. These nations come against Israel intending to wipe her from the face of the earth. No one stands with Israel against the armies of Gog and Magog but the God of heaven.

Where is the United States at this moment? Why are we not pictured as standing with our perennial ally Israel? The desertion of Israel by the United States was once deemed unthinkable, but no longer. Increasingly, our nation is catering to the oil-producing nations whose product gives them an inordinate hold over our contemporary lifestyle. These nations have an expressed hatred for Israel.

As if to prove my point, in words not even used when speaking of proven enemies like Iran and North Korea, Secretary of State

Hillary Clinton, with the apparent sanction of the administration, referred to Israel's proposal to build housing in its own capital city as "an insult to the United States."[33] The Anti-Defamation League's president, Abraham Foxman, observed, "We cannot remember an instance when such harsh language was directed at a friend and ally of the United States."[34]

While Clinton later offered reassurances that our bond with Israel is "unshakeable" and that our commitment to Israel's security is "absolute," there is no denying that there is a rending of that bond on the part of the United States.[35]

A further indication of this rift became acutely apparent with the unprecedented White House snubbing of Israeli prime minister Benjamin Netanyahu in a March 2010 visit to the United States. The president, angry over his failure to convince the prime minister to abandon the Jerusalem housing plan, chose not to dine with him and refused him the press briefing that normally accompanies visits by heads of state. According to the Israeli newspaper *Haaretz*, "The Prime Minister leaves America disgraced, isolated, and altogether weaker than when he came."[36]

If Israel's friends treat her in this way, it is no surprise that the evil thoughts of her enemies will one day draw them into war against her. What could produce thoughts evil enough for nations to amass armies against this tiny nation? Well, what does the Middle East have that the whole world needs? I think you know the answer: oil.

It is likely that oil is the "plunder and booty" spoken of in the Ezekiel passage above. The Middle East has rich deposits of oil because it was once an area rich with more lushness than any other place on the planet. The Garden of Eden was in the Middle East. If, as most scientists believe, oil is formed primarily from the decomposition of animal and vegetable matter, then this is the area where we might expect the greatest oil deposits. And that is indeed the case, as the following chart shows:

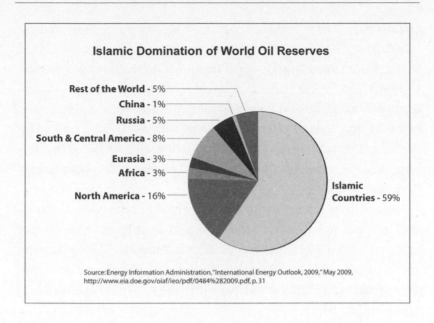

Islamic Domination of World Oil Reserves

Rest of the World - 5%
China - 1%
Russia - 5%
South & Central America - 8%
Eurasia - 3%
Africa - 3%
North America - 16%

Islamic Countries - 59%

Source: Energy Information Administration, "International Energy Outlook, 2009," May 2009, http://www.eia.doe.gov/oiaf/ieo/pdf/0484%282009.pdf, p. 31

This chart also reveals another statistic about the world's oil reserves—one that is a cause for serious concern: the majority of the reserves are held by Islamic nations. Almost 60 percent of all the oil in the world's top oil-producing nations is in reserve under nations that hate Israel and America. The increasing demand for oil in the world will give these hostile nations increasing leverage and power as oil-guzzling nations such as the U.S. become more and more careful about keeping relationships with these nations intact.

But the question arises, why would these nations want to attack Israel? I learned the probable answer when I met recently with the president of the Zion Oil and Gas company. He told me that his company has been granted licenses by the Israeli government to drill for oil in Israel. While the going has been tough and the cost high, don't be surprised if you hear in the near future that the nation of Israel has discovered oil in her own land. What could this mean in terms of end-time prophecies?

The present oil-rich nations desire to destroy Israel, and they have already tried it twice in modern history. Only Israel's superior military capacity, achieved through armaments and aid from the United States, has enabled Israel to repel attacks from these hostile nations. Consider what might happen as the U.S. grows increasingly dependent on Middle East oil and if Israel does discover massive deposits of oil on her land. Would not Israel's enemies jump on her for the "plunder and booty" of this newfound wealth, knowing that this time the U.S. would not come to her aid because of its utter dependence on their oil?

Even if Israel does not discover oil, would not the oil-rich nations that hate her use their oil as leverage to force Israel's oil-hungry allies such as the U.S. to step back as attempts are undertaken to annihilate their historical enemy? Either way, we can see why end-time prophecies predict a massive gathering of armies against Israel in the Middle East.

In Ezekiel 38:4 God tells these nations gathering against Israel with their evil plan that He will "turn you around [and] put hooks into your jaws." I believe that oil is the hook in the jaw. Since these nations are intent on their evil plan, God will allow their lust for wealth to lead them to their own destruction. It will be hunger for oil that will gather these nations to war against Israel. Ezekiel is pointedly clear about the motivation in the hearts of those who go up to the unwalled villages of Israel: "I will go up against a land of unwalled villages...to take plunder and to take booty, to stretch out your hand against the waste places that are again inhabited, and against a people gathered from the nations, who have acquired livestock and goods, who dwell in the midst of the land" (Ezekiel 38:11–12).

As author and speaker Terry James concludes, "How much of a stretch is it then to believe that the forces of Gog-Magog would one day consider this region a chief target for invasion? And carrying this logic to its biblically prophetic conclusion, is it any wonder that Armageddon, involving most every nation on earth, will take place in this very region to do battle for the great spoil—the liquid black gold—beneath the sand of the Middle East?"[37]

The Preoccupation with Materialism

Along with the proliferation of technology, the polarization of wealth, and the priority of oil, the Bible predicts that the end times will also be a time of preoccupation with materialism. Here is how the apostle Paul instructs his student Timothy concerning the "last days":

> But know this, that in the last days perilous times will come: For men will be lovers of themselves, lovers of money, boasters, proud, blasphemers, disobedient to parents, unthankful, unholy, unloving, unforgiving, slanderers, without self-control, brutal, despisers of good, traitors, headstrong, haughty, lovers of pleasure rather than lovers of God, having a form of godliness but denying its power. (2 Timothy 3:1–5)

Paul packs into this short passage nineteen characteristics that describe those who will be on the earth in the perilous end times before Jesus returns. These are not necessarily the characteristics of irreligious people; Paul tells us that these are people who have a form of godliness, but deny the power of it. They are religious people—people who will claim to love God but seem to love just about everything else instead. It is not within the purpose of this book to address all nineteen of these unholy characteristics, but the first two demand our attention because they give us signs of coming economic conditions in the last days.

The first item Paul notes is that in the last days people will be lovers of themselves. Love of self begins when we deny the Lord His supreme place in our lives. There is an old superstition that witches repeat the Lord's Prayer backward. First they recite, "Give us this day our daily bread" and "deliver us from evil," and then last of all, "Hallowed be thy name and thy will be done." In a sense, it seems to be the same prayer; it has the same content. But when you invert the prayer you invert its priorities, turning it into an altogether different prayer that places self first and God last.

That inversion shows how godlessness can begin so easily in godly people. Self-love can root itself invisibly in our hearts and increase until it dominates our very lives. Yet all the while we convince ourselves that we are still holding to God. There is no doubt that this is happening within the church today. There are those who have an outward profession of godliness but are actually practical atheists.

We see self-love more obviously in the secular world, where all the recent stories of financial misbehavior find their root in this one sin. The Martha Stewarts, the Bernie Madoffs, the Dennis Kozlowskis, the Kenneth Lays, the Bernard Ebberses of our generation were not thinking of anyone but themselves. "So what if people lose all their savings? So what if bankruptcies occur? So what if thousands are defrauded and hurt? If I come out ahead, all is well." That is the spirit of this age, and according to Paul, it is a sign of the approaching end times.

While I was working on this chapter, my literary agent and friend Sealy Yates asked me to read a manuscript written by one of his new authors. The author, David Platt, is the lead pastor of the 4,000-member congregation of the Church at Brook Hills in Birmingham, Alabama. The title of his book is certain to get your attention: *Radical: Taking Back Your Faith from the American Dream*. I must tell you that this was a most challenging and discomforting read. To show you what I mean, here is a paragraph from David Platt's new book:

When we pool our resources in our churches, what are our priorities? Each year in the United States, we spend more than $10 billion on church buildings. In America alone, the amount of real estate owned by institutional churches is worth over $230 billion. We have money and possessions, and we are building temples everywhere. Empires, really. Kingdoms. We call them houses of worship. But at the core, aren't they too often outdated models of religion that wrongfully define worship according to a place and wastefully consume our time and money when God has called us to be a people who spend our lives for the sake of His glory among the needy outside our gates?[38]

Earlier in his book, Dr. Platt clearly defines these needy outside our gates. Maybe I had seen these statistics before, but they never gripped my heart as when I read them there:

Today more than a billion people in the world live and die in desperate poverty. They attempt to survive on less than a dollar per day. Close to two billion others live on less than two dollars per day. That's half the world struggling to find food, water, and shelter with the same amount of money I spend on French fries for lunch. More than twenty-six thousand children today will breathe their last breath due to starvation or a preventable disease.... To put it in perspective, for the church I pastor, if this were my community, then every child eighteen years and younger in our county would be dead within the next two days.[39]

I pastor one of those large churches. We do reach out to touch the people outside our gates. We have established and support several ethnic congregations. We give 20 percent of our income to world missions. We have tried to be followers of the Great Commission and the Great Commandment. But the gap between what we are doing and what needs to be done is growing and often leaves us feeling powerless to be effective.

To keep from, in effect, "praying the Lord's Prayer backward," we must be continually vigilant over our priorities. Whom do we love first? Ourselves or others? Whom do we love most? Ourselves or our God? This vigilance over our loves must be ever more active as the last days approach when the order of the day is a rapidly increasing trend toward self-love.

It follows naturally that when you are a lover of yourself, you will also be a lover of money. Money gives one power to please self. And this brings us to Paul's second warning. He warned Timothy that in the last days, men will be lovers of money. The love of money is at the core of what motivates today's society. It fuels the engines that drive commercialism. It's the way people are judged, the standard by which achievement is measured.

Wilfred J. Hahn writes, "Doesn't it seem unimaginable that an inanimate thing like money, which at one time served only as a medium of exchange, should become something so large and complex, requiring legions of people to manage the myriad arrangement of who owes it and who owns it?... This whole phenomenon is evidence of just how controlling the monetary system has become."[40]

Thinking along the same lines, British philosopher Simon Critchley wonders: "What is money?... What does money really mean? What is the idea of money that we hold in our minds as we accept it, exchange it, squander it, or save it?" He goes on to say something that explains why many believe money is the most powerful "religion" of our day: "In the seemingly godless world of global finance capitalism, money is the only thing in which we really must have faith. Money is the one, true God in which we all believe.... And when it breaks down, as it has done so dramatically in the last year, then people experience something close to a crisis of faith."[41]

The eighteenth-century British cleric Robert South pulled no punches when he made a similar point: "There are not a few who believe in no God but Mammon, no devil but the absence of gold, no damnation but being poor, and no hell but an empty purse; and not a few of their descendants are living still."[42]

These men are merely confirming the words of Jesus, who said that when it comes to money, there can be no middle ground: "No one can serve two masters; for either he will hate the one and love the other, or else he will be loyal to the one and despise the other. You cannot serve God and mammon" (Matthew 6:24).

An Irish Dominican clergyman, Donagh O'Shea, clearly understood Jesus' point when he wrote these penetrating words:

Money means a lot of different things; it is much more than it appears to be. It is God's greatest rival. It is much more than the paper it seems to be, or the metal, or the plastic. It is our love of things; it is our escape from dependence on people; it is our security against death; it is our effort to control life....

It is easier to love things than to love people. Things are dead, so you can possess them easily....If you can't love people you will begin to love money. It will never hurt your feelings or challenge your motives, but neither will it ever respond to you—because it is dead....And after a while the problem will begin to show: you will begin to look dead yourself.... After a while you will be incapable of loving anyone, and then you might as well be dead....Money is neutral. But an extreme attachment to it is not neutral; it is a kind of opposite religion....The religion of God is the religion of love. The instinct of love is to share, to give away. But the instinct of Mammon is to accumulate.[43]

Please understand that neither Jesus nor Paul said you could not have money and still love God. Jesus said you could not love money and love God. Long ago I was taught that crises do not make us what we are; they reveal what we are. So what has our most recent financial crisis revealed about us? Wilfred J. Hahn answers this question in a way that you will immediately recognize as true:

> While other cultures would consider plagues, pestilences, and famine the worst that could be feared, our high-income societies consider one thing worse. The destruction of wealth. Our ultimate definition of disaster is a materialistic one, fixated as it is on the ups and downs of "cyberbit" financial asset values, home prices, cyclical patterns in employment and commerce, and other such things.[44]

Hahn has painted us an all-too-accurate picture. We can see evidence of its truth all around us today. When there is the slightest hiccup in the economy, it takes immediate and complete control of our lives. It dominates the discussion on talk radio. It fills the screen on CNN and Fox News. It's on the front page of *USA Today* and appears on the covers of all the major news magazines.

Yet in spite of the world's growing obsession with money, we Christians know that it is a false measure of true wealth and value. In his book *Desiring God*, John Piper starkly shows us the folly in treating financial wealth and its trappings as the ultimate value:

> Picture 269 people entering eternity in a plane crash in the Sea of Japan. Before the crash there is a noted politician, a millionaire corporate executive, a playboy and his playmate, a missionary kid on his way back from visiting grandparents. After the crash they stand before God utterly stripped of MasterCards, checkbooks, credit lines, image clothes, how-to-succeed books, and Hilton reservations. Here are the politician, the executive, the playboy, and the missionary kid, all on level ground with nothing, absolutely nothing in their hands, possessing only what they brought in their hearts. How absurd and tragic the lover of money will seem on that day—like a man who spends his

whole life collecting train tickets and in the end is so weighed down by the collection he misses the last train.[45]

This strong emphasis on money and the things it buys provides ample evidence that we are nearing the last days that Paul spoke of in his warning to Timothy. This and other signs are lining up just as he, Daniel, and Ezekiel predicted, and they are becoming more and more unmistakable. Global technology is proliferating, increasing our knowledge and mobility exponentially and setting us up for massive control by a central authority. The distance between the haves and have-nots is becoming a gaping chasm. Oil in the Middle East is becoming a source of power and arrogance for nations eager to annihilate Israel. And people are becoming alarmingly preoccupied with wealth and the good life. The warning signs could hardly be clearer.

Yet, it seems that few people are heeding these signs. Unfortunately, such obliviousness to impending disaster seems typical of our race. As Jesus told us:

And as it was in the days of Noah, so it will be also in the days of the Son of Man: They ate, they drank, they married wives, they were given in marriage, until the day that Noah entered the ark, and the flood came and destroyed them all. Likewise as it was also in the days of Lot: They ate, they drank, they bought, they sold, they planted, they built; but on the day that Lot went out of Sodom it rained fire and brimstone from heaven and destroyed them all. Even so will it be in the day when the Son of Man is revealed. (Luke 17:26–30)

This passage does not tell a story of debauchery at the end times as some have taught. Quite the contrary; the people who were living at the times of the Flood and the destruction of Sodom and Gomorrah were simply living their everyday lives. They ate, they drank, they married and were given in marriage. They bought, they sold, they planted, they built. These people went on with their love for the "good life" as if nothing unusual loomed on the horizon. They refused to heed the warnings and just kept on doing what they had always done until judgment descended and their window of opportunity closed forever.

Today the warning signs are clearer than ever before. This should grip all of us with a sense of urgency about examining our own lives and making necessary changes in our priorities. And it should spur us to a greater concern about the lives of those we know and love.

CHAPTER 8

The Collapse of the Global
Financial Market

October 29, 1929—they call it Black Tuesday—the day the stock market crashed and the Great Depression began. The Dow lost 23 percent of its value in one day. By the end of the following month, $100 billion was lost, leaving "financially ruined people of all economic backgrounds. Life savings were wiped out. Banks and businesses collapsed and unemployment soared."[1]

The Roaring Twenties, the decade that led up to the crash, was a time of wealth and excess. A speculative boom had taken hold late in the decade, leading hundreds of thousands of Americans to invest heavily in the stock market. A significant number even borrowed money to buy more stocks. By August 1929, brokers were routinely lending small investors more than two-thirds of the face value of the stocks they were buying. More than $8.5 billion was out on loan, more than the entire amount of currency circulating in the U.S. at the time.[2]

In the first chapter of this book, we chronicled America's recent financial meltdown, which many have compared to the 1929 crash. But let me assure you that neither the 1929 crash nor the recent global financial trauma even comes close to what God's Word says about the economic destruction slated for the future. Before we look at that future age, however, let's take a look back to an era that is not far behind us.

183

In the days before banks received government bailout funds, they were known to give out premiums, such as toasters and coffee pots, to entice new depositors. In the period from the Depression through the mid-1950s, many banks gave out a series of popular booklets on personal finances. The author of these booklets was the man who published the first American road atlas, George Samuel Clason. His parable-like stories, set in ancient Babylon, urged people to apply wisdom to their own finances gleaned from his title character, *The Richest Man in Babylon.*

The parables centered on a man named Bansir, a hardworking yet poor Babylonian chariot maker. Bansir is seeking to learn the secrets of Arkad, who was formerly poor like Bansir and his cronies but who became exceedingly rich. Clason reasoned that, although the city has crumbled to dust through the eons of time, "the wisdom of Babylon endures.... [It was] the cradle in which was nurtured the basic principles of finance, now recognized and used the world over."[3]

Old Testament and Middle East scholar Dr. Charles H. Dyer confirms Clason's evaluation:

> For nearly two thousand years, Babylon was the most important city in the world. It was the commercial and financial center for all of Mesopotamia, the center of a geographical "X" that linked the Orient with the Mediterranean and Egypt with Persia. Its scribes and priests spread its cultural heritage throughout the known world. The arts of divination, astronomy, astrology, accounting, and private commercial law all sprang from Babylon.[4]

As Dr. Dyer shows us, Clason's estimate of the influence of Babylon was dead-on. That influence did not end with the city's demise, nor have we yet seen the end of it. The city and its system lives on.

Earlier we noted that the first attempt at a world order is recorded in the first book of the Bible. It occurred in Babylon with the construction of the renowned Tower of Babel (see Genesis 11). Now, from the last book in the Bible, we are going to look at the final financial world order, which will also be located in Babylon. While the events we will be studying will occur toward the end of the Tribulation period, let me challenge you to consider them seriously. You may not think these events will affect you, but they will; their shadow is lengthening across the world even today.

Babylon no longer exists as a significant world city, but we know it will rise to power again because the Bible assumes it as fact. The eighteenth chapter of Revelation gives us some very specific information about Babylon as the rebuilt commercial capital of the world during the Tribulation period.

Why Babylon? Why would this ancient, once-powerful city, now obscure and gathering dust, rise again? Scientist and Bible scholar Dr. Henry Morris suggests some answers:

> Babylon is indeed a prime prospect for rebuilding, entirely apart from any prophetic intimation. Its location is the most ideal in the world for any kind of international center. Not only is it in the beautiful and fertile Tigris-Euphrates plain, but it is near some of the world's richest oil reserves.... Babylon is very near the geographical center of all of the earth's land masses. It is within navigable distances to the Persian Gulf and it is at the crossroads of the three great continents of Europe, Asia, and Africa. Thus there is no more ideal location anywhere for a world trade center, a world communication center, a world banking center... or especially a world capital!
>
> With all these natural advantages, it is not farfetched at all to suggest that the future financial capital of the ten-nation federation established at the beginning of the Tribulation should be built here. Arnold Toynbee, the greatest historian of modern

times, used to stress that Babylon would be the best place to build a future world cultural metropolis.[5]

The rebuilding of Babylon is not just the idle topic of scholarly books. When Saddam Hussein rose to power in Iraq, he conceived a grandiose scheme for the rebuilding of that ancient city. He promised that Babylon's grand palaces and legendary hanging gardens (one of the Seven Wonders of the Ancient World) would rise from the dust. Believing himself to be the reincarnation of King Nebuchadnezzar II, who had conquered Jerusalem 2,500 years earlier, Hussein invested more than $500 million toward his goal of restoring the ancient city of Babylon.

In 1987, while on a site visit to the ruins of Nebuchadnezzar's palace, Hussein asked how his guides were so certain of the date of its construction. The curator showed Hussein some of the original bricks, stamped with the name of Nebuchadnezzar II and the date that we now refer to as 605 BC. Hussein, not to be outdone, had bricks laid in his palace wall that read: "In the reign of the victorious Saddam Hussein, the president of the Republic, . . . the guardian of the great Iraq and the renovator of its renaissance and the builder of its great civilization, the rebuilding of the great city of Babylon was done in 1987."[6]

To further cement the implication of a relationship between himself and Nebuchadnezzar, Hussein had a seal struck depicting parallel images of both himself and the ancient ruler. The inscription was written in the wedge shapes of ancient cuneiform script as well as, strangely enough, English.

Hussein was consumed with reviving the glory days of Babylon under Nebuchadnezzar. He made Babylon "the focal point of Iraqi nationalism," and on September 22, 1987, he inaugurated the musical event known as the Babylon Festival. Saddam seemed determined to echo Nebuchadnezzar's bold proclamation: "Is not this

Nebuchadnezzar and Saddam Hussein

great Babylon, that I have built for a royal dwelling by my mighty power and for the honor of my majesty?" (Daniel 4:30).

Saddam's extravagant plans were interrupted by the U.S. invasion of Iraq in 2003. Despite his removal from power and subsequent execution, the work to rebuild Babylon continues.

How does a war-torn nation like Iraq come up with the funds to rebuild an ancient site? Obviously, some of the resources come from the exportation of oil. In early 2010, Iraqi oil exports were at the highest level in more than a decade. The government of Prime Minister Nouri al-Maliki announced plans to quadruple oil production to 2.15 million barrels per day by the end of 2010. The Iraqi government has issued long-term contracts with foreign oil companies to manage ten of Iraq's major oil fields. Al-Maliki aims to make Iraq a "preeminent producer that will rival, if not eclipse, Saudi Arabia and Russia" as the predominant world oil producers.[7]

Oil is not Iraq's only source of funds. Despite its own enormous budget deficit, the United States continues to pump reconstruction money into Iraq. This in spite of Iraq's estimated budget surplus in excess of $60 billion, little of which is being invested in rebuilding the nation.[8]

Today the United Nations Educational, Scientific, and Cultural Organization (UNESCO) is also pumping millions of dollars into Babylon. With the help of private donors, the UN hopes to turn Babylon into a thriving center of tourism and commerce. If everything goes according to plan, Babylon will be a cultural center complete with shopping malls, hotels, and maybe even a theme park.

In 2009 the U.S. State Department issued a media note announcing a $700,000 pledge to The Future of Babylon Project, explaining that "Babylon stands out among Iraq's rich contributions to humanity." The note went on to say that this project "exemplifies the American people's commitment to the preservation of human heritage and their respect for the cultural heritage of Iraq."[9]

An article in the British newspaper the *Independent* was titled, "Iraq's New Venture: Holidays in the Garden of Eden," and subtitled, "Iraq is trying to lure visitors to the land of Babylon with the slogan 'tourism not terrorism.'" The article goes on to say, "The cradle of civilisation, the land of Babylon and the Garden of Eden, will become a paradise for foreign tourists."[10]

The United States government is taking seriously the rise of the city of Babylon and the central place of Iraq in the future of the world. On January 5, 2009, the largest and, at $474 million, the most expensive U.S. Embassy in the world opened in Baghdad, not far from Babylon. The 104-acre, twenty-seven-building complex is situated on the banks of the Tigris River.[11] It includes 619 apartments for staff, restaurants, basketball and volleyball courts, and an indoor Olympic-sized swimming pool.[12]

This embassy, known as "Embassy Baghdad," is the largest of its kind in the world. It is the size of eighty football fields—as large as Vatican City—with a population of 5,500. It dwarfs U.S.

embassies elsewhere that typically cover about ten acres. The Baghdad embassy has its own defense force and is designed to be entirely self-sufficient.

We can see by these moves toward rebuilding Babylon that the city has a special interest in the eyes of the powers of the world. I believe these steps signal the beginning of the fulfillment of biblical prophecy. Henry Morris explains:

> Never has a great world city had such a meteoric rise as New Babylon, and never will one experience such a cataclysmic and total fall.... Babylon on the Euphrates has lain dormant and foreboding for centuries.... But mighty Babylon is not really dead.... Suddenly it will rise once again. Under the impact of overwhelming geopolitical needs, it will be authorized and implemented by the unprecedented building program undertaken by the federal ten-kingdom empire of the West, then pushed to dynamic completion by the Beast. Finally it will be inaugurated as the great world capital of the Beast, who will have become king of all the kingdoms of the globe.[13]

Babylon's Rebirth as the World Financial Center

This rebuilding of modern Babylon is of special interest to our present study because of the city's historic past and prophetic future. Nimrod, the first world dictator, tried to make Babylon the first world capital. And biblical prophecy tells us that the revived city is destined to be one of the three capitals of the Antichrist, the final world dictator.

According to the prophetic scheme outlined in Revelation, when the Antichrist takes control of the world, his government will function out of three major cities. From *Rome* he will rule the political world (see Revelation 17). From *Jerusalem* he will control the religious world after making a covenant with the Jews (see 2 Thessalonians

2:4). From *Babylon* he will direct his worldwide empire of economic and financial concerns (see Revelation 18).

Revelation 18:12–13 catalogs twenty-eight items that form the basis for end-time economic commerce. This list includes the various material possessions for which men and women have labored, schemed, and become enslaved throughout history, which makes the list symbolic of man's perennial pursuit of wealth. While John lists commodities that were significant to his day, it is amazing to see how timeless they still are today and obviously will be in that final day:

> Merchandise of gold and silver, precious stones and pearls, fine linen and purple, silk and scarlet, every kind of citron wood, every kind of object of ivory, every kind of object of most precious wood, bronze, iron, and marble; and cinnamon and incense, fragrant oil and frankincense, wine and oil, fine flour and wheat, cattle and sheep, horses and chariots, and bodies and souls of men. (Revelation 18:12–13)

Gold, silver, and precious stones come first. Whether this indicates a return to a gold/silver world economic system we cannot know. But as Henry Morris points out, we do know that

> precious metals and jewels...have always served as the measure of value and the basis of monetary systems. Especially in times of inflation, such as in the years of the tribulation, men will seek to protect their savings by investing in items of intrinsic value—gold, silver, gemstones, and pearls—and trade in such commodities as these has always been and will continue to be uppermost in the plans of international merchants.[14]

As world currencies (like the dollar) fall apart and continue to lose value, it may be that the entire world will revert to a gold/silver/

hard currency standard. The Arab gold dinar is currently being used as currency in nine countries, so there is definitely a pattern in place for trade in gold/silver. If Iraq suddenly began demanding payment for its oil in dinars, the influx of gold into that country would be huge. That probably won't happen, but as international debt continues to spur inflation, we can be sure that gold will play an increasingly important role in the world economy.

The rest of the commodities list includes things that are for show and personal adornment, followed by choice articles of rare and precious wood, metal, and ivory. Perfumes, assorted luxuries, and more substantial commodities such as horses and chariots also make up the inventory.

The prosperity of Babylon will attract merchants from all over the globe, people whose wealth will classify them as the great men of the world. As Henry Morris explains:

> The international bankers and the corporation directors and the mercantile barons and the shipping magnates and all their host of money-worshiping, power-seeking underlings, who once traversed their orbits around New York and Geneva, London and Paris, Moscow and Berlin, Johannesburg and Tokyo, now find it gloriously profitable to center it all in Great Babylon.[15]

In other words, Babylon is destined to rise again as the greatest center of financial power yet known to the world. But as we are about to see, it will not last.

The Destruction of Babylon

Babylon, from its first mention in Genesis as the site of the Tower of Babel, has always been synonymous with paganism, humanism, and rebellion. This infamous city is the second most frequently referenced city in the Bible. It is mentioned 295 times in 261 verses (NKJV), appearing first in Genesis 10 and last in Revelation 18. Babylon is mentioned thirty-one times in just one chapter—Jeremiah 51. It seems pretty obvious that Babylon will play a major role in God's end-time plan.

Jerusalem, the most frequently mentioned city in the Bible, stands against Babylon like the opposite pole of a magnet. References to Jerusalem are always positive, whereas references to Babylon are always negative. Jerusalem has always been God's city, His dwelling place, the center of worship and rule over God's people.

It should come as no surprise that Babylon was involved in the first assault on God's promise to give Abram and his descendants the Promised Land. As Charles H. Dyer explains,

> Genesis 14 describes an attack by an alliance of four kings from the east against five kings residing in the Land of Promise. Among the four kings who attacked Abram's land was Amraphel, king of Shinar (Babylon).... This was the first great test of God's promise and Abram's faith.... It was the initial threat against God's Promised Land, and God gave Abram victory.[16]

Just as the evil and rebellion that began in Babylon has characterized the city throughout the ages, it will continue to characterize it in the future. It was Babylon that ended Judah's existence as an independent nation, and it will continue to plague God's people even in times to come. Educator and prophetic scholar Dr. Ed Hindson writes, "End-time Babylon is symbolic of all evil, pride, oppression, and power which exalts itself against God. It will combine the best efforts of a collective humanity to rule itself without God. And it will fail!"[17]

The Bible is not squeamish about calling Babylon exactly what it is:

And on her forehead a name was written:
MYSTERY,
BABYLON THE GREAT,
THE MOTHER OF HARLOTS
AND OF THE ABOMINATIONS OF THE EARTH.
  (Revelation 17:5)

Because of Babylon's persistent effusion of evil, a time is coming when God will ultimately engineer its final destruction. In the final climax of world history, when eternity supersedes time, the polarization between Babylon and Jerusalem will be over. Babylon will be gone, and the New Jerusalem will descend from heaven as the capital city of the new earth and the eternal dwelling place of God and His people (see Revelation 21).

In his prophecy against Babylon, Jeremiah describes it as a place that will be desolate forever, a heap of ruins, a haunt of jackals, an object of horror and scorn, a desert and dry land, a place where no man lives and through which no man travels (see Jeremiah 51:26, 37, 43). Isaiah tells us that Babylon will be a desolate land that will never again be inhabited through all generations—a place where no Arab will pitch his tent and no shepherd will rest his flocks (see Isaiah 13:19–20).

Since some teach that the prophecies concerning Babylon's destruction have already been fulfilled, it is important to separate the *fall* of Babylon in history from the *destruction* of Babylon in the future. Persia did not destroy Babylon in 539 BC as some have taught. When Cyrus captured Babylon, he did it by subterfuge, not by military destruction (see Daniel 5). On the evening of Belshazzar's garish banquet, suddenly the hand of God appeared, writing on the wall. The message read: "God has numbered your kingdom, and finished it.... Your kingdom has been divided, and given to the Medes and Persians" (Daniel 5:26–28). That prophecy came true on that very night as the Medo-Persian army took over the city.

193

These conquerors did not destroy the city; they made it the secondary capital of the Persian Empire. When the Greeks conquered the Persians in 331 BC, Alexander the Great made Babylon his capital and died there.

Neither has Babylon ever been desolate, as Isaiah prophesied it would be in chapter 13 of his prophecy. In fact, Babylon exists today in central Iraq as the province of Babil, an area of 5,603 square kilometers containing eight cities with a combined population of 1,651,600.[18] While her population has vacillated over the centuries, it has nearly tripled since 1977 when its citizenry numbered 592,000.[19]

As we can see, in the centuries since the ancient empires, Babylon has faded into obscurity but not into oblivion. It has degenerated from a great city to its present status as an Iraqi province. But if we take the Bible seriously, we understand that Babylon must again rise to power in order to receive the judgment that Isaiah, Jeremiah, and the apostle John have prophesied. We know this will happen because the Bible often speaks of the future Babylon in terms of its grandeur. The Greek phrase used to describe the city in Revelation 18 is *ha megala polis*, which in English means "the megalopolis." This title leads us to believe that the population of the rebuilt city of Babylon just before its future destruction will be much greater than its current provincial population.

Babylon was likely the largest city in the world at the time of Jeremiah. By the time of the apostle John, however, it was no longer a large city. So, in the book of Revelation when John describes the vision he receives from God concerning the destruction of a prosperous mega-Babylon, he obviously speaks of a future event in a future city.

This future Babylon is described in Isaiah 13:19 as "Babylon, the glory of kingdoms, the beauty of the Chaldeans' [Iraqi's] pride." Such will be Babylon's status just before it is annihilated by a destruction so complete that it will never be inhabited again.

Is Babylon's Destruction Literal or Metaphoric?

One aspect of the prophecies concerning Babylon's destruction has generated a great deal of controversy among Bible scholars. Should we take these references literally or metaphorically? Is the Bible really referring to the destruction of the actual city? Or to the world economic system and humanistic philosophy that city epitomizes? Author and educator Dr. Mal Couch affirms the latter without dismissing the former. "In either case," he says, "the Scripture makes it clear that Babylon represents the worldwide, global, political and ecclesiastical world system of the end times."[20]

Some scholars see in Revelation 18:1–2 an indication of a dual metaphoric meaning: "After these things I saw another angel coming down from heaven, having great authority, and the earth was illuminated with his glory. And he cried mightily with a loud voice, saying, 'Babylon the great is fallen, is fallen.' Author/editor Dr. J. A. Seiss believed that the repetition of the phrase indicates two separate parts or stages of the fall—the undoing of Babylon as a religious entity and also as an economic entity.[21]

In the above passage from Revelation 18, John tells us that the prophecy concerning Babylon's destruction is delivered by an angel so powerful that he lights up the entire world. When this angel says, "Babylon is fallen, is fallen," he uses a phrase that describes an instantaneous action. This tells us that the destruction of the city or the system of Babylon will not be gradual, but instantaneous. Revelation 18 notes over and over the suddenness of the destruction that will come at the close of the Tribulation period:

- "Therefore her plagues will come in one day" (v. 8).
- "For in one hour your judgment has come" (v. 10).
- "For in one hour such great riches came to nothing" (v. 17).
- "For in one hour she is made desolate" (v. 19).

When God comes against Babylon, it will be with the suddenness and effectiveness of a spring trap. Note particularly verse 17, which tells us that whatever else Babylon's destruction means, it will certainly include an economic crash.

Why Will Babylon Be Destroyed?

Why is God determined to pour out His judgment upon the city of Babylon? In general, we have already seen ample reason. From the beginning, Babylon's philosophy and religion have been in diametric opposition to God, making it the exemplar of a worldview that has corrupted mankind throughout all ages.

But within this broad overview we can glean from the prophetic vision of John six specific and telling reasons why Babylon or its influences cannot be allowed to exist in God's kingdom. We will consider these one by one.

Babylon Will Be Destroyed Because of Her Sorceries

In Revelation 18:2 we read that "Babylon... has become a dwelling place of demons, a prison for every foul spirit, and a cage for every unclean and hated bird!"

In the days of Daniel the prophet, Babylon was the home of magicians, soothsayers, and astrologers who were members of King Nebuchadnezzar's brain trust. Revelation 18 shows us that this evil will intensify as the Babylonian system is overrun by the satanic influence of the Beast. Babylon will be the center of depravity where demonic spirits strive to gain control over every man's mind.

As the world descends into materialism, it tends to dismiss God. But in dismissing God, people do not eliminate the deep human need for a spiritual connection. When they push God out of the picture, the resulting vacuum is often filled by turning to occultism, mysticism, and contacts with the spirit world. As G. K. Chesterton is credited with saying, "The opposite of a belief in God is not a belief in nothing; it is a belief in anything."[22] Jesus warned that in such a vacuum of unbelief a person becomes vulnerable to multiple "unclean spirits" and thus is much worse off than when he believed (see Luke 11:24–25).

Babylon Will Be Destroyed Because of Her Seductions

Revelation 18 goes on to say this of Babylon: "For all the nations have drunk of the wine of the wrath of her fornication, the kings of the earth have committed fornication with her, and the merchants of the earth have become rich through the abundance of her luxury" (v. 3).

This is an echo of a prophecy from Jeremiah: "Babylon was a golden cup in the LORD's hand, that made all the earth drunk. The nations drank her wine; therefore the nations are deranged" (Jeremiah 51:7).

Babylon will be famous around the world as the most enlightened and liberated city on the planet. Her constitution will give free rein to all forms of immorality and depravity, making Las Vegas, Paris, and Hong Kong seem tame by comparison. Babylon will be a favorite getaway place for the richest and most powerful people of the world, seeking pleasures and activities not legally available in their hometowns. Thus the heads of nations and great corporations will be seduced to be unfaithful to God in every way possible.

Bible expositor John Phillips suggests: "The crime syndicate, already enormously wealthy and powerful, feudal, ruthless, and omnipresent, will move its headquarters to Babylon. There can be little doubt that the syndicate, controlling the vice traffic of the world and insinuating itself into all kinds of legitimate business, will ultimately look to the beast as its head."[23]

Babylon epitomizes the godless influence that will reign over man's social, political, cultural, and commercial life in the Tribulation. Nations, kings, and merchants will be intoxicated by it. The only way this worldwide sewer of evil can be stopped is for God to destroy it.

Babylon Will Be Destroyed Because of Her Sins

In addition to Babylon's judgment for her sorceries and her seductions, she will be judged because "her sins have reached to heaven, and God has remembered her iniquities" (Revelation 18:5).

The Greek word rendered *reached* in this passage literally means "to be glued together" or "welded together." The picture is graphic. The sins of Babylon have been piled one upon another as bricks in a building, an obvious allusion to the Tower of Babel, which was the inception of Babylon's wicked career. Just as Babylon's makers once put bricks one on top of another to build that physical tower, the city's rebuilders will pile her sins one upon another until they reach to God in heaven. Again, He will have to step in and topple the profane tower.

Babylon Will Be Destroyed Because of Her Self-Glorification

"In the measure that she glorified herself and lived luxuriously, in the same measure give her torment and sorrow; for she says in her heart, 'I sit as queen, and am no widow, and will not see sorrow'" (Revelation 18:7).

It is not hard to imagine the haughty arrogance and blasphemies as the city of Babylon is rebuilt. The word on the street will be that this city is even greater than the one built by Nebuchadnezzar. Such self-aggrandizing posturing and rebellion has been a characteristic of Babylon since its inception. According to the historian Josephus, Nimrod built the Tower of Babel in defiance of God and as a form of protection should God dare to flood the earth again. Nimrod planned to build a tower "too high for the waters to reach" and which was to be topped off by a platform where Nimrod could "scream his defiance and hatred toward God."[24]

As an aside, the recent renovations at Babylon are being slowed by—you guessed it—water. The group running The Future of Babylon project indicates that all that remains of the Tower of Babel today is rubble, which "is surrounded by standing water."[25]

At Babel God stepped in to prevent the human race from falling under the sway of an absolute tyrant over all the earth. But in the end times, this very place will provide a platform for the most evil tyrant the world has ever known. The pride of Nebuchadnezzar will live again in the ruler of the final Babylon. And like that ancient monarch, he will also view himself as immortal and invincible. But his towering pride will be toppled as sure as Nimrod's tower. Pride will be Babylon's undoing, as pride always is: "Pride goes before destruction, and a haughty spirit before a fall" (Proverbs 16:18).

Babylon Will Be Destroyed Because of Her Slavery

Above we addressed the catalog of economic commodities for which Babylon will become the world trade center. That list sadly concludes with "slaves, and souls of men" (Revelation 18:13 KJV). In other words, slavery will be prevalent in that wicked economy. Emotional slavery to material things will certainly be prevalent to an unprecedented degree in those days, but this is not the kind of slavery this passage specifies. This passage refers to the trafficking of men and women caught up in forced prostitution. International human trafficking and outright physical slavery will be part of the Babylonian prosperity.

In the final system of commerce that will characterize the Tribulation period, humans will not be thought of as beings created in the image of God. They will be dehumanized, seen as nothing more than highly developed animals—a commodity to own, to barter, and to sell.

According to English activist and professor of sociology Kevin Bales, although slavery is illegal throughout the world, today more than 27 million people are entrapped as slaves. This is a slavery linked to the global economy. The new slaves are not viewed as long-term investments as they once were. Their value is that they are cheap, require little care, and are disposable.[26] This outrageous practice will greatly increase in the Tribulation period. God will put an end to it with the final destruction of Babylon.

Babylon Will Be Destroyed Because of Her Sacrifices

As if any one of the previously listed five causes is not sufficient to deserve God's judgment, Babylon adds her sacrifices to her offenses. "And in her was found the blood of the prophets and saints, and of all who were slain on the earth" (Revelation 18:24). "I saw the woman, drunk with the blood of the saints and with the blood of the martyrs of Jesus" (Revelation 17:6).

Not only will Babylon be filled with demonic activity and occultism, which often involves the ritual sacrifice of animals, it will also be responsible for the martyrdom of the prophets and the saints of God. Many may be those who are persecuted for refusing to accept the mark of the Beast. Others no doubt will be executed simply for wearing the name of Christ and taking stands for morality, purity, and ethics against the odious tyranny of Satan, the Antichrist, and the False Prophet.

As John tells us in recording his vision, God will not forget the loyal and courageous sacrifice of those who die for His name:

I saw under the altar the souls of those who had been slain for the word of God and for the testimony which they held. And they cried with a loud voice, saying, "How long, O Lord, holy and true, until You judge and avenge our blood on those who dwell on the earth?" Then a white robe was given to each of them; and it was said to them that they should rest a little while longer, until both the number of their fellow servants and their brethren, who would be killed as they were, was completed. (Revelation 6:9–11)

The blood of the martyrs so ruthlessly shed by the oppression of Babylon will be avenged when God brings about His promised and final destruction of that city, which has become the world's symbol for wickedness and enmity against God's holy people.

Babylon's Destruction Comes

Block upon block, sin upon sin, Babylon's tower of iniquity will rise to the very presence of God, giving Him ample reason to act. "Therefore her plagues will come in one day—death and mourning and famine. And she will be utterly burned with fire, for strong is the Lord God who judges her" (Revelation 18:8). A few verses later, John describes the finality of Babylon's destruction:

Then a mighty angel took up a stone like a great millstone and threw it into the sea, saying, "Thus with violence the great city Babylon shall be thrown down, and shall not be found anymore. The sound of harpists, musicians, flutists, and trumpeters shall not be heard in you anymore. No craftsman of any craft shall be found in you anymore, and the sound of a millstone shall not be heard in you anymore. The light of a lamp shall not shine in you anymore, and the voice of bridegroom and bride shall not be heard in you anymore." (Revelation 18:21–23)

201

Note that in this passage the word *anymore* is used six times. That is the strongest term available in the Greek language to express "not at all." One writer has described the scene like this: "The angel's words announce most impressively the vanishing forever of all the joys and delights of the great city, the music and the song, the hum of industry, the brightness of its illumination and above all, the rejoicings of the bridegroom and bride, which in the Bible stand for the highest of all human joys."[27]

Never again will normal human joys exist in Babylon. What a picture of final desolation! When God judges a nation or a city or a system, the judgment is sure and swift and final.

At the height of Babylon's glory, the greatest kings of the earth will occupy her. But in one hour all their majesty and power will be gone. In this city will be the most fashionably dressed of all the world's people, but in one hour all the expensive and costly clothes will be gone. In this city the best musicians will live, but in one hour every note will be silenced.

The world's largest international corporations, banks, and financial institutions will be centered in Babylon. The most powerful heads of the world's commercial and financial enterprises will dwell in Babylon, but in one hour their financial dreams will be dashed. The globalism that once seemed to promise a managed, worldwide utopia will have created a web of interconnectivity, the failure of which will pull down the entire world.

At that moment of Babylon's destruction, the world's financial system will collapse. All global markets will crash. Banks will shut down. Corporations will be instantly bankrupt. Merchants will go out of business. All stocks in corporations will be instantly worthless. All currency will be nothing more than printed paper, good for little beyond fireplace kindling. Billions of people will be instantly out of work. Their bank accounts will no longer exist. The entire world will experience a financial meltdown multiple times worse than anything ever witnessed and far beyond anything the most pessimistic prognosticator could possibly imagine. Such a huge cataclysmic event will not go unnoticed.

World Reactions to the Destruction of Babylon

How will the world react to Babylon's fall? The apostle John gives us the reactions of three groups, each expressing cataclysmic shock by using the same woeful expression, "Alas, alas." That archaic word is seldom used today, but everyone understands it as an expression of calamity and grief. Let's explore why these three groups will utter that word.

The Kings of the Earth Will Mourn

> The kings of the earth who committed fornication and lived luxuriously with [Babylon] will weep and lament for her, when they see the smoke of her burning, standing at a distance for fear of her torment, saying, "Alas, alas, that great city Babylon, that mighty city! For in one hour your judgment has come." (Revelation 18:9–10)

The kings who thought all power was theirs are going to mourn because the great capital city of the Beast's financial empire has been destroyed. As prophetic author Walter K. Price explains, "These kings who wail at the fall of Babylon are the provincial rulers who administrate the world empire of the Antichrist, and whose domains are affected most by the sudden disruption of commerce."[28]

Apparently Babylon was the final hope of these kings. When Babylon is destroyed, they are utterly devastated and can do nothing but mourn their enormous financial loss.

The Merchants of the Earth Will Mourn

> And the merchants of the earth will weep and mourn over her, for no one buys their merchandise anymore.... The fruit that your soul longed for has gone from you, and all the things which are rich and splendid have gone from you, and you shall find them no more at all. The merchants of these things, who became rich by her, will stand at a distance for fear of her torment, weeping and wailing, and saying, "Alas, alas, that great city that was clothed in fine linen, purple, and scarlet, and adorned with gold and precious stones and pearls! For in one hour such great riches came to nothing." (Revelation 18:11, 14–17)

The word here translated as "merchants" is the Greek word *emporoi*. It refers particularly to wholesalers, or those who deal in large quantities of trade items. These merchants will be instantly ruined. They will lament because their commercial power base—the economic hub of the world—will be gone. The stock exchanges will crash and the banks will close their doors. Bankruptcy will permeate world economies. In that day the god of mammon will prove to be worthless. In one hour all economic well-being will vanish!

The Shipmasters of the Earth Will Mourn

The shipping magnates of the world and their employees will mourn along with the rulers and merchants.

> Every shipmaster, all who travel by ship, sailors, and as many as trade on the sea, stood at a distance and cried out when they saw the smoke of her burning, saying, "What is like this great city?" They threw dust on their heads and cried out, weeping and wailing, and saying, "Alas, alas, that great city, in which all who had ships on the sea became rich by her wealth! For in one hour she is made desolate." (Revelation 18:17–19)

I doubt that most Americans think much about the importance of overseas shipping today, but a casual glance at the country of origin for many of the products we buy shows that they arrived via ship. Shipping is more important to us than we think, and many economists watch it carefully.

The Baltic Dry Index is an economic measurement used to gauge the direction of the global economy. The BDI measures shipping of raw materials in twenty of the world's busiest trade routes by assessing daily what shippers are charging to ship various lots of goods in oceangoing vessels. If prices are rising, that means the demand for shipping space is increasing, which is a signal for a strong economy. If prices are falling, it means there is an excess of shipping capacity, indicating that world economies are in recession. So, a BDI going up is good for the economy, and a BDI going down is bad. The BDI is considered a "leading economic indicator" because it predicts future economic strength or weakness. Although the BDI is still below its February 2008 high, it has increased dramatically since January 2009.[29]

Despite current global economic conditions, in November 2009 the Persian Gulf States announced their plan for a $40 billion expansion that will "triple port capacity across the oil-rich region...to keep pace with rapid economic growth in the Gulf."[30]

We can expect this increase to continue. During the Tribulation, the Persian Gulf will be flooded with merchant ships coming from Babylon, the great center of world commerce. But one day as these ships enter the Gulf, the shipmasters will stare gaping and in shock at the enormous columns of smoke billowing from the inland city where their goods are going up in a blaze of fire. At that moment their ships' cargoes will be utterly worthless. The entire system upon which they had built their lives and their hopes will be gone, and they will cry out, "Alas, alas, that great city, in which all who had ships on the sea became rich by her wealth! For in one hour she is made desolate" (Revelation 18:19).

205

The Rejoicing in Heaven over the Destruction of Babylon

When Babylon is destroyed, the kings, the merchants, and the mariners of the earth will mourn. But in heaven the apostles and the prophets will rejoice. "Rejoice over her, O heaven, and you holy apostles and prophets, for God has avenged you on her!" (Revelation 18:20).

The apostles and prophets are urged to rejoice at Babylon's destruction because it was the system of that city that had martyred all of the apostles except John. It was that system that demanded, "Take the mark of the Beast, or starve." It was that system that had persecuted them, cut them to ribbons, boiled them in oil, hung them up to die, and sent them to the lions' den. It was that system that stood for everything that was against the God of heaven. One by one, they died, and it seemed as if nobody knew or cared.

But the God of heaven does not forget His own. "Vengeance is Mine," He promised (Romans 12:19). This is an echo of many such promises to His people: "Vengeance is Mine, and recompense; their foot shall slip in due time; for the day of their calamity is at hand, and the things to come hasten upon them" (Deuteronomy 32:35). " 'Vengeance is Mine, I will repay,' says the Lord. And again, 'The LORD will judge His people.' It is a fearful thing to fall into the hands of the living God" (Hebrews 10:30–31). The manner and timing of the repayment for man's wickedness is God's prerogative. The apostles and prophets rejoice, not over the deaths of those doomed to eternal hell, but because God's righteousness and justice have prevailed.

John records something startling: "Then a mighty angel took up a stone like a great millstone and threw it into the sea, saying, 'Thus with violence the great city Babylon shall be thrown down, and shall not be found anymore' " (Revelation 18:21). In ancient times the millstone symbolized commerce because the grinding of wheat exemplified the economic stability of the culture. The millstone sinking into the sea signaled the final end to life in Babylon and to the economy of the world.

But there is another possible application. Do you remember reading what the Lord said about those who offend little children? "Whoever causes one of these little ones who believe in Me to sin, it would be better for him if a millstone were hung around his neck, and he were drowned in the depth of the sea" (Matthew 18:6). The annihilation of this godless power, gorged with the blood of the prophets, the apostles, and the saints of God, is pictured as a great millstone thrown with violence into the sea, sinking into eternal oblivion.

Do you ever find yourself wondering if God has forgotten you? When you experience unfair treatment? When your evil adversaries seem to get the upper hand? When those who abuse the system advance while you miss yet another promotion? Do you ever say, as David did, "How long will the wicked triumph?" (Psalm 94:3).

This is one of the questions most often leveled at Christians. "If you have such a great God, why does He allow evil?" The Bible does provide answers to that question (see Job, Habakkuk, and Psalm 73). But the ultimate answer is this: God does not ignore iniquity. He does not trivialize transgressions or wink at wickedness. While we are not always able to trace the judgment of God in our immediate circumstances, He is faithful, and in His own time He will avenge all evil that has been done. The destruction of Babylon will be one of His loudest statements affirming that fact!

The book of Revelation is filled with surprises. More than one student of this apocalyptic book has noticed the presence of the word *mercy* sprinkled throughout those chapters that are essentially prophecies of God's wrath. It almost seems that the darkest moments of God's judgment are followed with parentheses of His abounding mercy.

Revelation 18, which we have been exploring in this chapter, is no exception. In verse 20 we read, "Rejoice over her, O heaven, and you holy apostles and prophets, for God has avenged you on her!" This verse follows the announcement of judgment on the city of Babylon, and in all of Revelation's chapters depicting terror and tears, it is the first call to rejoice. As the apostles, prophets, and saints look down upon the world they have left, they see the final ruin of the seductive system and vile city of Babylon, which had poured out its scorn upon them. Babylon has fallen never to rise again, and all heaven breaks out in a celebration of praise.

Our Response to the Destruction of Babylon

While kings, merchants, shipmasters, apostles, and prophets all react to the ultimate destruction of Babylon, there is one more entity that is called upon to respond. The literal Babylon historically and prophetically so exemplifies man-centered pride and depravity that it has become a lasting metaphor for evil and rebellion against God. The people of God in every generation are instructed to separate themselves from the sins and mind-set of godless Babylon. "And I heard another voice from heaven saying, 'Come out of her, my people'" (Revelation 18:4). The prophet Jeremiah warned: "Flee from the midst of Babylon, and every one save his life! Do not be cut off in her iniquity, for this is the time of the LORD's vengeance" (Jeremiah 51:6).

These passages make us realize that in this wicked, foul city, there will be Christians living. One author explains: "The appeal of salary and prestige will entice many capable Christian business and professional men...to participate in the planning and activation of this exciting and dynamic new metropolis.... No doubt many of these Christians will rationalize their move to Babylon by the opportunity thus afforded to 'have a witness' in the world's most important city."[31]

What such Christians fail to recognize is that effective witness is never mediated through compromise. God's message is not "Be like her, My people, thereby to appease and attract her," but rather "Come out of her, my people, that ye be not partakers of her sins" (Revelation 18:4 KJV).

There can be no dual citizenship in the polar opposite cities of Jerusalem and Babylon. Paul wrote,

> Do not be unequally yoked together with unbelievers. For what fellowship has righteousness with lawlessness? And what communion has light with darkness? And what accord has Christ with Belial? Or what part has a believer with an unbeliever? And what agreement has the temple of God with idols? For you are the temple of the living God. (2 Corinthians 6:14–16)

I believe this is God's present-day call to separate ourselves from the world and especially the world as it is increasingly exhibited in the churches. My friend Erwin Lutzer makes an important observation about the current sad condition within the American church compared with that of previous eras of church history:

> We have seen the Gospel neglected and even mocked by religious liberals and nominal Christians. What is different today is that the message of the cross is being ignored by those who claim to be saved by its message. At the very time when the Gospel must be proclaimed most clearly, we are hearing muffled voices even from some of the great evangelical pulpits of our land.... We have lost our intellectual and spiritual center and replaced it with consumerism, self-help, and the quest for personal advantage. We are self-absorbed rather than God-absorbed.[32]

As Dr. Lutzer indicates, many Christians today are trying to live with one foot in Jerusalem and the other in Babylon. But as Paul tells us, there can be no fellowship between the two cities. The time has come for those who love God to stop being lovers of self and worldly pleasures and to become single-focused lovers of God; to let go of a powerless form of godliness and to separate ourselves from the Babylonian worldview (see 2 Timothy 3:2, 5).

John calls us to separate from Babylon, "lest you share in her sins, and lest you receive of her plagues" (Revelation 18:4). This warning tells us that indulging in the practices of Babylon has consequences, for these practices and the plagues that accompany them are inevitably paired.

Aside from the accompanying plagues, Babylon's mighty towers and false spiritual powers can provide us with none of the security they promise. When we put our trust in financial investments, government security regulators, bank accounts, economic growth, or any other human device designed to provide protection, we can be sure they will ultimately fail us.

On the other hand, shunning Babylon and remaining in God's city is paired with blessing. The apostle Paul reminds us of Ezekiel's promise to those who obey God's call: "I will dwell in them and walk among them. I will be their God, and they shall be My people" (2 Corinthians 6:16; cf. Ezekiel 37:23, 27).

No tribulation, trial, distress, persecution, famine, loss, peril, or sword can ever separate us from the love of Christ (see Romans 8:35). In fact, nothing "shall be able to separate us from the love of God which is in Christ Jesus our Lord" (Romans 8:39).

Unlike the bedrock of the world system, which shifts as frequently as the tectonic plates below Southern California, God's promises are the sure and solid rock of our faith and future. While we can grieve at the tragic choices so many make in choosing Babylon over Jerusalem, our reaction to the destruction of Babylon must be celebration that good will finally triumph and that the perennial enemy of God will no longer be able to inflict evil upon God's people.

CHAPTER 9

God's Ultimate New World Order

Last year I managed to overpay my California state taxes and was due to receive a refund. You can imagine my surprise when my refund arrived in the form of an IOU! The accompanying documentation said the state would redeem the IOU sometime after October 2, 2009, but it would require filing additional papers. I finally got my refund at the beginning of 2010.

Before I could recover from the shock of the IOU, I was notified that the state of California had decided to raise the withholding rate by 10 percent in order to keep the government from going bankrupt. State officials are saying it is a "loan" rather than a tax rate increase. Frankly, I am somewhat uncomfortable "loaning" them any more money!

Those of you who don't live in our fair state are not much better off. As a nation, we collectively contributed $2.1 trillion in taxpayer-generated revenues in 2009; the government projects that figure will grow to $2.2 trillion in 2010. How are those tax dollars to be spent? More than 32 percent, or $715 billion, will go to provide for our common defense and international security.[1] What if I told you that an ultimate new world order was on its way that would zero out all military expenses and do away with war entirely?

In 2010, our government budget calls for spending $708 billion for Social Security payments to 36 million retired workers and 6.4 million surviving spouses and children. How do you think our economic situation would change if none of these expenditures were necessary?

Another 34 percent of America's 2010 tax revenues—or $753 billion—is designated to go to Medicare, Medicaid, and children's health insurance programs. What would it be like if somehow we could eliminate all sickness and thus all need for health care?

Still another $482 billion (22 percent) will go for safety-net programs to assist the nation's poor and moderate-income families.[2] What if no citizen was hungry, no one was ever oppressed, and government entitlement programs were completely unnecessary?

The statistics in the paragraphs above do not tell even half the story. They reflect only the expenditures of our own nation. When you multiply the cost of addressing such problems in all the nations of the world, the total is staggering.

What if all these expenditures of all the nations were simply no longer needed? By now you are probably thinking I have been reading too much fiction. But the fact is, a time is coming when the needs for all these entitlement expenses will be eliminated. It will truly be a new world order.

Since Adam and Eve were evicted from the Garden of Eden, political philosophers, theologians, and artists have dreamed of an eventual golden age—an age in which righteousness and peace would prevail. A utopian age when one could live in harmony with his Maker, family, and society, and opposition and war would cease. Poets have written about it, folk-singers have sung about it, politicians have promised it, prophets have forecasted it, and the world has cried out for it.

We are made to be kingdom builders (see Genesis 1:28). But history demonstrates that when we try to build without God as King, our "utopias" become hell on earth. We've already studied what happened when Nimrod and others tried to establish a new world order, and we continue to witness the futility of the United Nations in their awkward and ineffective attempts at world peace. Yet we have good reason for hope.

The Coming "Golden Age"

The Bible makes it abundantly clear that a golden age is coming when all man-caused problems and imbalances will be history. As author and former Billy Graham associate John Wesley White writes,

> God's word assures us that a golden age lies just beyond Armageddon—an age of unprecedented peace and prosperity. An idyllic age, it will not be a democracy, a monarchy, or a socialist state. It will be a theocracy. Christ will be Lord and King over all the earth. What the Antichrist will have failed to do with militaristic and computer surveillance, Jesus Christ will do by His omniscience, omnipotence, and omnipresence.[3]

An earthly kingdom is coming, and the King's name is Jesus. The Bible does not merely hint at this coming event; it is a major theme. Dwight Pentecost, who has devoted his entire life to the study of prophecy, writes: "A larger body of prophetic Scripture is devoted to the subject of the millennium, developing its character and conditions, than any other one subject. This millennial age, in which the purposes of God are fully realized on the earth, demands considerable attention."[4]

This coming age is referred to variously as "times of refreshing" (Acts 3:19); "times of restoration" (Acts 3:21); "the day of Jesus Christ" (Philippians 1:6); and "the fullness of the times" (Ephesians 1:10). But it is best known as the Millennium. The English word *millennium* is made up of two Latin words: *mille*, which means a thousand; and *annum*, which means a year. So, the word *millennium* simply means a period of one thousand years.

Considerable news and some degree of hysteria surrounded the coming of "Y2K," the common term denoting our entry into the

2000s. As a result, the word *millennium* became well known around the world. Chicago planned and planted its Millennium Park. London built its Millennium Bridge across the Thames. Cedar Point Amusement Park boasts its Millennium Force roller coaster, the world's first to exceed 300 feet in height. There are millennium hotels all over the world, millennium high schools, and millennium banks. There is even a Millennium Princess Barbie. A look at the business listings in any phone book will show dozens of millenniums—Millennium Brokerage, Millennium Apartments, and Millennium Nails (whatever that is). Numerous companies go by the name Millennium Consultants.

Of course, the best Millennium consultants are the Old Testament prophets. According to their forecasts, the biblical Millennium has nothing to do with a calendar change. It will begin immediately following the return of Christ to the earth. One of these prophets put it like this: "Then the LORD will go forth and fight against those nations, as He fights in the day of battle.... And the LORD shall be King over all the earth. In that day it shall be—'The LORD is one,' and His name one" (Zechariah 14:3, 9).

Immediately after the Rapture of the church (see 1 Corinthians 15:50–52; 1 Thessalonians 4:16–17), when all Christians are taken to heaven to be with Jesus, there will be a seven-year period of Tribulation, a time the Old Testament refers to as "the time of Jacob's trouble" (Jeremiah 30:7). The Tribulation period will conclude with the Battle of Armageddon. Jesus Christ will return from heaven with His saints and angels, and He will defeat the Antichrist and his armies. The Antichrist and the False Prophet will be cast alive into the lake of fire, and their followers will be killed (see Revelation 19:20–21). Satan will be incarcerated in the bottomless pit for a thousand years (see Revelation 20:1–3). Then the Old Testament saints and the Tribulation saints will be resurrected, and they, joined by the saints of the church who lived before and at the time of the

Rapture, will reign with Christ for a thousand years (see Revelation 20:4–6). For ten centuries, Jesus Christ will rule with absolute authority over the entire world.

With all the importance attached to the Millennium, some are surprised to discover that the word does not appear once in the entire Bible. But then again, neither does the word *Trinity*. Both of these words have been chosen to describe and define solid biblical truths. When teaching, preaching, or writing, the single word *Trinity* is less cumbersome than having to say, "God existing in three persons." The word *millennium* means exactly the same thing as the biblical phrase "one thousand years," but it, too, provides a more efficient way to communicate quickly. While the term is not in the Bible, it is utterly biblical.

Six times in the first seven verses of Revelation 20, the phrase "a thousand years" is used to describe some aspect of Christ's kingdom. We are told that Satan will be bound for a thousand years, and that he will not be able to deceive the nations during that entire period of time. The martyred saints of the Tribulation will reign with Christ in His kingdom for a thousand years. At the end of the thousand years, Satan will be released from his prison to attempt one last battle between good and evil (see Revelation 20:7–10).

Why Is a Millennium Needed?

Many people are skeptical or at least puzzled about the Millennium because they cannot see its purpose. Why would God choose to insert a ten-century reign of perfection between the twin traumas of the Tribulation and the Final Rebellion—the last showdown with Satan? We will spend the next several pages answering this important question.

The Millennium Will Remove Satan from the Earth

The imprisonment of this archenemy of God and man is the first notable event of the Millennium. As the apostle John tells us: "He laid hold of the dragon, that serpent of old, who is the Devil and Satan, and bound him for a thousand years; and he cast him into the bottomless pit, and shut him up, and set a seal on him, so that he should deceive the nations no more till the thousand years were finished" (Revelation 20:2–3).

The Bible teaches that the world is "oppressed by the devil" (Acts 10:38), and "under the sway of the wicked one" (1 John 5:19). In fact, in several places the New Testament refers to Satan as "the ruler of this world" (John 12:31), a title he won by default from Adam, who succumbed to Satan's temptation and disobeyed God. But Satan's rule will end. "The Son of God was manifested, that He might destroy the works of the devil" (1 John 3:8).

At the cross and by the Resurrection, Jesus cemented the right to destroy the devil's work. In the Millennium, Satan will be imprisoned in the bottomless pit, and Jesus will set right all that the devil has perverted and destroyed since creation.

Dr. Harry Ironside said, "There's coming a day when men will no longer be deceived and led astray by the great tempter who, ever since his victory over our first parents in Eden, has been the persistent and malignant foe of mankind."[5]

Will people sin in the Millennium? It surprises many to learn that the answer is yes, they will sin. There are two reasons: First, while the people in the Millennium will be Christians, they will not be perfect any more than we are perfect as Christians today. They will still have the sinful natures we inherited from Adam, which will not be removed until they are resurrected. Second, the Millennium is a long period of time, and the millennial dwellers will have many children. Not all of these descendants will retain the faith of their believing parents.

Over the length of ten centuries, evil will be present in the world. But it will not be the same kind of evil we know today. Sin during the millennial period will not be the result of satanic temptation; it will be the result of our own sinful nature. Satan will be locked up in the special prison God has prepared for him. His hierarchy of demons will be neutralized. In the Millennium no one will be able to mimic the words of the 1970s comic Flip Wilson, whose character Geraldine was famous for saying, "The devil made me do it."

Thomas Jones, in his book *Sober Views of the Millennium*, wrote: "To have the great enemy of our salvation banished from the earth, and confined in hell, will be of itself an immense benefit....Were the Millennium to consist of nothing more than this deliverance, it would produce the most marvelous change in the condition of mankind."[6]

The Millennium Will Reward the People of God

The Bible speaks of a prophetic future in which Christians will be greatly rewarded immediately following the Rapture. Every Christian will stand before the judgment seat of Christ to be rewarded for his life of service while on earth. Several Scriptures teach this truth:

- For we shall all stand before the judgment seat of Christ. (Romans 14:10)
- For we must all appear before the judgment seat of Christ, that each one may receive the things done in the body, according to what he has done, whether good or bad. (2 Corinthians 5:10)
- Behold, the Lord GOD shall come with a strong hand, and His arm shall rule for Him; behold, His reward is with Him, and His work before Him. (Isaiah 40:10)

And we have these words from Jesus:

- For the Son of Man will come in the glory of His Father with His angels, and then He will reward each according to his works. (Matthew 16:27)
- Behold, I am coming quickly, and My reward is with Me, to give to every one according to his work. (Revelation 22:12)

In other places the New Testament speaks of these rewards as "crowns," which indicates that ruling is involved. Referring to the New Testament saints, Jesus said, "Do not fear, little flock, for it is your Father's good pleasure to give you the kingdom" (Luke 12:32). Paul echoed this idea in three passages: "Do you not know that the saints will judge the world?...Do you not know that we shall judge angels?" (1 Corinthians 6:2–3). "If we endure, we shall also reign with Him" (2 Timothy 2:12).

Daniel tells us that the Old Testament saints will participate in the future rule of the earth: "But the saints of the Most High shall receive the kingdom, and possess the kingdom forever, even forever and ever.... Then the kingdom and dominion, and the greatness of the kingdoms under the whole heaven, shall be given to the people, the saints of the Most High" (Daniel 7:18, 27).

As the following passage shows, the Tribulation saints will also participate:

Then one of the elders answered, saying to me, "Who are these arrayed in white robes, and where did they come from?" And I said to him, "Sir, you know." So he said to me, "These are the ones who come out of the great tribulation, and washed their robes and made them white in the blood of the Lamb."...Then I saw the souls of those who had been beheaded for their witness to Jesus and for the word of God, who had not worshiped the beast or his image, and had not received his mark on their foreheads or on their hands. And they lived and reigned with Christ for a thousand years. (Revelation 7:13–14; 20:4)

Christ will return to defeat His enemies at the Battle of Armageddon. Immediately after His victory, Christ will establish His kingdom and the redeemed saints from throughout all historical periods—Old Testament, New Testament, and Tribulation—will reign with Him.

Our reward for faithfulness during this life will be a greater opportunity to serve in the earthly kingdom of Jesus Christ. The idea of being assigned a duty as a reward can be a disconnect to some Christians. But as Randy Alcorn explains:

Service is a reward, not a punishment. This idea is foreign to people.... We think that faithful work should be rewarded by a vacation for the rest of our lives. But God offers us something very different: more work, more opportunities, increased responsibilities, along with greater abilities, resources, wisdom and empowerment. We will have sharp minds, and strong bodies, clear purpose, and unabated joy. The more we serve Christ now, the greater our capacity will be to serve Him in Heaven.[7]

Before we leave this point, I want to respond to an objection that is often raised about our ruling and serving in the Millennium. If the saints are going to judge the world and the angels, and the twelve apostles are going to rule over the twelve tribes of Israel, and if David is going to be resurrected to serve alongside Jesus Christ (see Jeremiah 30:9; Ezekiel 37:24), won't there be a problem with the commingling of resurrected and nonresurrected beings during the Millennium? Theologian John F. Walvoord provides a valid response to this objection:

The objection...is of course denied by the simple fact that our Lord in His resurrection body was able to mingle freely with His disciples. Though there evidently was some change in their relationship, he could still talk with them, eat with them, and be subject to physical contact with them....Though the free mingling of resurrected and non-resurrected beings is contrary to our present experience, there is no valid reason why there should not be a limited amount of such association in the millennial earth.[8]

The Millennium Will Validate the Prophets' Predictions

Most of the biblical information concerning the Millennium comes to us through the prophets Isaiah, Jeremiah, Ezekiel, Daniel, Joel, Amos, Micah, and Zechariah. As they speak of Christ's coming kingdom, they foresee a time when "all kings shall fall down before Him; all nations shall serve Him" (Psalm 72:11); and when "His dominion shall be 'from sea to sea, and from the River to the ends of the earth'" (Zechariah 9:10). The predictions of these prophecies have not been realized at any time in the world's history. Only in the Millennium will they find their ultimate fulfillment.

In considering how these prophecies will be fulfilled, it is important to understand that the political, economic, and religious structure that we know today will be totally altered in the Millennium. No longer will any city—Washington, D.C.; New York; London; Beijing; or Babylon—be the political center. The focus of all life will be Jerusalem in the land of Israel.

Every important news release will dateline from Jerusalem. Jerusalem will be the seat of the new global government. It is from that city King Jesus will reign.

Some people wonder why is it important that Jesus reign for a time in a completely earthly kingdom. Prophetic scholar Charles C. Ryrie answers:

Because *Christ* must be triumphant in the same arena where He was seemingly defeated. His rejection by the rulers of this world was on this earth (1 Corinthians 2:8). His exaltation

220

must also be on this earth. And so it shall be when He comes again to rule this world in righteousness. He has waited long for His inheritance; soon He shall receive it.[9]

In that day Jerusalem will regain the glory it displayed in the days of King David, but magnified beyond imagination. Jerusalem will experience the glory of the Lord in such a way that the city itself will be glorious. Despite all its current issues, most people today find their first glimpse of Jerusalem breathtaking. But nothing will compare to the glory of millennial Jerusalem, and no other capital city will rival it. It will be "the City of Truth," "the Holy Mountain" (Zechariah 8:3). It will be the seat of power and authority for one thousand years until the arrival of the New Jerusalem, which will come down from heaven as promised in Revelation 3:12 and 21:2.

Jerusalem today is a divided city in a divided land. An aerial view of the city exposes a serpentine concrete security wall that restricts the free movement between the Israeli and Palestinian-held sections. But more than just a wall separates Jerusalem's citizens. Jewish, Arab, and Christian, they differ from one another linguistically, religiously, politically, and historically. Under the terms of the Oslo Accords of 1993, they are also divided and their mobility is constricted by the color of their identity cards. Towns to which Jesus traveled easily from Jerusalem, such as Bethlehem and Bethany, are off-limits to certain citizens. Travel is restricted and monitored by a series of checkpoints.[10]

The Jerusalem of the Millennium will be an altogether different place. That wall of division will be removed—probably as one of the first casualties of the massive earthquake that will transform the topography of Jerusalem when Jesus' foot touches the Mount of Olives on His second coming to earth (see Zechariah 14:3–4).

On that day there will be no need of a security wall. The Lord Jesus will reign with an iron hand, and no enemy will stand against His power. Man-made boundary demarcations will be useless, as the city will expand to an unprecedented area and population.

More important, there will be no need of barriers to restrict travel into or out of the city. The Highway of Holiness will be open for the redeemed (see Isaiah 35:8–9). People of every nation, language, and ethnicity will journey to Jerusalem to seek the Lord, eager to accompany a Jewish person to the place of prayer (see Zechariah 8:21–23).

Many of our favorite Christmas passages will find their ultimate fulfillment in the millennial period. If you read Isaiah's Christmas prophecy carefully, you will notice that only the first two clauses actually belong to Christmas. The rest will not be fulfilled until Jesus comes back to set up His kingdom on earth.

> For unto us a Child is born, unto us a Son is given [Christmas]; and the government will be upon His shoulder. And His name will be called Wonderful, Counselor, Mighty God, Everlasting Father, Prince of Peace. Of the increase of His government and peace there will be no end, upon the throne of David and over His kingdom, to order it and establish it with judgment and justice from that time forward, even forever. The zeal of the LORD of hosts will perform this [Millennium]. (Isaiah 9:6–7)

The same is true of the angel Gabriel's words to Mary. They speak of that which is to happen both in the near and distant futures. The first sentence speaks of Christmas, while the rest of the passage refers to the Millennium: "And behold, you will conceive in your womb and bring forth a Son, and shall call His name JESUS. He will be great, and will be called the Son of the Highest; and the Lord God will give Him the throne of His father David. And He will reign over the house of Jacob forever, and of His kingdom there will be no end" (Luke 1:31–33).

The Millennium will be the time in which a vast number of both Old Testament and New Testament prophecies will find their fulfillment.

The Millennium Will Answer the Disciples' Prayer

Jesus instructed His disciples to pray the following prayer: "Our Father in heaven, hallowed be Your name. Your kingdom come. Your will be done on earth as it is in heaven.... Deliver us from the evil one" (Luke 11:2, 4). What does it mean to pray for God's kingdom to come?

In the beginning, the Garden of Eden was the kingdom of God on earth. But, as we noted above, Satan usurped that kingdom through the default of Adam. So in this prayer Jesus taught His disciples— which includes us—to pray for the reestablishment of the kingdom of God on earth—for the world again to be under God's reign, establishing His will here "as it is in heaven."

We will not see the ultimate fulfillment of this prayer of Jesus until the Millennium when Christ reigns in power and glory (see Psalm 2:6–12; Isaiah 11:4; 42:4; Jeremiah 23:3–6; Daniel 2:35–45; Zechariah 14:1–9). Only then will God rule and reign over every dimension of existence. Sin's power will be mitigated, and Satan will be incarcerated in hell. Not until then will we be finally delivered from the power and even the presence of the Evil One.

The Millennium Will Reveal the Rebellion in the Heart of Man

The Millennium will answer, once and for all, the age-old question of whether man's sin stems from nurture or from nature. For one thousand years of unbroken peace and prosperity, Christ will rule from Jerusalem with an iron rod. At the end of this age of perfect bliss, Satan will be loosed for a short time to demonstrate that even in a perfect environment, unredeemed men will turn against God and rebel.

Dr. Walvoord asks, "Why is the millennial kingdom necessary in God's plan for the human race? The answer seems to be that the Millennium is the final illustration of the grace of God and man's need of salvation. The Millennium demonstrates that the death of Christ is essential for man's salvation."[11]

Pictures of God's Ultimate World Order

What will life in the Millennium be like? How will conditions, health, economics, and society as a whole differ from what we know today? The Bible is not silent on these questions. It gives us at least seven outstanding characteristics of that future reign of Christ over the earth. In this section we will explore these one by one.

The Millennium Will Be a Time of Peace

Today people are praying for peace, marching for peace, and even dying for peace. But in spite of all the talk and action, " 'There is no peace,' says my God, 'for the wicked' " (Isaiah 57:21).

On October 1, 2009, Dr. Victor Davis Hanson, Distinguished Fellow in History at Hillsdale College, gave a lecture at Hillsdale College on the subject of war. Here is an excerpt from that speech:

> The first point I want to make is that war is a human enterprise that will always be with us. Unless we submit to genetic engineering, or unless video games have somehow reprogrammed our brains, or unless we are fundamentally changed by eating different nutrients—these are possibilities brought up by so-called peace and conflict resolution theorists—human nature will not change. And if human nature will not change—and I submit to you that human nature is a constant—then war will always be with us. Its methods or delivery systems—which can be traced through time from clubs to catapults and from flintlocks to nuclear weapons— will of course change. In this sense war is like water. You can pump water at 60 gallons per minute with a small gasoline engine

or at 5000 gallons per minute with a gigantic turbine pump. But water is water—the same today as in 1880 or 500 BC. Likewise war, because the essence of war is human nature.[12]

Hanson's observation resoundingly confirms that of the New Testament book of James: "Where do wars and fights come from among you? Do they not come from your desires for pleasure that war in your members? You lust and do not have. You murder and covet and cannot obtain. You fight and war" (4:1–2).

Peace is a matter of the heart. It is because the heart of fallen man tends toward evil that all attempts at peace throughout history have ultimately failed. Isaiah summarizes the futility of man's efforts: "The way of peace they have not known, and there is no justice in their ways; they have made themselves crooked paths; whoever takes that way shall not know peace" (Isaiah 59:8).

But the Millennium will be a time when the angels' message of "peace on earth" will be realized. The psalmist describes the Lord as the One who "makes wars cease to the end of the earth; He breaks the bow and cuts the spear in two; He burns the chariot in the fire.... In His days the righteous shall flourish, and abundance of peace, until the moon is no more" (Psalm 46:9; 72:7).

Writing of this time, Isaiah says, "The work of righteousness will be peace, and the effect of righteousness, quietness and assurance forever. My people will dwell in a peaceful habitation in secure dwellings, and in quiet resting places" (Isaiah 32:17–18). The prophet Zechariah adds, "I will cut off the chariot from Ephraim and the horse from Jerusalem; the battle bow shall be cut off. He shall speak peace to the nations; His dominion shall be 'from sea to sea, and from the River to the ends of the earth' " (Zechariah 9:10).

Isaiah gives us one of the most amazing peace passages I have ever read. It is an extraordinary description of the peace that will exist between the nations in the Millennium:

Then the LORD will be known to Egypt, and the Egyptians will know the LORD in that day, and will make sacrifice and offering; yes, they will make a vow to the LORD and perform it.... In that day there will be a highway from Egypt to Assyria [Iraq], and the Assyrian will come into Egypt and the Egyptian into Assyria, and the Egyptians will serve with the Assyrians. In that day Israel will be one of three with Egypt and Assyria—a blessing in the midst of the land, whom the LORD of hosts shall bless, saying, "Blessed is Egypt My people, and Assyria the work of My hands, and Israel My inheritance." (Isaiah 19:21, 23–25)

In an earlier chapter, I spoke of a statue given to the United Nations by what was formerly the Soviet Union. Inscribed upon it is a sentiment expressed by Old Testament prophets: "They shall beat their swords into ploughshares" (see Isaiah 2:4 and Micah 4:3).

The leaders of the atheistic Soviet Union apparently did not realize that the fulfillment of that inscription would not come until the day when Christ rules the earth. Only then will there be no war. Kingdoms will be unified. All man-made implements of mechanized warfare will be eliminated. Dr. M. R. DeHaan has written:

The Bible is replete with prophecies of a coming age of peace and prosperity. It will be a time when war will be utterly unknown. Not a single armament plant will be operating, not a soldier or sailor will be in uniform, no military camps will exist, and not one cent will be spent for armaments of war, not a single penny will be used for defense, much less for offensive warfare. Can you imagine such an age, when all nations shall be at perfect peace, all the resources available for enjoyment, all industry engaged in the articles of a peaceful luxury?[13]

This millennial peace will be so pervasive that it will extend even to the animal kingdom. As Isaiah describes it,

The wolf also shall dwell with the lamb, the leopard shall lie down with the young goat, the calf and the young lion and the fatling together; and a little child shall lead them. The cow and the bear shall graze; their young ones shall lie down together; and the lion shall eat straw like the ox. The nursing child shall play by the cobra's hole, and the weaned child shall put his hand in the viper's den. They shall not hurt nor destroy in all My holy mountain, for the earth shall be full of the knowledge of the LORD as the waters cover the sea. (Isaiah 11:6–9)

Clearly, only God could bring about such dramatic transformations, both on the geopolitical front and in the nature of animals. Complete peace under the reign of Jesus Christ is one characteristic of the millennial golden age.

The Millennium Will Be a Time of Prosperity

God has given us bodies, which come equipped with certain physical needs and a great capacity for pleasure. God intended for those needs to be met and for humans to find joy in meeting them. He placed Adam in the lush environment of Eden and gave him a wife for love and companionship. God continually provided food from the earth, dew on the ground, stars in the sky, and beauty in the natural world. Today He continually "gives us richly all things to enjoy" (1 Timothy 6:17).

In the present world, Satan's influence has skewed nature—including human nature—inflicting upon humanity famines, natural disasters, greed, and oppression, which often deprive people of their basic needs. During the Millennium this will change. God will provide for us in abundance, and no evil will impair our ability to receive and enjoy all He gives. The entire world will be turned into a kind of paradise that will resurrect the joys of Eden.

John F. Walvoord says, "In the Millennium, all want will be eliminated. Prosperity will characterize all parts of the world. The curse which descended upon the physical world because of Adam's sin apparently is lifted during the Millennium.... The world in general will be delivered from its unproductiveness which characterized great portions of the globe."[14]

The prophets foretell a prosperity in the Millennium that will be unlike anything ever seen since the Garden of Eden. Isaiah, for example, says, "The wilderness and the wasteland shall be glad for them [the earth's inhabitants], and the desert shall rejoice and blossom as the rose; it shall blossom abundantly and rejoice, even with joy and singing.... For waters shall burst forth in the wilderness, and streams in the desert. The parched ground shall become a pool, and the thirsty land springs of water" (Isaiah 35:1–2, 6–7).

Just as some desert areas have been converted into productive land through modern irrigation technology, the Bible says that in the Millennium all desert land will be transformed into fertile territory.

Ezekiel's prophecies are filled with descriptions of the prosperity of the Millennium:

> I will make them and the places all around My hill a blessing; and I will cause showers to come down in their season; there shall be showers of blessing. Then the trees of the field shall yield their fruit, and the earth shall yield her increase.... I will call for the grain and multiply it, and bring no famine upon you. And I will multiply the fruit of your trees and the increase of your fields.... The desolate land shall be tilled instead of lying desolate in the sight of all who pass by. So they will say, "This land that was desolate has become like the garden of Eden." (Ezekiel 34:26–27; 36:29–30, 34–35)

Joel prophesies that during the coming kingdom age, the Jews will be so prosperous that their "threshing floors shall be full of wheat, and the vats shall overflow with new wine and oil" (Joel 2:24).

One of the most visual pictures of millennial prosperity comes from the prophet Amos: " 'Behold, the days are coming,' says the LORD, 'when the plowman shall overtake the reaper, and the treader of grapes him who sows seed' " (Amos 9:13).

Amos is telling us that the earth will be so fertile that there will be no barren "dead space" of winter between harvesting and planting. Of course Amos, like the other prophets we've quoted, is using terms that fit the day in which he wrote. Visualizing the contemporary fulfillment to his prophecy, here's Amos's prophecy updated as I see it happening in the coming Millennium: A farmer driving a new Case IH Combine harvester is hard at work bringing in a grain harvest that covers lush fields as far as the eye can see. Following immediately behind him is another farmer on a John Deere 8R tractor pulling a twenty-four-row tiller/planter.

If you are a suburbanite and agricultural analogies don't help you visualize the millennial prosperity, maybe the following story will.

On a *CBS Evening News* segment called "The American Spirit," correspondent Rich Schlesinger reported the philanthropy of Doris Buffett, the sister of Warren Buffett. Her brother's management of her inherited wealth has made her extremely rich, but making more money is not her goal. The octogenarian is striving to "give away the money she has left in the time she has left."

For most of us, that would not take too much effort. But after giving away more than $80 million, Buffett told Schlesinger, "We'd give away money during the month and then the bank statement would come and I'd have more money than I started out the month with, so it seemed like we were on a treadmill after a while."[15] The woman was literally making more money than she could give away. Most of us would like to know where you get one of those treadmills!

My point in relating Doris Buffett's story is this: her experience may well depict what is prophesied for the Millennium. It will be a time of more abundance than we can imagine in our present world of struggle and scarcity.

Carl G. Johnson summarizes what the Bible says about the prosperity of the Millennium:

> God will give abundant and timely rainfall; trees will bear fruit; the earth will be very fertile, people will no longer die from hunger and malnutrition; there will be no more famine; grain will be increased; former desolate land will become so productive that it will be compared to the Garden of Eden; the threshing floor of the granaries will be full of wheat; wine and oil will fill the vats to overflowing; people will have more than sufficient to eat; they will plant gardens and eat from them; each man will have his own fruit orchard and vineyard to enjoy, the planted seed will always produce, and the skies will be noted for dew rather than scorching heat or bitter cold.[16]

The Millennium Will Be a Time of Physical Health

In the Millennium Christ will do for all what He did for the sick and handicapped He encountered in the Gospels. He will remove all sickness, deformities, and handicaps. In the golden age of His reign there will be no blindness, deafness, or dumbness—no need for eyeglasses, hearing aids, speech therapy, wheelchairs, or crutches. We have that promise from two Old Testament prophets:

> In that day the deaf shall hear the words of the book, and the eyes of the blind shall see out of obscurity and out of darkness.... And the inhabitant will not say, "I am sick."... Then the eyes of the blind shall be opened, and the ears of the deaf shall be unstopped. Then the lame shall leap like a deer, and the tongue of the dumb sing.... "For I will restore health to you and heal you of your wounds," says the LORD. (Isaiah 29:18; 33:24; 35:5–6; Jeremiah 30:17)

The Millennium Will Be a Time of Purity

During the Millennium, a new level of moral purity will characterize the people. As Isaiah and Ezekiel declare, "He who is left in Zion and remains in Jerusalem will be called holy.... And they shall teach My people the difference between the holy and the unholy, and cause them to discern between the unclean and the clean" (Isaiah 4:3; Ezekiel 44:23).

In the Millennium it will be much easier for morality, ethics, and worship of the true God to prevail because under the perfect reign of Jesus Christ, many of the causes of evil will be eliminated. As Isaiah tells us, everyone will be aware of the presence of the Lord: "They shall not hurt nor destroy in all My holy mountain, for the earth shall be full of the knowledge of the LORD as the waters cover the sea" (Isaiah 11:9).

The idols that tempted Israel away from God throughout Old Testament history will not be present in the Millennium. As the prophet Zechariah tells us, " 'It shall be in that day,' says the LORD of hosts, 'that I will cut off the names of the idols from the land, and they shall no longer be remembered' " (Zechariah 13:2). Nor, presumably, will the inhabitants be tempted by the modern idols of money, fame, self-actualization, or obsessive pleasure-seeking. In the abundance of the golden age, everyone will have these blessings at hand. There will be no need to strive for them or allow them to distract us from the worship of God.

As we have noted, Satan will be bound, making it impossible for him or his demonic spirits to tempt us. Nor will there be occultists leading people to seek transcendence by communicating with evil spirits. Zechariah goes on to say the Lord "will also cause the [false] prophets and the unclean spirit to depart from the land" (Zechariah 13:2).

I noted earlier that this millennial kingdom age is not a period of sinlessness. Even in that blessed time there will be people who dare to defy the will of God. But here is the difference: those offenders will never get on a court docket for trial, for no defense lawyer would stand a chance of winning a case against the Lord Jesus Christ, who will be both Prosecutor and Judge. Against Him there will be no defense! The Lord, who knows our thoughts as well as our deeds, will be the righteous Judge. As the prophet Amos relates, it will be a time when justice will "run down like water, and righteousness like a mighty stream" (Amos 5:24).

The Millennium Will Be a Time of Prolonged Life

In the golden age people will live to a greatly advanced age, and children will not die before their time. In fact, Isaiah says that a man who is one hundred years old will be considered a child. "No more shall an infant from there live but a few days, nor an old man who has not fulfilled his days; for the child shall die one hundred years old" (Isaiah 65:20).

People will live to see the completion of their plans and enjoy the results of their efforts. As Isaiah explains, "They shall not build and another inhabit; they shall not plant and another eat; for as the days of a tree, so shall be the days of My people, and My elect shall long enjoy the work of their hands" (Isaiah 65:22).

Addressing the subject of longevity in the golden age, Robert J. Little of Moody Bible Institute had this to say:

During this period no one shall die in infancy, nor will anyone die of old age, since the span of life will be greatly increased, and medicine will be available for any illness. One who shall die at the age of 100 at that time will be considered to have died as a child. . . . Death will not be from what we now call "natural causes," but will be the result of the judgment of God. Psalm

101:8 has been rendered, "Morning by morning, I will destroy all the wicked of the land, that I may cut off all wicked doers from the city of the Lord." This has been taken to mean that every morning there will be a summary judgment of all wickedness since, under conditions which shall exist then, there will be no incentive to sin. It seems that one who commits a transgression will have until the following morning to repent and make the matter right.[17]

It appears that during the millennial period, the lifespan that characterized the world in the days before the Flood will return, and people will live to be hundreds of years old. As Zechariah reports, venerable Methuselahs will be a common sight in the new age. "Old men and old women shall again sit in the streets of Jerusalem, each one with his staff in his hand because of great age" (Zechariah 8:4).

Jeremiah tells us that in the golden age there will also be an enormous increase in the birthrate. "I will multiply them, and they shall not diminish; I will also glorify them, and they shall not be small" (Jeremiah 30:19). Zechariah affirms this abounding fertility with this appealing tidbit of prophetic color: "The streets of the city shall be full of boys and girls playing in its streets" (Zechariah 8:5).

With the combination of a high birthrate, extreme longevity, the elimination of sickness, and the enhancement of personal health, the world's population in the Millennium will explode. But this will not create the environmental concerns we experience today because, as we have already noted, the earth itself will be so fertile that there will be no want or lack of any thing.

The Millennium Will Be a Time of Personal Joy

The Millennium will be an exhilarating era of happiness, contentment, and joy. It will be the answer to many ancient and anguished prayers from the many who have struggled to find joy in this fallen world of pain and tragedy. Isaiah describes how these prayers will be answered in the golden age:

> You have multiplied the nation and increased its joy; they rejoice before You according to the joy of harvest, as men rejoice when they divide the spoil.... Therefore with joy you will draw water from the wells of salvation.... The whole earth is at rest and quiet; they break forth into singing.... And the Lord GOD will wipe away tears from all faces.... You shall have a song as in the night when a holy festival is kept, and gladness of heart as when one goes with a flute.... For you shall go out with joy, and be led out with peace; the mountains and the hills shall break forth into singing before you, and all the trees of the field shall clap their hands. (Isaiah 9:3; 12:3; 14:7; 25:8; 30:29; 55:12)

If Isaiah makes the Millennium seem like a thousand-year celebration, it's because that's essentially what it will be. Every day will bring a Christmas-like elation of peace, well-being, and goodwill. Joyful feelings that come to us only at certain seasons and in our best moments will be a permanent feature of the Millennium.

The Millennium Will Be a Time of Praise and Worship

Throughout the Millennium, the worldwide dominion of the Lord will include all peoples of all nations. As Daniel tells us, "His kingdom is an everlasting kingdom, and all dominions shall serve and obey Him" (Daniel 7:27). Christ will reign over the earth from the greatly enlarged and enhanced Jerusalem, and Israel, vastly expanded, will be considered the center of the earth. The people of the world will happily journey to the Holy City to worship and sacrifice to Christ the King:

And it shall come to pass that everyone who is left of all the nations which came against Jerusalem shall go up from year to year to worship the King, the LORD of hosts, and to keep the Feast of Tabernacles. And it shall be that whichever of the families of the earth do not come up to Jerusalem to worship the King, the LORD of hosts, on them there will be no rain. (Zechariah 14:16–17)

"And it shall come to pass that from one New Moon to another, and from one Sabbath to another, all flesh shall come to worship before Me," says the LORD. (Isaiah 66:23)

The center of worship in the Millennium will be the temple. This will not be Solomon's temple rebuilt or Herod's upgrade and remodeling of Zerubbabel's temple. This will be an altogether new and glorious temple constructed especially for use during the thousand-year reign of Christ. Ezekiel devotes seven chapters of his prophecy to the description of this temple and the details of the worship that will take place within its walls (see Ezekiel 40–46).

Some scholars struggle with the reality of a temple in the Millennium because the worship within it involves the offering of animal sacrifices. They argue that if Christ's death was the final, once-for-all sacrifice for sins (see Hebrews 7:27; 9:26, 28), there can be no purpose in animal sacrifices in the Millennium. John F. Walvoord speaks to their concerns: "The answer lies in the fact that the millennial sacrifices will constitute a memorial of Jesus' death, much as observing the Lord's Supper is a reminder of His death (Luke 22:19; 1 Corinthians 11:26). Also, just as the Old Testament sacrifices looked forward symbolically to Christ's death, so the sacrifices of the millennial kingdom will look back in remembrance to His sacrifice on the cross."[18]

According to Franklin Logsdon, this observance of animal sacrifices will serve another important purpose:

When the saints of all ages, and especially the saved Jews, see King Immanuel in all His transcendent majesty and resplendent glory, they might in awe and wonderment, in joy and rejoicing, forget utterly that it was He who once was impaled between earth and heaven on the old rugged cross in ignominy and shame. The few blood offerings will constitute the memorial and will remind all of the basis for all eternal blessing.[19]

Throughout the ages men have made numerous attempts to envision and create a new world order—an idyllic utopia—in which the evils that plague this fallen world are banished. All have failed for the simple reason that man contains within himself the source of his own problems. Our sinful nature makes it impossible for us to construct or maintain a perfect environment. As Jeremiah said, "O LORD, I know the way of man is not in himself; it is not in man who walks to direct his own steps" (Jeremiah 10:23).

We cannot create our own utopia, but as we have shown in this chapter, a utopia can be in our future—one created by God Himself. The utopia we all hope for is part of our eternal inheritance. Jesus urges us to take hold of that inheritance now, in our hearts, and some day soon in our resurrected bodies. He invites us into this new world He is creating for us: "Come, you blessed of My Father, inherit the kingdom prepared for you from the foundation of the world" (Matthew 25:34).

Randy Alcorn provides us with an insightful closure for this topic. In his book *Heaven*, he amplifies Christ's invitation in a way that vividly shows how deeply it should appeal to each one of us:

God hasn't changed His mind; he hasn't fallen back to Plan B or abandoned what He originally intended for us at the creation of the world. When Christ says "take your inheritance, the kingdom prepared for you since the creation of the world," it's as if he's saying, "This is what I wanted for you all along. This is what I went to the cross and defeated death to give you. Take it, rule it, exercise dominion, enjoy it, and in doing so, share my happiness."[20]

CHAPTER 10

Keep Your Head in the Game and Your Hope in God

Gatlinburg, Tennessee, is a family friendly tourist town that serves as the gateway to the Great Smoky Mountains National Park. It is known for its rustic hotels, quaint shops, and popular restaurants, all surrounded by green-clad hilltops and Smoky Mountain peaks. Few people take time to trace the back roads around Gatlinburg; but those who turn onto Campbell Lead Road, just off the bypass from Pigeon Forge, drive by a remarkable house sprawled at the end of a sloping, winding drive. It's a 16,512-square-foot superchalet nestled on the side of a mountain. The three-story living room offers lofty windows and fabulous views of the Smoky Mountain beauty. It is a massive home—and empty.

It belonged to Dennis Bolze, a middle-aged stock trader who apparently bilked clients out of millions of dollars in an elaborate Ponzi scheme. Some say he's the hillbilly version of Bernie Madoff. Having been forced into bankruptcy, Bolze very well may be swapping his chalet for a jail cell. The real losses, however, are those of his victims. One victim, Virginia Borham, a recently widowed woman who worked for years as a secretary in Europe, lost the bulk of her life savings.

"I don't know what my future is going to be now," said Ms. Borham, "because I have only enough income to pay my rent. Literally, I am living on the charity of friends."[1] Like many others, Virginia

Borham thought her investments were sure and her money was safe; and now it's gone.

The loss of one's personal financial stability can and does happen for many reasons other than being cheated or making bad investments. Money seems to have a way of getting away from us. The Bible says, "Cast but a glance at riches, and they are gone, for they will surely sprout wings and fly off to the sky like an eagle" (Proverbs 23:5 NIV). We've always known that money has wings, but only lately have we begun to comprehend its wingspan. Our financial security can vanish in an instant. As we have explored in this book, events occurring today portend a bleak economic outlook for this nation and, indeed, for the world. All of us are sure to be affected, and many of us have already felt the pinch.

If you have stood helplessly by and watched your savings and investments shrink to the point that you must scale back your retirement plans, you're in good company. Millions of people have recently suffered losses in pension accounts, retirement funds, and investment income. Many have suffered loss of wealth trying to help children, family, and friends in these distressing times. Others have drained their savings during prolonged bouts of unemployment or because of catastrophic illness and crippling medical bills.

In this last chapter I want to turn away from the bleak picture of the global economic future and speak directly to you about what you can do now to prepare and either avoid or ease the stress to your own finances. We cannot escape what is happening in the world. As I have said, we are now seeing the looming shadow being cast by biblically predicted catastrophic events, and we cannot avoid living under that shadow. We may experience difficulties due to the global economic and political disintegration, but we know that we are in God's hands. Not only can we trust Him for our future well-being; He has also given us sound financial principles that can rule our economic lives in a way that stabilizes our personal finances and gets us through tough times.

So, in spite of the coming global economic Armageddon, we Christians need not despair. We have good reason for hope. That hope is what I want to show you in this chapter. I am not so presumptuous as to offer you specific financial advice. I simply want to give you sound, proven, workable principles from the Bible that can see you through the coming economic shadows now creeping across the world.

The Biblical Approach to Money

The Bible doesn't see money and riches exactly as we do. In fact, Scripture shows that God's perspective on wealth is the opposite from that of most of us. He's not overly concerned about our building massive wealth here on earth, but He's highly concerned that we build a solid foundation for our spiritual future. No surprise there; we've heard that from the pulpit all our lives. But it's easy to get caught up in the societal race for wealth and tend to forget the perspective of Scripture.

In many places the Bible warns that money is as transient as a butterfly. Proverbs 27:24 says that "riches are not forever." Through His prophet Haggai, the Lord told the backslidden Israelites that they were earning wages only to put the money into a bag with holes (see Haggai 1:6). Paul warns us not to trust in wealth, which is uncertain (see 1 Timothy 6:17), and Jesus said, "Do not lay up for yourselves treasures on earth, where moth and rust destroy and where thieves break in and steal" (Matthew 6:19). He wasn't forbidding us to be prudent savers or to plan for the future. He was simply saying our permanent wealth is eternal, but the dollar, the pound, and the euro are not.

In his book *Just Walk Across the Room: Simple Steps Pointing People to Faith*, Bill Hybels tells about an experience that underscored the difference between the temporary and the permanent:

I was sitting in a meeting one time when the speaker suddenly unfurled a roll of stickers in his hand. "There is something we must all understand," he said as he walked across the front of the room. Periodically, he would stop and put a red sticker on a tiny replica of a house, and a red sticker on a Hot Wheels car, and a red sticker on a dollhouse-sized desk that represented our vocational lives.

"You may not be able to tell from where you're sitting, but each red sticker has a single word on it," he said. "The word is 'temporary.' And these things I'm putting them on are all temporary. They will fade away, turning cartwheels like leaves in the wind when this world ends.

"If you are living for these things, then you are living a life of temporary pleasure, temporary satisfaction, and temporary fulfillment." He continued walking around the room, now silent as he labeled everything in sight with red stickers. I watched his hands declare the fate of the best this world has to offer as those stickers made their way to the goods in front of us.

Temporary. Temporary. Temporary.

"There is only *one* thing in this room that is not temporary," he continued. "There is only one thing that you can take with you into the next world."

He called someone up to join him on the stage, and he placed a blue sticker on her lapel. "When you get to the end of your life and take in your last breath," he said, "what do you want your life to have been about?" . . .

No earthly commodity is going to make it from this world into the next. Not land, not homes, not bank accounts, not titles, not achievements. Only *souls*. Friends, Jesus Christ taught that every human being would be resurrected to spend an eternity in community with God in heaven or in isolation from God in hell. And because Jesus understood these eternal realities and believed them to the core of His being, He focused His attention on the only entity that would extend into the next reality: people.

I don't know what the final assessment of my earthly life will be once I am gone. But I know this much: my quest while I am here is to seek people out and point them toward faith in God. I've tried enough approaches in my five decades of living to know that to invest yourself in anything other than people is to settle for the pursuit of a lesser vision—that ugly ensnaring trap of the temporal.[2]

Solomon, the wisest man who ever lived, seems to agree with Hybels. In his memoirs, the often-neglected book of Ecclesiastes, King Solomon had much to say about money, even devoting an entire chapter to the dispensing of his monetary wisdom. He began by saying five things about money and greed:

- The more we have, the more we want (see Ecclesiastes 5:10).
- The more we have, the more we spend (see Ecclesiastes 5:11).
- The more we have, the more we worry (see Ecclesiastes 5:12).
- The more we have, the more we lose (see Ecclesiastes 5:13–14).
- The more we have, the more we leave behind (see Ecclesiastes 5:14–17).

Then Solomon went on to say two things about money and God:

- First, the power to earn money comes from God. "Here is what I have seen: It is good and fitting for one to eat and drink, and to enjoy the good of all his labor in which he toils under the sun all the days of his life *which God gives him*; for it is his heritage" (Ecclesiastes 5:18, emphasis added).
- Second, the power to enjoy money also comes from God. "As for every man to whom God has given riches and wealth, and given him power to eat of it, to receive his heritage and rejoice in his labor—*this is the gift of God*. For he will not dwell unduly on the days of his life, because God keeps him busy with the joy of his heart" (Ecclesiastes 5:19–20, emphasis added).

Solomon's insights about money echo God's instructions to the people of Israel as they were about to enter the Promised Land: "And you shall remember the LORD your God, for it is He who gives you power to get wealth, that He may establish His covenant which He swore to your fathers, as it is this day" (Deuteronomy 8:18).

Based on this perspective that money, its uses, and the benefits of it are gifts from God, let me suggest a four-point formula for financial survival during these days of economic confusion.

Keep Your Head in the Game

My youngest son, Daniel, was the quarterback on his high school football team. During one of the games in his junior year, he took a vicious hit from the opposing linebacker, which resulted in a concussion. At the time, we did not know it was a concussion, and so the coach let him go back into the game.

During the final quarter of the contest, Daniel threw for a touchdown and ran for another, but afterward he did not remember any of it. His teammates told me later that he could not remember the plays to call in the huddle, so they would just go to the line of scrimmage and improvise. Daniel told me that he could not remember anything that happened after his head injury, but he kept on playing, and only his teammates knew that anything was wrong.

Daniel's experience reminds me of the way many people are functioning financially today. Outwardly, they are playing the game. But if you get close enough to them, you realize they have no idea what the game is all about. They have no plays to call, and while they might bumble into doing some things right, they are living every moment in jeopardy of taking a hit that will put them on the sidelines, perhaps for the rest of their lives.

You've probably heard friends say, "I don't even listen to the news anymore. It's all so depressing; I just ignore it." Or, "What's the use of trying to keep up with the mess we're in? There's nothing I can do about any of it, so I have just decided to ignore it all and go on with my life." These are two actual quotes from people I have talked to in recent days, and I think they represent the attitudes of a huge segment of our population.

This attitude is a major mistake, and it demonstrates an irresponsible approach to financial management that can result in disaster. In his book *The New Economic Disorder*, Larry Bates wrote:

> We are creatures of comfort and as such have grown accustomed to our comfort zones. We will never be moved to anything unless our comfort zones are invaded. I can tell you that, if you lack understanding and knowledge of the times, your comfort zones are about to be wrecked. Our standard of living, incredible compared to the rest of the world, and our ease of life have literally disconnected from reality.[3]

Yes, we have enjoyed our comfort zones, and many have talked themselves into believing that life will go on being comfortable to the end. But recently the discomfort level has suddenly skyrocketed, and some have decided that the game is basically over. Now they are going through the motions of living with no idea where life is taking them. While we can understand their frustration and sense of futility, it is hard to mesh these attitudes with the information we find in the Word of God. He has included several key verses in His Book for such a time as this: "It is high time to awake out of sleep" (Romans 13:11). "Therefore let us not sleep, as others do, but let us watch and be sober" (1 Thessalonians 5:6).

Like the Old Testament sons of Issachar, we need to develop an "understanding of the times," so that like them, we will know what we ought to do (1 Chronicles 12:32). On one occasion, Jesus reprimanded the Pharisees and the Sadducees, saying, "You know how to discern the face of the sky, but you cannot discern the signs of the times" (Matthew 16:3).

As we have shown in this book, we are living in very fragile times. The truth is, these are unprecedented times. We are charting new territory almost every day. In fact, things are changing so quickly that some of the chapters in this book have been updated five or six times. Far from giving us cause to turn off the news in despair, the rapid changes in our times actually increase our urgent need for diligence in staying aware of what is going on.

When I began to see the great fluctuations and changes in national and global economics, I jumped into the game and began to learn all I could about the financial world. I am far from being an expert; there is much about economics that I will never comprehend. But what I have done is this: I have gotten my head into the game! I have become a student, and I am the better for it.

In his book *What Your Money Means and How to Use It Well*, author Frank J. Hanna talks about the four things he does in his business and in his private life to handle not only finances, but anything else in the way it should be handled:

1. Find out the truth about how things are now.
2. Discover the truth about how they're supposed to be.
3. Figure out how to change things from how they are now to how they're supposed to be.
4. Make myself want to change them enough that I'll do what's necessary to bring about that change.[4]

Every important decision in life starts with finding the truth. When you know the truth, you have someplace to go. Without the truth, there can be no meaningful journey, simply because progress is impossible unless there is a fixed point toward which you can progress. So first of all, let's agree that we need to know the truth about sound finance. That means keeping our heads in the financial game and becoming students of economics.

There was a time or two other than when my son was playing football with a concussion that his coach felt his focus was not as sharp as it could be. I remember hearing the coach yell, "Daniel, get your head in the game!" I know I am not your coach, but I feel the need to "yell" if you will allow it: When it comes to your financial future, you desperately need to get your head in the game!

If you have not already begun that process, I hope you will do so now. I hope this book has opened your eyes to a few things about the future and the national and international economy that you did not know. But don't stop the learning process with this book. There are other books to read, knowledgeable people to consult, and helpful seminars to attend. In this generation of instant information, knowledge about any subject is only a click away. All it takes to access it is simply the desire to get your head in the game.

And whatever you do, don't forget the best resource of all: the Bible. Although it was never intended to be a book about finances, you will discover many timeless and helpful principles salted away in the pages of this great Book. I will share a few of them with you later in this chapter.

Keep Your House in Order

You and I can do nothing about the problems we see in the world economic order. I think that sense of helplessness is the reason so many people despair and turn off the news. But we are not helpless. There are things we can do to insulate ourselves significantly against the worst of any economic disaster that may come. We cannot control world economics, but we can do much to control our own. In this section I will offer you a few pointers in that direction.

Take a Personal Inventory

As I said above, until you know the real truth about any situation, you cannot know for sure what to do. Affecting the future starts with knowing the truth.

One of the most important things Donna and I have done as a couple during these last few months has been to take a financial inventory of our lives. With the help of professional planners, we began the process of finding out exactly where we are financially. This has been a good experience for us, but it has not been without some surprises. Frankly, we have been so busy with our lives and our ministries that we have not always kept our heads in the game as we should have.

We are on target to change all of that, and I encourage you to do the same. You may resist this exercise out of the fear of what you will discover. But almost no financial situation is totally without hope. If there are real problem areas in your financial picture, it's much better to know of them than to leave them buried like land mines, waiting to destroy you. You will never change what you do not acknowledge.

Minimize Your Indebtedness

Years ago the late Lewis Grizzard wrote a newspaper column in which he told of a former coworker who received a letter from one of his creditors:

> "They're mad at me about the fact that I missed a payment," said the coworker. "The way I pay my bills is I put them all in a hat. Then I reach into the hat without looking and pull out a bill. I keep doing that until I'm out of money. There are always a few bills left in the hat, but at least everybody I owe has a chance of being paid out of the hat. I wrote the people back and told them if they sent me another nasty letter I wouldn't even put them in the hat anymore."[5]

Apparently there are a lot of folks today who are leaving unpaid bills in the hat. The total U.S. consumer debt, which includes credit card and non credit card debt (but not mortgage debt), reached $2.45 trillion as of March 2010.[6]

The Bible does not forbid indebtedness, but it warns about its misuse. For instance, Proverbs points out that the borrower is in danger of becoming a servant to the lender (see Proverbs 22:7). Six times Proverbs warns against cosigning on another's notes (see Proverbs 6:1–2; 11:15; 17:18; 20:16; 22:26; 27:13).

One of the best ministries we have at the church that I pastor is called Crown Financial Ministries. Those who have graduated from this eleven-week, in-depth study have reduced their personal debt by an average of 38 percent, increased their savings by 27 percent, and increased their giving by 72 percent! For those of you struggling to balance your budget, pay your bills, or establish a plan for your finances, I highly recommend that you visit the Crown Financial Web site and start turning your debt around today.[7]

Manage Your Money

Some of my friends who know I have been working on this book have asked if I have any investment advice for them. My answer is no. For me to attempt such a thing would be foolish and arrogant. That's a scary question even in times of financial stability, let alone in today's market chaos.

While I would not advise anyone on investments, I have discovered that when I stay focused on what the Bible actually says, I can give some pretty good general advice on the placement and use of money we possess. The following Scriptures speak for themselves and need no amplification from me. This list is by no means exhaustive, but it illustrates the powerful things the Bible has to say about money and finances. These truths come from the 126 financial principles found in the New Testament and more than 2,350 Bible verses that speak to the subject of finances and material possessions.

1. The Desire Principle:

   • "It's obvious, isn't it? The place where your treasure is, is the place you will most want to be, and end up being.... You can't worship two gods at once. Loving one god, you'll end up hating the other. Adoration of one feeds contempt for the other. You can't worship God and Money both" (Matthew 6:19–21, 24 The Message).

2. The Discernment Principle:

   • "Remove falsehood and lies far from me; give me neither poverty nor riches—feed me with the food allotted to me; lest I be full and deny You, and say, 'Who is the LORD?' Or lest I be poor and steal, and profane the name of my God" (Proverbs 30:8–9).

3. The Discussion Principle:

   • "Listen to counsel and receive instruction" (Proverbs 19:20).
   • "In the multitude of counselors there is safety" (Proverbs 11:14; also see 24:6).

4. The Discipline Principle:

   • "A faithful man will abound with blessings, but he who hastens to be rich will not go unpunished.... A man with an evil eye hastens after riches, and does not consider that poverty will come upon him" (Proverbs 28:20, 22).

5. The Depreciation Principle:

   • "Do not lay up for yourselves treasures on earth, where moth and rust destroy and where thieves break in and steal; but lay up for yourselves treasures in heaven, where neither moth nor rust destroys and where thieves do not break in and steal" (Matthew 6:19–20).

6. The Due Diligence Principle:

   • "For which of you, intending to build a tower, does not sit down first and count the cost, whether he has enough to finish it—lest, after he has laid the foundation, and is not able to finish, all who see it begin to mock him" (Luke 14:28–29).

7. The Diversification Principle:

   • "Give a serving to seven, and also to eight, for you do not know what evil will be on the earth" (Ecclesiastes 11:2).

8. The Descendant Principle:

   • "A good man leaves an inheritance to his children's children, but the wealth of the sinner is stored up for the righteous" (Proverbs 13:22).
   • "But if anyone does not provide for his own, and especially for those of his household, he has denied the faith and is worse than an unbeliever" (1 Timothy 5:8).
   • "For the children ought not to lay up for the parents, but the parents for the children" (2 Corinthians 12:14).

9. The Devotion Principle:

- "Honor the LORD with your possessions, and with the firstfruits of all your increase; so your barns will be filled with plenty, and your vats will overflow with new wine" (Proverbs 3:9–10).
- "So let each one give as he purposes in his heart, not grudgingly or of necessity; for God loves a cheerful giver" (2 Corinthians 9:7).

Follow the advice given in this sampling of wise and practical principles from the Bible and your finances will stay afloat in the worst of economic storms.

Keep Your Heart in Your Faith

For the last several months, I have been spending a great deal of time in the Old Testament book of Daniel. Not only is this one of the most important prophetic books of the Bible, it also records the courageous experiences of Daniel and his Jewish friends during the years of their captivity.

While little of what we read of Daniel's life pertains directly to economics, his unwavering conviction and dedication to the truth of God forms an underlying foundation of trusting one's security in all matters to the only power that is ultimately dependable in seeing us through any kind of crisis. As the shadows of the end times begin to encroach, not only upon our finances but upon all facets of our lives, I find the example of Daniel extremely inspiring. And I want to share with you some of what I've learned from him.

These were difficult years for Daniel. God was revealing to His prophet information about the future that was overwhelming, just as much of what we've shown in this book about the world's imminent future is overwhelming. As he began to internalize what God was telling him, Daniel broke down emotionally. The descriptive terms that tell of Daniel's agonized responses remind me of things I have heard people say during these days of frightening financial fallout:

> I, Daniel, was grieved in my spirit within my body, and the visions of my head troubled me....My thoughts greatly troubled me, and my countenance changed....And [I] fainted and was sick for days....[I] was mourning three full weeks. I ate no pleasant food, no meat or wine came into my mouth, nor did I anoint myself at all....And no strength remained in me; for my vigor was turned to frailty in me, and I retained no strength....I turned my face toward the ground and became speechless....Because of the vision my sorrows have overwhelmed me. (Daniel 7:15, 28; 8:27; 10:2–3, 8, 15–16)

Daniel had faith in God, but he was not prepared for the dark visions of the future that God gave him. He temporarily lost heart. These words from the seventh through the tenth chapters of Daniel clearly show the anguished pressure he was feeling as he began to get his heart back into his faith. These were very difficult days, and there was no way to get through them but to go through them.

Does that sound familiar? If our responses to the ominous economic and political news of today produce similar anguish, it simply shows our need to get our hearts into our faith.

The book of Daniel is a great read for Christians of our generation whose faith may tend to be shaken by current news headlines. It reveals the kind of life we should aspire to live when we are under pressure. In each of the twelve chapters of Daniel's prophecy, we find incidents that show us how to keep our hearts in our faith when we might be overwhelmed by the powers that seem to be aligned against us. Here are just a few of them.

In the first chapter we learn that Daniel was among a group of young Jews from noble families who were brought to Babylon by

King Nebuchadnezzar. At the outset, Daniel had to decide whether to go along just to get along or to stand up for what he believed. The record shows that Daniel "purposed in his heart that he would not defile himself with the portion of the king's delicacies, nor with the wine which he drank" (Daniel 1:8). Daniel risked his life for his convictions, and God blessed him for it.

In chapter 3, Daniel's three friends refused to bow down to Nebuchadnezzar's idol, and the king threatened to burn them alive. We reviewed their response in an earlier chapter, but it is worth repeating simply to be inspired yet again by their conviction and courage:

> O Nebuchadnezzar, we have no need to answer you in this matter. If that is the case, our God whom we serve is able to deliver us from the burning fiery furnace, and He will deliver us from your hand, O king. But if not, let it be known to you, O king, that we do not serve your gods, nor will we worship the gold image which you have set up. (Daniel 3:16–18)

In chapter 4, Daniel interpreted one of King Nebuchadnezzar's dreams. The interpretation exposed the ruthless wickedness of the king and foretold God's judgment upon him. At the conclusion of his interpretation, Daniel confronted the king with these words: "Therefore, O king, let my advice be acceptable to you; break off your sins by being righteous, and your iniquities by showing mercy to the poor" (Daniel 4:27). Imagine standing before the most powerful man on earth and telling him that he is a sinner and needs to repent!

In chapter 5, Daniel confronts Nebuchadnezzar's grandson Belshazzar. In the first part of the chapter, the story of Nebuchadnezzar's judgment is repeated and Daniel says to Belshazzar, "But you his son, Belshazzar, have not humbled your heart, although you knew all this. And you have lifted yourself up against the Lord of heaven...."

And you have praised the gods of silver and gold . . . and the God who holds your breath in His hand and owns all your ways, you have not glorified" (Daniel 5:22–23).

Before that very evening was over, Daniel revealed the judgment concealed in the mysterious handwriting on the banquet room wall: Belshazzar's kingdom was to be divided between the Medes and the Persians, and "Belshazzar, king of the Chaldeans, was slain" (Daniel 5:30).

In chapter 6 we are told that Daniel refused to obey the royal statute that said no prayer or petition was to be offered to "any god or man for thirty days" (v. 7) except to Darius, king of the Medes. Instead of complying, Daniel went to his own house and prayed to the God of heaven: "Now when Daniel knew that the writing was signed, he went home. And in his upper room, with his windows open toward Jerusalem, he knelt down on his knees three times that day, and prayed and gave thanks before his God, as was his custom since early days" (6:10).

Some writers have described Daniel's conduct as an act of defiance against the king. It was not that at all. Daniel simply went home and did what he had always done. In other words, he did not let the pronouncement of the king or the plot of his enemies change the course of his life. He would not be bullied into denying his God.

Because of his faithfulness to God, Daniel was thrown into a den of hungry lions. But, as Daniel reported later, "My God sent His angel and shut the lions' mouths, so that they have not hurt me, because I was found innocent before Him; and also, O king, I have done no wrong before you" (6:22).

This incident reveals a real challenge for us today. Whether we are pressured into bowing to political correctness, multiculturalism, or ecumenicalism, we cannot allow ourselves to be pushed off course. We must continue to keep our hearts in our faith and be God's people, holding up His standard and obeying His will no matter what the consequences. Increasingly today the political powers apply financial pressure to those who resist their efforts to enforce political correctness. Our businesses may be boycotted, or we may be threatened with being fired from our jobs. Financial pressure has a way of softening our resolve. If we are not vigilant, we begin to make small concessions to societal pressure, compromising God's truth in order to align ourselves with cultural norms in an effort to strengthen our sense of immediate security. That's where the example of Daniel can really help us.

In chapter 8, Daniel was given an astonishing vision of the Antichrist so frightful that he "fainted and was sick for days." But read what the Bible says he did next: "Afterward I arose and went about the king's business" (v. 27). This may not be as dramatic as some of the events we have already cited, but it is perhaps the most important of all. Daniel was trusted with great insight into the future, but he did not allow this lofty calling to take him away from his daily responsibilities. He arose and went about the king's business.

This is a great rallying cry for these days of financial hardship and economic and political confusion. We must not give up in despair and helplessness. We must not, as some have foolishly done, sell our homes, abandon our lives, and camp on a mountaintop waiting for the Lord to come. Like Daniel, we need to get the facts, and then get up and get about the King's business—the business of doing the will of God.

Chapter 11 of Daniel foretells the story of Antiochus IV Epiphanes and his brutal assault against Israel. In the middle of the narrative describing this attack, we read these wonderful words: "But the people who know their God shall be strong, and carry out great exploits. And those of the people who understand shall instruct many" (vv. 32–33).

In one of the most horrendous moments in Israel's long history of suffering, the people who knew their God stood their ground. In every generation and in every situation, God has His people. When we put our hearts into our faith, we join this courageous band of brothers and sisters. Standing together we give courage and strength to one another, ensuring companionship and support as the world moves toward the incvitable chaos of the end times.

In the magazine *Evangel*, J. K. Gressett writes about a man named Samuel S. Scull who settled on a farm in the Arizona desert with his wife and children:

One night a fierce storm struck with rain, hail, and high wind. At daybreak, feeling sick and fearing what he might find, Samuel went out to survey the loss.

The hail had beaten the garden and truck patch into the ground; the house was partially unroofed, the henhouse had blown away, and dead chickens were scattered about. Destruction and devastation were everywhere.

While standing dazed, evaluating the mess and wondering about the future, he heard a stirring in the lumber pile that was the remains of the henhouse. A rooster was climbing up through the debris, and he didn't stop climbing until he had mounted the highest board in the pile. That old rooster was dripping wet, and most of his feathers were blown away. But as the sun came over the eastern horizon, he flapped his bony wings and proudly crowed.

That old wet, bare rooster could still crow when he saw the morning sun. And like that rooster, our world may be falling apart, we may have lost everything, but if we trust in God, we'll be able to see the light of God's goodness, pick ourselves out of the rubble, and sing the Lord's praise.[8]

Though the world may seem to be crashing down around us, it really changes neither our basic duty nor our ultimate security. We know the truth. We know who we are and to whom we belong. We are God's people, living under His grace and assured by His promises that whatever happens, we are in His strong and dependable hands. Lions' dens, fiery furnaces, storms that crash our world down around our heads don't matter. Our task is still the same: greet the approaching sunrise with joy. The sun will come up. It always does for those who love the Lord.

Keep Your Hope in God

Not long ago, I saw a bumper sticker that carried this profound message:

KNOW GOD—KNOW HOPE
NO GOD—NO HOPE

These simple words summarize the final message of this chapter and this book. If you are looking for the kind of hope you need for difficult days, you will find that hope only in God.

During the difficult days of World War II, a young Jewish girl in the Warsaw ghetto of Poland managed to escape over the wall and hide in a cave. Tragically, she died in that cave shortly before the Allied army broke into the ghetto to liberate the prisoners. But before she died, she scratched on the wall some powerful words that sound like a creed:

I believe in the sun, even when it is not shining.
I believe in love, even when I cannot feel it.
I believe in God, even when He is silent.

This young girl endured dark days and great trauma in her life, but she maintained hope in the face of apparent hopelessness. Her last statement about God comes very close to describing what many today have been experiencing. Through faith and hope, we can know

God is there even though the growing shadow cast by coming events may obscure a clear vision of Him.

It may be that as you have read what I have written in this book, you are wondering whether there is any hope. Perhaps you find yourself feeling like Job, who asked, "Where then is my hope? As for my hope, who can see it?" (Job 17:15). To be sure, there may be many causes for discouragement. But there are far more reasons for hope. Every generation since Adam has faced calamity. Within its epochs, the Bible records a long history of wars, plagues, famines, corruption, depravity, and suffering. Yet God is still in control. He has a plan, and His Bible is a book of hope. When we walk in fellowship with God, we find ourselves lifted by the irresistible updraft of biblical hope.

If we maintain this hope, nothing can destroy our real security or our joy. The psalmist wrote, "Why are you cast down, O my soul? And why are you disquieted within me? Hope in God, for I shall yet praise Him for the help of His countenance" (Psalm 42:5).

Commenting on this passage, Dr. Martyn Lloyd-Jones said,

> The first thing we have to learn is what the Psalmist learned—we must take ourselves in hand. This man was not content just to lie down and commiserate with himself. He does something about it. He takes himself in hand—he talks to himself....I say that we must talk to ourselves instead of allowing "ourselves" to talk to us!...Have you realized that most of your unhappiness in life is due to the fact that you are listening to yourself instead of talking to yourself?[9]

The good doctor is right. We must learn to preach to ourselves. We must learn to encourage ourselves in the Lord. We must learn to search out and claim God's promises for our present needs and future fears. We must ask the Holy Spirit to make these verses so real in our minds that the hope we draw from them will lift our spirits like giant balloons of spiritual helium.

In many places the Bible makes it clear that even in the darkest hours, we have good reason for hope. The psalmist said, "I will hope continually, and will praise You yet more and more" (Psalm 71:14).

Solomon said, "The hope of the righteous will be gladness" (Proverbs 10:28).

Jeremiah wrote, "Blessed is the man who trusts in the LORD, and whose hope is the LORD. For he shall be like a tree planted by the waters, which spreads out its roots by the river" (Jeremiah 17:7–8).

And in the book of Lamentations, "This I recall to my mind, therefore I have hope....His compassions fail not. They are new every morning; great is Your faithfulness. 'The LORD is my portion,' says my soul, 'Therefore I hope in Him!' ...It is good that one should hope and wait quietly" (3:21–26).

Paul calls God "the God of hope" (Romans 15:13) and assures us that "hope does not disappoint, because the love of God has been poured out in our hearts by the Holy Spirit who was given to us" (Romans 5:5).

The writer of Hebrews gives us a great visual of the kind of hope we have in God when he writes: "This hope we have as an anchor of the soul, both sure and steadfast, and which enters the Presence behind the veil, where the forerunner has entered for us, even Jesus, having become High Priest forever according to the order of Melchizedek" (6:19–20).

According to Isaiah 40:3, those who hope in the Lord shall renew their strength and mount up with wings like eagles. In a world in which we're beset by burdens big and small, we have these strong gusts of hope, catching our wings and sending us soaring heavenward as God's hopeful, joyous people.

Alexander Solzhenitsyn was a man who knew how to hang on to hope. He became an icon of perseverance through his suffering as a political prisoner in Russia where he was forced to work twelve hours a day at hard labor while existing on a starvation diet. The story is told of a time when he became gravely ill. Although the doctors predicted his death was imminent, his captors did not spare him from his daily forced labor.

One afternoon he stopped working, even though he knew the guards would beat him severely. He just could not go on any longer. At that precise moment another prisoner, a fellow Christian, approached him. With his cane the man drew a cross in the sand. Instantly, Solzhenitsyn felt all the hope of God flood his soul. In the midst of his despair, that emblem of hope where Christ fought and won the victory over sin gave Solzhenitsyn the courage to endure that difficult day and the grueling months of imprisonment that were before him.[10]

The next time you feel hopeless, take your finger and draw a cross in the sand. Or take your pen and draw one on paper and remember what it means. It means that there was a day when hopelessness encountered a Person on a cross. And three days later, the Lord Jesus banished all hopelessness by rising from the dead, offering true hope to all who would believe and receive it. When we hang on to hope, we can go through anything.

As Christians, we should never place our hope in the systems of this world. The real hope that Christ gave us does not depend on the shifting sand of politics and economics. If you long to have this hope for life after death, you will find it in Jesus Christ and in Him alone.

Archbishop Desmond Tutu, the leading figure in the fight to end apartheid in South Africa, suffered greatly at the hands of the racists in his country. When an interviewer asked if he was hopeful about the future of South Africa, he replied, "I am always hopeful, for a Christian is a prisoner of hope."[11]

Financial pressures have one great benefit. They push us to new levels of faith, forcing us to be utterly dependent on God. And that dependence is solidly justified, for the Bible is filled with promises that God will meet the needs of His children. No matter how dark the horizon may seem, we who trust in the Lord need not fear at all. Psalm 23 says that if the Lord is our Shepherd, we shall not lack. Jesus counseled us to study birds and flowers, for the God who cares for them will care for us (see Matthew 6:25–34). The psalmist said, "I have been young, and now am old; yet I have not seen the righteous forsaken, nor his descendants begging bread" (Psalm 37:25).

Paul told his readers, "My God shall supply all your need according to His riches in glory by Christ Jesus" (Philippians 4:19). And in another letter, "God is able to make all grace abound toward you, that you, always having all sufficiency in all things, may have an abundance for every good work" (2 Corinthians 9:8).

We can only lose hope if we take our eyes off the God of Hope. In his book *Disappointment with God*, author Philip Yancey tells a story that perfectly summarizes this principle and provides a fitting ending to this book:

Once a friend of mine went swimming in a large lake at dusk. As he was paddling at a leisurely pace about a hundred yards offshore, a freak evening fog rolled in across the water. Suddenly he could see nothing: no horizon, no landmarks, no objects or lights on shore. Because the fog diffused all light, he could not even make out the direction of the setting sun.

For thirty minutes he splashed around in panic. He would start off in one direction, lose confidence, and turn ninety degrees to the right. Or left—it made no difference which way he turned. He could feel his heart racing uncontrollably. He would stop and float, trying to conserve energy, and force himself to breathe slower. Then he would blindly strike out again.

At last he heard a faint voice from shore. He pointed his body toward the sounds and followed them to safety.

All of us can relate to this story. Recently it seems as if we have been forced to live life in an increasingly dense fog. All the familiar surroundings that we once knew are shrouded and clouded, and we do not know which way to go. If we are honest, we are often scared and sometimes desperate, longing for some direction from God.

But if we will just stay quiet and trust in Him, we will hear the sounds from the shore and we will know which way to go.[12]

Notes

Introduction

1. Caroline Baum, "Greek Contagion Myth Masks Real Europe Crisis," *Bloomberg Businessweek*, 9 May 2010, http://www.businessweek.com/news/2010-05-09/greek-contagion-myth-masks-real-europe-crisis-caroline-baum.html (accessed 10 May 2010).
2. James Kanter and Judy Dempsey, "Europeans Move to Head Off Spread of Debt Crisis," *New York Times.com*, 7 May 2010, http://www.nytimes.com/2010/05/08/business/global/08drachma.html?th&emc=th (accessed 8 May 2010).
3. *Merriam-Webster's Collegiate Dictionary*, 11th ed., s.v. "Armageddon."
4. Geoff Colvin, "This Isn't Armageddon," *CNN Money.com,* 3 October 2008, http://money.cnn.com/2008/09/25/news/economy/colvin_economy.fortune/index.htm (accessed 3 June 2010). Allan Roth, "The Stock Market—One Year after Armageddon," *CBS MoneyWatch.com*, 9 March 2010, http://moneywatch.bnet.com/investing/blog/irrational-investor/the-stoc-market-one-year-after-armageddon/1188 (accessed 25 March 2010).
5. Kimberly Schwandt, "Boehner: 'It's Armageddon,' Health Care Bill Will 'Ruin Our Country,'" *FOX News.com*, 20 March 2010, http://congress.blogs.foxnews.com/2010/03/20/boehner-its-armageddon-health-care-bill-will-ruin-our-country/ (accessed 23 March 2010).

6. Mark Moring, "It's the End of the World, and We Love It," *Christianity Today*, March 2010, 44–45.

7. Ibid., 45.

8. U.S. Department of Labor/Bureau of Labor Statistics, Economic News Release, "Regional and State Employment and Unemployment Summary," 21 May 2010, http://www.bls.gov/news.release/laus.nr0.htm (accessed 3 June 2010).

9. U.S. Department of Labor/Bureau of Labor Statistics, Economic News Release, "Employment Situation Summary," 5 April 2010, http://www.bls.gov/news.release/pdf/empsit.pdf (accessed 26 April 2010); U.S. Department of Labor/Bureau of Labor Statistics, Economic News Release, 4 June 2010, http://www.bls.gov/news.release/empsit.nrO.htm (accessed 4 June 2010).

10. Charles Abbott and Christopher Doering, "One of Seven Americans Short of Food," Reuters.com, 16 November 2009, http://www.reuters.com/article/idUSTRE5AF42220091116 (accessed 3 June 2010).

11. Stephanie Armour, "Underwater Mortgages Drain Equity, Dampen Retirement," *USA Today.com*, 24 March 2010, http://www.usatoday.com/money/economy/housing/2010-03-24-1Aunderwater25_CV_N.htm (accessed 25 March 2010).

12. Mary Williams Walsh, "Social Security to See Payout Exceed Pay-In This Year," *New York Times*, 25 March 2010, A1.

13. Rex Nutting, "We Saved the World from Disaster, Fed's Bernanke Says," *MarketWatch.com*, 21 August 2009, http://marketwatch.com/story/we-saved-the-world-from-disaster-bernanke-says-2009-08-21-10100 (accessed 21 August 2009).

14. Joachim Starbatty, "Euro Trashed," *New York Times.com*, 28 March 2010, http://www.nytimes.com/2010/03/29/opinion/29Starbatty.html (accessed 3 June 2010).

15. Ibid.

16. Ibid.

17. "Recession," Times Topics, *New York Times.com*, http://topics.nytimes.com/top/reference/timestopics/subjects/r/recession_and_depression/index.html (accessed 23 October 2009).

18. Jennifer Ryan, "U.K. Recession Probably Ended in Third Quarter, Survey Shows," *Bloomberg.com*, 23 October 2009, http://www.bloomberg.com/apps/news?pid=20601085&sid=aOT10AMC-15U (accessed 23 October 2009).

19. Philip Webster, Gráinne Gilmore, and Suzy Jagger, "Shock as Figures Show Britain Is Still in Recession," *The Times*, 24 October 2009, http://business.timesonline.co.uk/tol/business/economics/article6888402.ece (accessed 24 October 2009).

20. Bill Draper, "Volcker Says US Markets Need More Supervision," Associated Press, 23 October 2009, http://abcnews.go.com/Business/wireStory?id=8902450 (accessed 22 June 2010).

21. http://abcnews.go.com/PollingUnit/Politics/economic-recovery-abc-news-washington-post-poll/story?id=8891003&page=3 (accessed 9 June 2010).

22. Bill Bonner, "Don't Count on China," *Fleet Street Invest.com*, 26 August 2009, http://www.fleetstreetinvest.co.uk/daily-reckoning/bill-bonner-essays/china-rescue-world-ecnonmy-54115.html (accessed 26 August 2009).

CHAPTER 1. The Fall of the American Economy

1. Brian Ross, *The Madoff Chronicles: Inside the Secret World of Bernie and Ruth* (New York: Hyperion Books, 2009), 162. See also "Report: Madoff's Sister Among Scammed Victims," *FOX News.com*, 11 January 2009, http://www.foxnews.com/story/0,2933,479154,00.html (accessed 23 February 2010).

2. Ross, *Madoff Chronicles*, 144.

3. William Bonner and Addison Wiggin, *The New Empire of Debt: The Rise and Fall of an Epic Financial Bubble* (Hoboken, NJ: John Wiley & Sons, 2009), 291–294, 313–315.

4. "Losers," *WORLD*, 2 January 2010, 32.

5. Robert Pear, "Recession Drains Social Security and Medicare," *New York Times.com*, 12 May 2009, http://www.nytimes.com/2009/05/13/us/politics/13health.html (accessed 23 February 2010).

6. Edmund L. Andrews, "Payback Time: Wave of Debt Payments Facing U.S. Government," *New York Times.com*, 22 November 2009, http://www.nytimes.com/2009/11/23/business/23rates.html (accessed 23 November 2009).

7. Richard Wolf, "Rash of Retirements Pushes Social Security to Brink," *USA Today.com*, 8 February 2010, http://www.usatoday.com/news/washington/2010-02-07-social-security-red-retirements_N.htm (accessed 8 February 2010).

8. Charles Goyette, *The Dollar Meltdown: Surviving the Impending Currency Crisis with Gold, Oil, and Other Unconventional Investments* (New York: Penguin Group, 2009), 29.

9. Joseph E. Stiglitz and Linda J. Bilmes, *The Three Trillion Dollar War: The True Cost of the Iraq Conflict* (New York: W. W. Norton & Company, 2008).

10. Joel Belz, "Up, Up and Up: On Almost Every Front, It's Been an Inflationary Year," *WORLD*, 19 December 2009, 6.

11. U.S. Department of State, "The Growth of Government in the United States," *About.com*, http://economics.about.com/od/howtheuseconomyworks/a/gov_growth.htm (accessed 23 February 2010).

12. Ibid.

13. Solomon Fabricant, "The Rising Trend of Government Employment," National Bureau of Economic Research, Inc., Occasional Paper 29: June 1949.

14. See Declan McCullagh, "It's a Good Time to Work for Uncle Sam," *CBS News.com*, 12 May 2009, http://www.cbsnews.com/blogs/2009/05/12/business/econwatch/entry5007862.shtml (accessed 3 February 2010), and "In U.S., 35% Would Rather Work for Gov't Than for Business," *Gallup*, 29 January 2010, http://www.gallup.com/poll/125426/In-U.S.-35-Rather-Work-Govt-Than-Business.aspx (accessed 29 January 2010).

15. Dennis Cauchon, "For Feds, More Get 6-Figure Salaries," *USA Today.com*, 11 December 2009, http://www.usatoday.com/news/washington/2009-12-10-federal-pay-salaries_N.htm (accessed 4 February 2010).

16. Andrews, "Payback Time."

17. Goyette, *The Dollar Meltdown*, 33–35.

18. Pamela Villarreal, "Social Security and Medicare Unfunded Liabilities," 2009 Social Security and Medicare Trustees Reports, *National Center for Policy Analysis: Social Security and Medicare Projections: 2009*, Brief Analysis No. 662, 11 June 2009.

19. Goyette, *The Dollar Meltdown*, 36.

20. Mark Knoller, "National Debt Tops $13 Trillion For First Time," *CBS News/Political Hotsheet.com*, 2 June 2010, http://www.cbsnews.com/8301-503544_162-20006618-503544.html(accessed 2 June 2010).

21. Lawrence Kadish, "Taking the National Debt Seriously," *Wall Street Journal.com*, 11 October 2009, http://online.wsj.com/article/SB10001424 052748 704429304574467071019099570.html (accessed 20 October 2009).

22. "Major Foreign Holders of Treasury Securities Holdings," December 2009, http://www.treas.gov/tic/mfh.txt (accessed 15 December 2009).

23. Jeanne Sahadi, "$4.8 trillion—Interest on U.S. debt," *CNN Money.com*, 20 December 2009, http://money.cnn.com/2009/11/19/news/economy/debt_interest/index.htm (accessed 11 February 2010).

24. Doug Andrew, "The US Economy Is a Sinking Ship and David Walker," *Missed Fortune.com* 7 May 2009, http://blog.missedfortune.com/2009/05/economy-sinking-ship-david-walker/(accessed 3 June 2010).

25. Andrews, "Payback Time."

26. Bonner and Wiggin, *New Empire of Debt*, 201.

27. "History and Fun Facts," http://www.hasbro.com/monopoly/en_US/discover/ history.cfm (accessed 6 October 2009).

28. "Strategy Guide—Rules," http://www.hasbro.com/monopoly/en_US/discover/strategy/rules.cfm (accessed 4 February 2010).

29. Larry Bates, *The New Economic Disorder* (Lake Murray, FL: Excel Books, 2009), 7.

30. Ibid., 13.

31. Erwin W. Lutzer, *When a Nation Forgets God: 7 Lessons We Must Learn from Nazi Germany* (Chicago: Moody Press, 2009), 38.

32. Constantino Bresciani-Turroni, *The Economics of Inflation: A Study of Currency Depreciation in Post-War Germany* (Florence, KY: Routledge, 2003), 80.

33. Bonner and Wiggin, *New Empire of Debt*, 27.

34. Bresciani-Turroni, *Economics of Inflation*, 404.

35. Bonner and Wiggin, *New Empire of Debt*, 46.

36. Ibid., 28.

37. U.S. Department of the Treasury, "FAQs: Currency/Denominations," http://www.ustreas.gov/education/faq/currency/denominations .shtml#q3 (accessed 20 October 2009).

38. Adapted from http://www.dailycognition.com/index.php/2009/03/ 25/what-1-trillion-dollars-looks-like-in-dollar-bills.html (accessed 16 October 2009).

39. "The Buzz: Need-to-Know News/Dollar Signs," *WORLD*, 15 August 2009, http://www.worldmag.com/articles/15710 (accessed 11 February 2010; subscription needed).

40. Kadish, "Taking the National Debt Seriously."

41. Devon Maylie, "Spot Gold Hits Record High Above $1250/oz." *Wall Street Journal.com*, 8 June 2010, http://online.wsj.com/article/BT -CO-20100608-703527.html (accessed 8 June 2010).

42. D. Edmond Hiebert, *The Epistle of James* (Chicago: Moody Press, 1992), 259–260.

43. Homer A. Kent Jr., *Faith that Works: Studies in the Epistle of James* (Grand Rapids: Baker, 1986), 171.

44. John MacArthur, *The MacArthur New Testament Commentary: James* (Chicago: Moody Press, 1998), 245.

45. Wilfred Hahn, "Last Day Change of Seasons," *The Midnight Call*, April 2007, 28.

46. Andy Serwer, "The Decade from Hell," *Time*, 7 December 2009, 30.

47. S. Mitra Kalita, "Americans See 18% of Wealth Vanish," *Wall Street Journal.com*, 13 March 2009, http://online.wsj.com/article/ SB123687371369308675.html (accessed 7 June 2010).

48. Brett Arends, "Can Vanished Real Estate Wealth Come Back?" *Wall Street Journal.com*, 20 August 2009, http://online.wsj.com/article/ SB125079838400747341.html (accessed 17 February 2010).

49. Associated Press, "Retirement Account Losses Near $2 Trillion," *MSNBC.com*, 7 October 2008, http://www.msnbc.msn.com/id/ 27073061/ (accessed 17 February 2010).

50. Jackie Calmes, "U.S. Budget Gap Is Revised to Surpass $1.8 Trillion," *New York Times.com*, 12 May 2009, http://www.nytimes .com/2009/05/12/business/economy/12budget.html (accessed 26 February 2010).

51. Associated Press, "U.S. Budget Deficit Hit Record $1.4 Trillion in 2009," *FOXNews.com*, 7 October 2009, http://www.foxnews.com/ politics/2009/10/07/budget-deficit-hit-record-trillion/ (accessed 8 February 2010).

52. "U.S. Posts 19th Straight Monthly Budget Deficit," *Reuters.com*, 12 May 2010, http://www.reuters.com/article/idUSTRE64B53W20100512 (accessed 25 May 2010).

53. Alexandra Twin, "Stocks Crushed," 29 September 2008, http:// money.cnn.com/2008/09/29/markets/markets-newyork/index.htm (accessed 24 February 2010).

54. "Factbox—U.S., European Bank Writedowns, Credit Losses," *Reuters.com*, 5 November 2009, http://www.reuters.com/article/ idCNL554155620091105?rpc=44 (accessed 24 February 2010).

55. Saul Relative, "Bill Gates Is Forbes Richest Man in the World... Again," *Associated Content.com*, 12 March 2009, http://www .associatedcontent.com/article/1557001/bill_gates_is_forbes _richest_man_in.html?cat=3 (accessed 24 February 2010).

56. Serwer, "The Decade from Hell," 32.

57. Robert Frank and Amir Efrati, "'Evil' Madoff Gets 150 Years in Epic Fraud," *Wall Street Journal.com,* 30 June 2009, http://online.wsj.com/ article/SB124604151653862301.html (accessed 11 February 2010).

58. David Jeremiah, *What in the World Is Going On?* (Nashville: Thomas Nelson Publishers, 2008), 130.

59. Ibid., 138.

60. Al Mohler, "A Christian View of the Economic Crisis," *Christianity Today.com*, 29 September 2008, http://www.christianitytoday.com/ ct/2008/septemberweb-only/140-12.0.html (accessed 12 March 2010).

CHAPTER 2. The New World Order

1. H. G. Wells, *The New World Order* (London: Secker & Warburg, 1940), 104, 26, 33.

2. "Jimmy Carter: Voyager Spacecraft Statement by the President," http://www.presidency.ucsb.edu/ws/index.php?pid=7890 (accessed 29 September 2009).

3. George Herbert Walker Bush, "Address before a Joint Session of the Congress on the Persian Gulf Crisis and the Federal Budget Deficit," 11 September 1990, http://bushlibrary.tamu.edu/research/public _papers.php?id=2217&year=1990&month (accessed 26 August 2009).

4. George Herbert Walker Bush, "Address Before a Joint Session of the Congress on the State of the Union," 29 January 1991, http://bushlibrary.tamu.edu/research/public_papers.php?id=2656&year =1991&month=01(accessed 4 June 2010).

5. George Herbert Walker Bush, "Address Before a Joint Session of the Congress on the Cessation of the Persian Gulf Conflict, 1991-03-06, http://bushlibrary.tamu.edu/research/public_papers.php?id=2767 &year=1991&month=3(accessed 4 June 2010).

6. Henry Kissinger, "A Chance for a New World Order," *New York Times.com*, 12 January 2009, http://www.nytimes.com/2009/01/ 12/opinion/12iht-edkissinger.1.19281915.html?_r=2 (accessed 9 December 2009).

7. Henry Kissinger, "An End to Hubris," *The Economist.com*, 19 November 2008, http://www.economist.com/displaystory.cfm?story -id=12575180 (accessed 23 July 2009).

8. Drew Zahn, "Kissinger: Obama Primed to Create 'New World Order,'" WorldNetDaily, 6 January 2009, http://www.wnd.com/ index.php?pageId=85422 (accessed 23 July 2009).

9. "Barack Obama's New World Order," *Time.com*, 3 April 2009, http://www.time.com/time/world/article/0,8599,1889512,00.html (accessed 11 November 2009).

10. "Barack Obama Is 'President of the World,'" *CNN Politics.com*, 5 November 2008, http://edition.cnn.com/2008/POLITICS/11/

05/international.press.reaction/index.html (accessed 25 February 2010).

11. Michael Fullilove, "Barack Obama: President of the World," *Brookings*, 4 February 2008, http://www.brookings.edu/articles/2009/0204_obama_fullilove.aspx (accessed 25 February 2010).

12. Michael Scherer, "Barack Obama's New World Order," *Time.com*, 3 April 2009, http://www.time.com/time/world/article/0,8599,18889512,00.html#ixzz0gZNrvuj8 (accessed 25 February 2010).

13. Andrew Grice, "This Was the Bretton Woods of Our Times," *The Independent*, 4 April 2009, http://www.independent.co.uk/opinion/commentators/andrew-grice/andrew-grice-this-was-the-bretton-woods-of-our-times-1662231.html (accessed 8 December 2009).

14. Benedict VXI, "Caritas in Veritate," Encyclical Letter, 29 June 2009, http://www.vatican.va/holy-father/benedict-xvi/encyclicals/documents/hf-ben-xvi-enc-20090629-caritas-in-veritate-en.html (accessed 26 August 2009).

15. "Editorial: Green World Government," *Washington Times*, 27 October 2009, http://washingtontimes.com/news/2009/oct/27/green-world-government/ (accessed 31 October 2009).

16. Laura Blumenfeld, "Soros's Deep Pockets vs. Bush," *Washington Post*, 11 November 2003, A30.

17. Paul B. Farrell, "Warning: Crash dead ahead. Sell. Get liquid. Now.," *MarketWatch.com*, 25 May 2010, http://www.marketwatch.com/story/crash-is-dead-ahead-sell-get-liquid-now-2010-05-25?reflink=MW_news_stmp (accessed 25 May 2010).

18. PR Newswire, "George Soros Unveils New Blueprint for World Financial System," 28 October 2009, http://www.prnewswire.com/news-releases/george-soros-unveils-new-blueprint-for-world-financial-system-66799482.html (accessed 30 October 2009).

19. "WSJ Claims It Surpasses *USA Today* as Top-Selling Paper," *NYI.com*, 15 October 2009, http://ny1.com/7-brooklyn-news-content/features/107360/wsj-claims-it-surpasses-usa-today-as-top-selling-paper (accessed 15 October 2009).

20. Craig Parshall, "Nimrod and Globalism at Shinar," *Israel, My Glory*, January/February 2010, 16.

21. C. H. Mackintosh, *Genesis to Deuteronomy* (Neptune, NJ: Loizeaux Brothers, 1980), 57.

22. Eugene H. Peterson, *The Message* (Colorado Springs: NavPress, 2002), 34.

23. John Ankerberg, John Weldon, Dave Bresse, and Dave Hunt, *One World: Bible Prophecy and the New World Order* (Chicago: Moody Press, 1991), 17.

24. C. Theodore Schwarze, *The Program of Satan* (Chicago: Good News Publishers, 1947), 192.

25. Adapted from Robert Dallek, *Lone Star Rising: Lyndon Johnson and His Times, 1908–1960* (New York: Oxford Press, 1991), 275.

26. "Dag Hammarskjöld: A Room of Quiet," *United Nations.org*, http://www.un.org/Depts/dhl/dag/meditationroom.htm (accessed 25 February 2010).

27. "What Is the Meditation Room?" Fact Sheet #19, Public Inquiries Unit, Department of Public Information, United Nations.

28. Alex Grobman, *Nations United: How the United Nations Undermines Israel and the West* (Green Forest, AZ: Balfour Books, 2006), 62.

29. "List of Wars 1945–1989," http://en.wikipedia.org/wiki/List_of_wars_1945%E2%80%931989 (accessed 26 February 2010). "List of Wars 1990–2002," http://en.wikipedia.org/wiki/List_of_wars_1990%E2%80%932002 (accessed 26 February 2010). "List of Wars 2003–Current," http://en.wikipedia.org/wiki/List_of_wars_2003%E2%80%93current (accessed 26 February 2010).

30. Kofi Annan, "Secretary-General's Remarks at Inauguration of the Holocaust History Museum at Yad Vashem," 15 March 2005, http://www.un.org/apps/sg/sgstats.asp?nid=1349 (accessed 25 February 2010).

31. Slobodan Lekic, "Ahmadinejad's UN Speech: 'The American Empire' Is Nearing Collapse," *Huffington Post.com*, 23 September 2008, http://www.huffingtonpost.com/2008/09/23/ahmadinejads-un-speech-th_n_128707.html (accessed 8 December 2009).

32. "From Globalization to Global Peace?" *Vision.org*, Summer 2009, http://www.vision.org/visionmedia/article.aspx?id=18193 (accessed 26 August 2009).

33. Grant Jeffrey, *Shadow Government: How the Secret Global Elite Is Using Surveillance against You* (Colorado Springs: Waterbrook Press, 2009), 173. War statistics from Michael Kidron and Dan Smith, *The War Atlas Conflict: Armed Peace* (London: Pan Books, 1983), 5.

34. Grant Jeffrey, *Shadow Government*, 5.

35. Debbie Elliot, "Carter Helps Monitor Nicaragua Presidential Election," *National Public Radio.com*, 5 November 2006, http://www.npr.org/templates/story/story.php?storyId=6439233 (accessed 27 August 2009).

36. John Lennon, "Imagine," 1971, http://www.answers.com/topic/imagine-performed-by-various-artists (accessed 29 September 2009).

37. Francis A. Schaeffer, *How Should We Then Live?: The Rise and Decline of Western Thought and Culture* (Old Tappan, NJ: Fleming H. Revell Company, 1976), 246–247.

38. Berit Kjos, "Part 2: The Emerging New World Order," 25 June 2006, http://www.crossroad.to/articles2/006/migration-2.htm (accessed 26 February 2010).

39. Bruce Judson, *It Could Happen Here* (New York: HarperCollins, 2010), 81–82, 162.

40. Max Lucado, *Fearless: Imagine Your Life without Fear* (Nashville: Thomas Nelson Publishers, 2009), 106–107.

CHAPTER 3. The New Global Economy

1. William Bonner and Addison Wiggin, *The New Empire of Debt: The Rise and Fall of an Epic Financial Bubble*, 2d ed. (Hoboken, NJ: John Wiley & Sons, Inc., 2009), 295.

2. Erwin W. Lutzer, *When a Nation Forgets God: 7 Lessons We Must Learn from Nazi Germany* (Chicago: Moody Press, 2009), 37.

3. David Jeremiah, *The Handwriting on the Wall* (Nashville: Thomas Nelson Publishers, 1992), 151–152.

4. Lutzer, *When a Nation Forgets God*, 41.

5. Adapted from William Jasper, *Global Tyranny Step by Step* (Appleton, WI: Western Islands Publishers, 1992), 281.

6. *Merriam-Webster's Collegiate Dictionary*, 11th ed., s.v. "globalization."

7. G. Edward Griffin, "Transcript of Interview of Newshour's Ask the Expert," *Financial Sense Online*, 28 October 2006, http://www .financialsense.com/transcriptions/2006/1018griffin.html (accessed 6 October 2009).

8. Charles Goyette, *The Dollar Meltdown* (New York: Portfolio, 2009), 108.

9. Neil Shah, "As Budget Deficit Grows, So Do Doubts on the Dollar," *Wall Street Journal.com*, 26 August 2009, http://online.wsj .com/article/SB125122938682957967.html (accessed 18 February 2009).

10. Roger C. Altman, "The Great Crash, 2008: A Geopolitical Setback for the West," *Foreign Affairs*, January/February 2009, http://www .foreignaffairs.com/articles/63714/roger-c-altman/the-great-crash -2008 (accessed 5 October 2009).

11. "Why the Dollar Is Toast," Rich Dad Education, 14 October 2009, http://www.richdadeducationblog.com/2009/10/why_the_dollar _is_toast.php (accessed 16 February 2010).

12. Wilfred J. Hahn, "Dollar Demise: Prophetic Significance of a One-World Currency," *Midnight Call*, October 2009, 27.

13. Larry Kudlow, "Save the Greenback, Mr. President,"*CNBC.com*, 9 October 2009, http://www.cnbc.com/id/33246832 (accessed 13 October 2009).

14. Daniel Wilson, "China, India battle for gold market supremacy," *Commodity online.com*, 26 May 2010, http://www.commodityonline .com/news/China-India-battle-for-gold-market-supremacy-28533 -3-1.html (accessed 26 May 2010).

15. Lyubov Pronina, "Medvedev Shows Off Sample Coin on New 'World Currency' at G-8," *Bloomberg.com*, 10 July 2009, http:// www.bloomberg.com/apps/news?pid=20601083&sid=aeFVNYQp ByU4 (accessed 31 July 2009).

16. Adapted from Shai Oster, "China, Russia Sign Deals during Putin Visit," *Wall Street Journal.com*, 13 October 2009, http:// online.wsj.com/article/sB125542273198682053.html?mod=WSJ _hpp_MIDDLTopStories (accessed 13 October 2009).

17. Harsh Joshi and Andrew W. Peaple, "Asia's great currency race," *Wall Street Journal.com,* 25 May 2010, http://online.wsj.com/article/SB1 000142405274870402620457526597100405664.html?mod=WSJ _Markets_section_Heard (accessed 26 May 2010).

18. Barrie McKenna and Andy Hoffman, "Calls Rise for a New Global Currency," *The Globe and Mail*, 17 November 2009, http://www .theglobeandmail.com/report-on-business/calls-rise-for-new-global -currency/article1367156/ (accessed 20 November 2009).

19. John Maynard Keynes, *The Economic Consequences of the Peace* (New York: Harcourt, Brace, and Howe, 1920), 148–149.

20. Mark Hitchcock, *Cashless: Bible Prophecy, Economic Chaos, & the Future Financial Order* (Eugene, OR: Harvest House, 2009), 9–10.

21. Craig Parshall, "Racing toward the New World Order," *Israel, My Glory*, January/February 2009, 15.

22. "Group of 20/Times Topics, *New York Times.com*, 25 September 2009, http://topics.nytimes.com/top/reference/timestopics/organizations/g/ group_of_20/index.html (accessed 16 February 2010).

23. Gordon Brown, "The Special Relationship of Going Global," 1 March 2009, http://www.timesonline.co.uk/tol/comment/columnists/guest _contributors/article5821821.ece (accessed 16 February 2010).

24. Financial Security Board, http://www.financialstabilityboard.org/ about/overview.htm (accessed 15 February 2010).

25. "European Union," http://www.fact-index.com/e/eu/european _union.html (accessed 22 February 2010).

26. David Jeremiah, *What in the World Is Going On?* (Nashville: Thomas Nelson Publishers, 2008), 62.

27. Parmy Olson and Miriam Marcus, "Bringing the Banking Mess to Broadway," *Forbes.com*, 16 October 2008, http://www.forbes.com/ 2008/10/16 europe-summit-investors-update-markets-equity-ex_po _mtm_1016markets39.html.

28. United Nations Conference on Trade and Development, "Annex Table A.I.12. The Top 50 financial TNC's ranked by Geographical Spread Index," http://www.unctad.org/sections/dite_dir/docs/ wir2009top50_geospread_en.pdf (accessed 28 September 2009).

29. Erica Harvill, "MasterCard Worldwide to Strengthen Global Economic Connections with MonySend Platform," MasterCard Worldwide News Release, 914-249-6848, http://www.prnewswire.com/news-releases/mastercard-worldwide-to-strengthen-the-global-economic-connections-with-moneysend-platform-70257742.html (accessed 22 February 2010).

30. Wilfred J. Hahn, "Collapse of Financial Institutions," in *How to Overcome the Most Frightening Issues You Will Face This Century* (Crane, MO: Defender, 2009), 285.

31. Joseph Stiglitz, "Wall Street's Toxic Message," *Vanity Fair.com*, July 2009, http://www.vanityfair.com/politics/features/2009/07/third-world-debt200907 (accessed 5 October 2009).

32. *Merriam-Webster's Collegiate Dictionary*, 11th ed., s.v. "mendacious; mendacity."

33. Eugene H. Peterson, *The Message*, 1971.

34. Drawn from Anna Bartholomew, "Get Rich? Get Real," *Reader's Digest.com*, http://www.rd.com/advice-and-know-how/get-rich-quick-schemes-and-scams/article12641.html (accessed 22 March 2010).

35. C. S. Lewis, *Screwtape Letters*, in *The Complete C. S. Lewis Signature Classics* (New York: HarperCollins Publishers, Inc., 2002), 143.

36. Bonnie Miller Rubin, "Homeless Students: Increasingly, Families Taking Shelter Anywhere They Can," *Chicago Tribune.com*, 28 October 2009, http://archives.chicagotribune.com/2009/oct/28/travel/chi-homeless-studentsoct28 (accessed 22 February 2010).

37. Rachelle Younglai, "Congress to Probe Compensation at AIG, Others, *Reuters*, 14 October 2009, http://reuters.com/article/news One/idUSTRE59D40k20091014 (accessed 15 October 2009).

38. "'I Warned Nic Cage to Cool It,'" *New York Post.com*, 19 November 2009, http://www.nypost.com/f/print/pagesix/warned_nic_cage_to_cool_it_dTgQtdAwOKv6CaFIh6ivVI (accessed 18 February 2010).

39. Rita Delfiner, "Foreclosing Act of Nicolas Cage," *New York Post .com*, 14 November 2009, http://www.nypost.com/p/news/national/foreclosing_act_on_cage_Tjo4CEH8Zc8SIysM4zifRJ (accessed 17 February 2010); Lauren Beale, "Foreclosure auction of Nicolas Cage's mansion is a flop," *Los Angeles Times.com*, 8 April 2010,

http://articles.latimes.com/2010/apr/08/business/la-fi-cage
-foreclosure8-2010apr08 (accessed 26 May 2010).

40. John Ortberg, *When the Game Is Over, It All Goes Back in the Box*
(Grand Rapids: Zondervan, 2007), 197–198.

CHAPTER 4. From Crisis to Consolidation

1. Damien McElry and Paul Anast, "Greece Crisis: Three Bank Workers Killed in Street Protests," *Telegraph.co.uk*, 5 May 2010, http://
www.telegraph.co.uk/travel/destinations/europe/greece/7682628/
Greece-crisis-three-bank-workers-killed-in-street-protests.html
(accessed 5 May 2010).

2. Derek Gatopoulos and Elena Becatoros, "3 Dead as Anti-Austerity
Riots Erupt in Athens," *Yahoo! News.com*, 5 May 2010, http://
news.yahoo.com/s/ap/20100505/ap_on_bi_ge/eu_greece_financial
_crisis (accessed 5 May 2010).

3. Brian M. Carney, "A Tale of Three Cities," *Wall Street Journal.com*,
3 May 2010, http://online.wsj.com/article/SB10001424052748704
342604575221862829605190.html?mod=WSJ_Opinion_LEFTTop
Opinion (accessed 4 May 2010).

4. Bureau of Labor Statistics, "Economic News Release/Employment
Situation Summary," 7 May 2010, http://www.bls.gov/news.release/
empsit.nr0.htm (accessed 7 May 2010).

5. Christine Hauser, "U.S. Adds 290,000 Jobs in April: Rate Rises
to 9.9%," *New York Times.com*, 7 May 2010, http://www.nytimes.
com/ 2010/05/08/business/economy/08jobs.html (accessed 7 May
2010).

6. Charles Dickens, *A Tale of Two Cities* (New York: Macmillan Company, 1922), 3.

7. Brian M. Carney, "A Tale of Three Cities."

8. Erwin Lutzer, *When a Nation Forgets God: 7 Lessons We Must
Learn from Nazi Germany* (Chicago: Moody Press, 2010), 47.

9. David M. Walker, *Comeback America* (New York: Random House,
2010),28.

10. State of Connecticut Department of Banking, "ABC's of Banking,"

http://www.ct.gov/DOB/cwp/view.asp?a=2235&q=297892 (accessed 17 March 2010).

11. "U.S. Bank, NA, of Minneapolis, Minnesota, Assumes All of the Deposits of Nine Failed Banks in Arizona, California, Illinois and Texas," Press Release: Federal Deposit Insurance Corporation, 30 October 2009, http://www.fdic.gov/news/news/press/2009/pr09195 .html (accessed 17 March 2010).

12. Federal Deposit Insurance Corporation, "Failed Bank List," http:// www.fdic.gov/bank/individual/failed/banklist.html (accessed 23 April 2010).

13. Tamara Keith, "2009 Ends with Fewer Banks in Business," *National Public Radio*, 29 December 2009, http://www.npr.org/templates/ story/story.php?storyId=121998631 (accessed 23 March 2010).

14. Eric Dash, "4 Big Banks Score Perfect 61-Day Run," *New York Times.com*, 12 May 2010, http://www.nytimes.com/2010/05/12/ business/12bank.html?th&emc=th (accessed 12 May 2010).

15. "Democrats Push Ahead on Finance Bill," *New York Times.com*, 12 March 2012, http://dealbook.blogs.nytimes.com.

16. Barack Obama, "Remarks by the President on Wall Street Reform," 22 April 2010, http://www.whitehouse.gov/the-pres-office/remarks -president-wall-street-reform (accessed 23 April 2010).

17. Michael Corkery, "Geithner: Even Conservatives Heart Financial Overhaul," *Blogs Wall Street Journal.com*, http://blogs.wsj .com/deals/2010/03/22/geithner-even-conservatives-heart-financial -overhaul/(accessed 3 June 2010).

18. Alexandra Twin, "Glitches Send Dow on Wild Ride," *CNN Money .com*, 6 May 2010, http://money.cnn.com/2010/05/06/markets/ markets_newyork/index.htm?hpt=T3 (accessed 11 May 2010).

19. Michael P. Regan and Rita Nazareth, "Dow Plunges Most Since 1987 Before Paring Losses; Euro Tumbles," *Bloomberg Businessweek .com*, 6 May 2010, http://www.businessweek.com/news/2010-05 -07/u-s-asia-stocks-tumble-as-debt-concern-spurs-electronic-rout .html (accessed 6 May 2010).

20. Twin, "Glitches Send Dow."

21. Robert Kiyosaki, "The End Is Near," Conspiracy of the Rich Online

Exclusive Update #42, ConspiracyOfTheRich.com, 7 May 2010 (accessed 11 May 2010).

22. Rex Nutting, "Time for Fed to Disprove PPT," *MarketWatch.com*, 5 January 2010, http://www.marketwatch.com/story/time-for-fed-to-disprove-ppt-conspiracy-theory-2010-01-05 (accessed 11 May 2010).

23. Ibid.

24. Wilfred Hahn, "Food Crisis and the Coming Anti-Joseph," *Rapture Ready Newsletter*, 25 April 2008, http://www.raptureready.com/featured/hahn/h8.html (accessed 19 May 2010).

25. Ibid.

26. Nahum M. Sarna, *JPS Torah Commentary* (Philadelphia: Jewish Publication Society, 1989), 322–323.

27. Henry M. Morris, *The Genesis Record* (Grand Rapids: Baker Books, 1976), 641.

28. R. Kent Hughes, *Genesis: Beginning & Blessing* (Wheaton: Crossway Books, 2004), 535.

29. Ibid., 534.

30. Morris, *The Genesis Record*, 640.

31. Wilfred J. Hahn, "Last-Day Oppressors: Honored Elites & an Indebted World Order," *Eternal Value Review,* June 2010, http://www.eternalvalue.com/adownload/EVR_06_2010.pdf (accessed 2 June 2010).

32. Griffith Thomas, *Genesis: A Devotional Commentary* (Grand Rapids: Eerdmans Publishing, 1946), 453.

33. Jay W. Richards, *Money, Greed and God: Why Capitalism Is the Solution and Not the Problem* (New York: Harper Collins Publishers, 2009), 19.

34. Ibid., 18, 19.

35. Mark Kramer et al., Jonathan Murphy, translator, *The Black Book of Communism* (Cambridge: Harvard University Press, 1999), 133–135.

36. Walker, *Comeback America*, 29.

37. Leslie Kwoh, "Study Shows 43 Percent of American Have Less Than $10k Saved for Retirement," *The Star-Ledger*, 10 March 2010, http://www.nj.com/news/index.ssf/2010/03/study_shows_americans_with_lit.html (accessed 18 March 2010).

38. Niccolò Machiavelli, *The Prince*, translated by W. K. Marriott, 1908, chapter 18, in the public domain, http://www.constitution.org/mac/prince18.htm (accessed 4 June 2010).

39. C. S. Lewis, taken from his essay "Equality," 11 February 1944, http://diwanggising.multiply.com/journal/item/64/Equality_An_Essay_by_CS_Lewis_1944 (accessed on 11 May 2010).

40. Fred Lucas, "Obama's Nominee to Run Medicare: 'The Decision Is Not Whether or Not We Will Ration Care—The Decision Is Whether We Will Ration Care With Our Eyes Open.'" *CBS News.com,* 24 May 2010, http://www.cnsnews.com/news/article/66465 (accessed 3 June 2010).

41. Joshua Rhett Miller, "Georgia Mayor Hopes to End Flap over Prayer Before Meals at Senior Center," *FOX News.com*, 10 May 2010, http://www.foxnews.com/us/2010/05/10/georgia-mayor-hopeful-end-prayer-flap-meals/ (accessed 14 May 2010).

42. David A. Raush, *A Legacy of Hatred* (Chicago: Moody Publishers, 1984), 72.

43. Lutzer, *When a Nation Forgets God*, 50, 53.

44. Aesop, "The Ass and the Old Shepherd," http://classics.mit.edu/Aesop/fab.3.3.html (accessed 12 May 2010).

CHAPTER 5. Satan's CEO

1. *Merriam-Webster's Collegiate Dictionary*, 11th ed., s.v. "CEO."

2. John Phillips, *Exploring the Future: A Comprehensive Guide to Bible Prophesy* (Grand Rapids: Kregel Publications, 2003), 272.

3. John F. Walvoord, *The Thessalonian Epistles* (Findlay, OH: Dunham Publishing Co., 1955), 117.

4. *The Anchor Bible: I Maccabees*, Jonathan A. Goldstein, transl. (New York, NY: Doubleday, 1976), 198, 206.

5. Marilyn Sewell, "The Hitchens Transcript," *Portland Monthly Magazine.com*, January 2010, http://www.portlandmonthlymag.com/arts-and-entertainment/category/books-and-talks/articles/christopher-hitchens/1/ (accessed 15 March 2010).

6. Phillips, *Exploring the Future*, 269.

7. Ibid.

8. A. W. Pink, *The Antichrist* (Grand Rapids: Kregel Publishing, 1988), 79.

9. Phillips, *Exploring the Future*, 277.

10. Walvoord, *Thessalonian Epistles*, 129.

11. Joel Rosenberg, "An Evil Wind Is Blowing: U.N. Approves Anti-Semitic Resolution," *Flash Traffic*, 6 November 2009.

12. David Jeremiah, *Escape the Coming Night* (Nashville: Word Publishing, 1990), 157–158.

13. Mark Hitchcock, *Cashless: Bible Prophecy, Economic Chaos, & the Future Financial Order* (Eugene, OR: Harvest House Publishers, 2009), 137.

14. Solomon Zeitlin, *The Rise and Fall of the Judean State*, vol. 1 (Philadelphia: Jewish Publications Society, 1962), 92.

15. *Anchor Bible*, 206–207.

16. Josephus, *Antiquities*, 7.5.4.

17. Ibid.

18. Adapted from "Hanukkah," *History.com*, http://www.history.com/topics/hanukkah (accessed 31 March 2010).

CHAPTER 6. "The Mark of the Beast"

1. Grant R. Jeffrey, *Shadow Government: How the Secret Global Elite Is Using Surveillance against You* (Colorado Springs: WaterBrook Press, 2009), 18.

2. Steve Connor, "Professor Has World's First Silicon Chip Implant," *Independent News*, 26 August 1998, www.independent.co.uk/news/professor-has-first-silicon-chip-implant-1174101.html (accessed 27 October 2009).

3. Positive ID Corp. "About Us," http://www.positiveidcorp.com/about-us.html (accessed 3 June 2010).

4. John Phillips, *Exploring Revelation* (Neptune, NJ: Loizeaux Brothers, 1991), 171.

5. Wilfred Hahn, "The False Prophet: Last and Final Economic Guru," *Midnight Call*, January 2010, 22.

6. Blaise Pascal, *Pensées*, translated by W. F. Trotter, http://www .leaderu.com/cyber/books/pensees/pensees.html (accessed 25 February 2010).

7. Ray Stedman, "When Men Become Beasts," http://www.raystedman .org/revelation/4205.html (accessed on 6 October 2009).

8. Arnold G. Fruchtenbaum, *The Footsteps of the Messiah* (Tustin, CA: Ariel Ministries, 2002), 250–251.

9. "Bel Air Homes for Sale," http://www.luxury-homes-condos-for -sale.com/Bel_Air.htm (accessed 25 February 2010).

10. Henry M. Morris, *The Revelation Record* (Wheaton: Tyndale House Publishers, 1983), 256.

11. Jeffrey, *Shadow Government*, 154.

CHAPTER 7. Financial Signs of the End Times

1. Robert Kiyosaki, *Rich Dad's Conspiracy of the Rich* (New York: Hachette Book Group, 2009), 39.

2. "The Things We Do for Love," recorded by 10cc.

3. "Ben-Gurion Airport Revolutionizes Security with Unipass Biometric System," *The Jerusalem Post.com*, 5 January 2010, http://www .jpost.com/Home/Article.aspx?id=165291 (accessed 28 March 2010).

4. Jamie B. Cheaney, "The Tower of Google," *WORLD*, 13 March 2010, http://www.worldmag.com/articles/16457 (accessed 16 March 2010; subscription needed).

5. Ibid.

6. Robert Samuelson, "The Cashless Society Has Arrived," *Real Clear Politics.com*, 20 June 2007, http://www.realclearpolitics.com/ articles/2007/06/the_cashless_society_has_arriv.html (accessed 7 October 2009). Also in: Robert Samuelson, "The Vanishing Greenback," *Newsweek*, 25 June 2007.

7. Tim Webb, "Cashless Society by 2012, Says Visa Chief," *The Independent*, 11 March 2007, http://www.independent.co.uk/news/ business/news/cashless-society-by-2012-says-visa-chief-439676 .html (accessed 7 October 2009).

8. Samuelson, "Cashless Society Has Arrived."

9. Coco Ballantyne, "Dirty Money: Can the Flu Be Passed on Dollar Bills?" *Scientific American.com*, 5 January 2009, http://www.scientificamerican.com/blog/60-second-science/post.cfm?id=dirty-money-can-the-flu-bepassed-o-2009-01-05 (accessed 8 October 2009).

10. Samuelson, "Cashless Society Has Arrived."

11. "Mobile Personal Point-of-Sale Terminal," 10 March 2010, http://www.freepatentsonline.com/y2010/0057620.html (accessed 16 March 2010).

12. Richard Mullins, "More Than Half of All 12-Year-Olds Have Cell Phones," Media General News Service, 1 September 2009, http://www2.tricities.com/tri/news/local/consumer/article/more_than_half_of_all_12-year-olds_have_cell_phones/31603/29 (accessed 16 March 2010).

13. John Horrigan, "Home Broadband Adoption 2009," *Pew Research .org*, 28 May 2009, http://pewresearch.org/pubs/1254/home-broadband-adoption2009 (accessed 18 June 2009) and John Horrigan, "Wireless Internet Use," *Pew Research.org*, 22 July 2009, http://www.pewinternet.org/Reports/2009/12-Wireless-Internet-Use.aspx (accessed 8 October 2009).

14. CTIA Media, "100 Wireless Facts," http://www.ctia.org/advocacy/research/index.cfm/AID/10377 (accessed 31 August 2009).

15. Colin Gibbs, "Rich Carriers Got Richer in Q," *Gigaom.com*, 6 November 2009, http://gigaom.com/2009/11/06/rich-carriers-got-richer-in-q3/ (accessed 16 March 2010).

16. John Ribeiro, "India's Rural Mobile Phone Users Hit 100 Million," *PCWorld.com*, 13 July 2009, http://www.pcworld.com/businesscenter/article/168354/indias_ruralmobile_phone_users_hit_100_million.html (accessed 31 August 2009).

17. "Number of Cell Phone Users in North Korea Hits 20,000," *China Post*, 7 April 2009, http://www.chinapost.com.tw/business/asia/borea/2009/04/07/203299/Number-of.htm (accessed 31 August 2009).

18. James Riley, "The World Now Has 4 Billion Mobile Phone Users," iTWire.com, 20 August 2009, http://www.itwire.com/it-industry

-news/market/27107-the-world-now-has-4-billion-mobile-phone-users (accessed 16 March 2010); "Number of Cell Phone Subscribers to Hit 4 Billion This Year, UN Says," *UN News Centre*, United Nations.org, 26 September 2008, http://www.un.org/apps/news/story.asp?NewsID=28251 (accessed 31 August 2009).

19. "Apple Announced Over 100,000 Apps Now Available on the App Store," Apple.com, 4 November 2009, http://www.apple.com/pr/library/2009/11/04appstore.html (accessed 16 March 2010).

20. Jim Bruene, "How Many iPhone Banking Apps Will There Be?" *Netbanker.com*, 12 November 2009, http://www.netbanker.com/2009/11/how_many_iphone_banking_apps_will_there_be.html (accessed 16 March 2010).

21. David Weliver, "The Best 15 Financial iPhone Apps," 28 April 2009, http://moneyunder30.com/bes-15-financial-iphone-apps (accessed 16 March 2010).

22. Lance Whitney, "USAA App Lets iPhone Users Deposit Checks," *CNET News*, 11 August 2009, http://news.cnet.com/8301-13579_3-10307182-37.html (accessed 16 March 2010).

23. Jim Bruene, "New Online Banking Report Available: The Case for Mobile Banking," 15 March 2010, http://www.netbanker.com/2010/03/new_online_banking_report_available_the_case_for_mobile_banking.html (accessed 16 March 2010).

24. Emmie V. Abadilla, "Smart Money Eyes 38.5 M Cell Phone Users," *Manila Bulletin.com*, 30 August 2009, http://www.mb.com.ph/articles/218353/smart-money-eyes-385-m-cellphone-users (accessed 31 August 2009).

25. Terrence O'Brien, "25% of Facebook Users Access the Service Via Mobile Phones," 6 September 2009, http://www.switched.com/bb2009/09/06/25-of-faceboob-users-access-the-service-via-mobile-phones/ (accessed 8 October 2009).

26. "Cellular Telephone Use and Cancer Risk," FactSheet, National Cancer Institute of U.S. National Institutes of Health, 9 September 2009, http://www.cancer.gov/cancertopics/factsheet/Risk/cellphones (accessed 16 March 2010), and "No Cell Phone, Brain Tumor Link,

Study Says," Reuters, MSNBC.com, 3 December 2009, http://www .msnbc.msn.com/id/34265692 (accessed 16 March 2010).

27. Quoted in A. E. Schaefer, *Observation from Exploring Needs in National Nutrition Programs*, http://ajph.aphapublications.org/cgi/ reprint/56/7/1088.pdf (accessed 16 March 2010).

28. Mark Hitchcock, *Cashless: Bible Prophecy, Economic Chaos & the Future Financial Order* (Eugene, OR: Harvest House, 2009), 100.

29. Mark Jurbowitz, "Bonus Coverage," Pew Research Center Publications, 30 October 2009.

30. James Randerson, "World's Richest 1% Own 40% of All Wealth, UN Report Discovers," *Guardian News*, 6 December 2006, http://www .guardian.co.uk/money/2006/dec/06/business.internationalnews (accessed 28 October 2009).

31. Ibid.

32. Wilfred J. Hahn, *Global Financial Apocalypse Prophesied* (Crane, MO: Defender, 2009), 319.

33. Paul Richter, "Hillary Rodham Clinton's Harsh Words Stun Israel," *Los Angeles Times.com*, 14 March 2010, http://articles.latimes .com/2010/mar/14/world/la-fg-us-israel14-2010mar14 (accessed 15 March 2010).

34. Ibid.

35. Andrew Quinn, "U.S. Affirms 'Unshakeable' Bond with Israel," *Reuters.com.* 16 March 2010, http://www.reuters.com/article/ idUSTRE62F52V20100316 (accessed 16 March 2010).

36. Sandy Smith, "Obama Dinner Snub of Netanyahu Reveals Depth of US-Israel Rift," http://www.huliq.com/8738/92206/obama-dinner -snub-netanyahu-reveals-depth-us-israel-rift (accessed 14 April 2010).

37. Terry James, *The American Apocalypse* (Eugene, OR: Harvest House Publishers, 2009), 147–148.

38. David Platt, *Radical: Taking Back Your Faith from the American Dream* (Colorado Springs: Multnomah Books, 2010), 118.

39. Ibid., 93.

40. Wilfred J. Hahn, *The Endtime Money Snare: How to Live FREE* (West Columbia, SC: Olive Press, 2002), 144.

41. Simon Critchley, "Coin of Praise," *New York Times.com*, 30 August 2009, http://happydays.blogs.nytimes.com/2009/08/30/in-cash-we -trust/ (accessed 31 August 2009).

42. Robert South, quoted in *A Dictionary of Thoughts: Being a Cyclopedia of Laconic Quotations from the Best Authors of the World, Both Ancient and Modern*, ed. Tyron Edwards (Detroit: F. B. Dickerson Co., 1908), 616.

43. Donagh O'Shea, "God and Mammon," *Jacob's Well.com*, http://www.goodnews.ie/jacobswelljuly.shtml (accessed 1 October 2009).

44. Wilfred J. Hahn, *Global Financial Apocalypse Prophesied* (West Columbia, SC: Olive Press, 2009), 60.

45. John Piper, *Desiring God* (Portland: Multnomah, 1986), 156.

CHAPTER 8. The Collapse of the Global Financial Market

1. "October 29, 1929: 'Black Tuesday,'" *CNN.com*, 10 March 2003, http://www.cnn.com/2003/US/03/10/sprj.80.1929.crash/ (accessed 20 April 2010).

2. "Stock Market Crash," *Ancestry*, vol. 25, no. 4, July–August 2007, 27.

3. George Samuel Clason, *The Richest Man in Babylon*, Kindle, 2806, 83–97, 56–65.

4. Charles H. Dyer, *The Rise of Babylon* (Chicago: Moody Publishers, 2003), 21.

5. Henry M. Morris, *The Revelation Record* (Wheaton: Tyndale House, 1983), 348–349.

6. Neil MacFarquhar, "Hussein's Babylon: A Beloved Atrocity," *New York Times.com*, 19 August 2003, http://www.nytimes.com/2003/08/19/world/hussein-s-babylon-a-beloved-atrocity.html (accessed 26 January 2009).

7. "Energy Resources: Iraq Oil Sales Up But Plans 'Unrealistic,'" *United Press International*, 5 March 2010, http://www.upi.com/Science_News/Resource-Wars/2010/03/05/Iraq-oil-sales-up-but -plans-unrealistic/UPI-98181267816651/ (accessed 12 March 2010).

8. Associated Press, "Iraq Oil Revenue Soars, Creating Huge

Surplus," *MSNBC.com*, 11 March 2008, http://www.msnbc.msn
.com/id/23578542/ (accessed 12 April 2010).

9. U.S. Department of State, "The Future of Babylon Project," 7 January
2009, http://www.state.gov/r/pa/prs/2009/01/1134648.htm (accessed
15 January 2009).

10. "Iraq's New Venture: Holidays in the Garden of Eden," *The Independent*, 1 August 2008, http://www.independent.co.uk/news/
world/middle-east/iraqs-new-venture-holidays-in-the-garden-of
-eden-882635.html (accessed 15 January 2009) and "Iraq: Ready to
Fly," http://www.airport-technology. com/features/feature59101/ (accessed 17 November 2009).

11. "New American Embassy Opens in Baghdad," *CNN.com*, 5 January
2009, http://www.cnn.com/2009/WORLD/meast/01/05/iraq.main/
index.html (accessed 15 January 2009).

12. "Opening Soon in Baghdad: Largest U.S. Embassy in the World
with Restaurants, 619 Apartments," *World Tribune.com*, 18 April
2008, http://www.worldtribune.com/worldtribune/WTARC/2008/
ss_iraq0068_04_18.asp (accessed 20 April 2010).

13. Henry M. Morris, *The Revelation Record* (Wheaton: Tyndale House,
1983), 351.

14. Ibid., 363.

15. Ibid., 354.

16. Dyer, *Rise of Babylon*, 51.

17. Ed Hindson, *End Times: The Middle East & the New World Order*
(Wheaton: Victor Books, 1991), 110.

18. "City Population/Iraq," http://www.citypopulation.net/Iraq.html (accessed 12 April 2010).

19. Ibid.

20. Mal Couch, *Dictionary of Premillennial Theology* (Grand Rapids:
Kregel Publications, 1996), 57.

21. J. A. Seiss, *The Apocalypse: Lectures on the Book of Revelation*
(Grand Rapids: Zondervan, 1967), 407.

22. Edward B. Fiske, "Malcolm Muggeridge: A Life," Book Review in
Theology Today, July 1981, http://theologytoday.ptsem.edu/jul1981/
v38-2-bookreview14.htm (accessed 14 June 2010).

23. John Phillips, *Exploring Revelation: An Expository Commentary* (Grand Rapids: Kregel Publications 2001), 222.

24. C. Theodore Schwarze, *The Program of Satan* (Chicago: Good News Publishers, 1947), 105.

25. John Noble Wilford, "After Years of War and Abuse, New Hope for Ancient Babylon," *New York Times.com*, 22 March 2010, http://www.nytimes.com/2010/02/23/science/23babylon.html (accessed 23 March 2010).

26. Kevin Bales, *Disposable People: New Slavery in the Global Economy* (Berkeley and Los Angeles: University of California Press, 1999), 8, 14–15.

27. Quoted in Donald Grey Barnhouse, *Revelation* (Grand Rapids, MI: Zondervan, 1985), 345.

28. Walter K. Price, *The Coming Antichrist* (Chicago: Moody Press, 1974), 181.

29. "BDI Economic Report," 20 January 2010, http://www.bdi.eu/BDI _english/images_content/KonjunkturStandortUndWettbewerb/ Economic_Report_Issue_01_20_January_2010_small.pdf (accessed 20 April 2010).

30. Jeff Cox, "Where's the Economy Headed? Insiders Watch This Key Index," *CNBC.com*, 26 August 2009, http://www.cnbc.com/ id/32567374 (accessed 10 November 2009) and Peter Shaw-Smith of Zawya Dow Jones, "Focus: Gulf States' $40Bln Port Plan Face Economic Head Winds," *Wall Street Journal.com*, 3 November 2009, http://www.online.wsj.com/article/BT-CO-20091103-702597.html (accessed 10 November 2009).

31. Morris, *The Revelation Record*, 357.

32. Erwin Lutzer, *When a Nation Forgets God* (Chicago: Moody, 2010), 136–137.

CHAPTER 9. God's Ultimate New World Order

1. Table S-1. Budget Totals, "Budget of the US Government FY2011," *GPO Access.gov*, http://www.gpoaccess.gov/usbudget/fy11/pdf/ summary.pdf (accessed 1 June 2010); "Policy Basics: Where Do Our

Federal Tax Dollars Go?" Center on Budget and Policy Priorities, 13 April 2009, http://www.cbpp.org/cms/index.cfm?fa=view&id=1258 (accessed 23 November 2009).

2. Table S-1. Budget Totals, "Budget of the US Government FY2011," *GPO Access.gov*, http://www.gpoaccess.gov/usbudget/fy11/pdf/ summary.pdf (accessed 1 June 2010).

3. John Wesley White, "The Millennium," *The Triumphant Return of Christ*, ed. William James, Essays in Apocalypse II (Green Forest, AK: New Leaf Press, 1993), 325.

4. J. Dwight Pentecost, *Things to Come* (Grand Rapids: Zondervan, 1958), 476.

5. H. A. Ironside, *Revelation: An Ironside Expository Commentary* (Grand Rapids: Kregel Publishing, n.d.), 193.

6. Thomas Jones, *Sober Views of the Millennium* (London: Seley and Burnside, 1835), 5.

7. Randy Alcorn, *Heaven* (Wheaton, IL: Tyndale House Publishers, 2005), 226.

8. John F. Walvoord, *The Millennial Kingdom* (Findlay, OH: Dunham Publishing Co., 1959), 329–330.

9. Charles Ryrie, *Basic Theology* (Wheaton, IL: Victor Books, 1986), 511.

10. Adapted from Mindy Belz, "What Do Palestinians Want?" *WORLD*, 10 April 2010, 30–35.

11. John F. Walvoord, *End Times* (Nashville: Word Publishers, 1998), 204.

12. Victor Davis Hanson, *Imprimis*, November 2009, vol. 38, no. 11, p. 1.

13. M. R. DeHaan, *The Great Society* (Radio Bible Class, 1965), 7–8.

14. Walvoord, *Millennial Kingdom*, 317–318.

15. Richard Schlesinger, "Doris Buffett Goes for Broke to Help City," *CBS News.com*, 4 December 2009, http://www.cbsnews.com/ stories/2009/12/04/eveningnews/main5893628.shtml (accessed 9 December 2009).

16. Carl G. Johnson, *Prophecy Made Plain* (Chicago: Moody Press, 1972), 185.

17. Robert J. Little, *Here's Your Answer* (Chicago: Moody Press, 1967), 113–114.

18. Walvoord, *End Times*, 203.
19. S. Franklin Logsdon, *Profiles of Prophecy* (Grand Rapids: Zondervan Publishing, 1970), 105.
20. Alcorn, *Heaven*, 100.

CHAPTER 10. Keep Your Head in the Game and Your Hope in God

1. Erica Estep, "Portuguese Investor Lost Life Savings in Alleged Gatlinburg Ponzi Scheme," *Wate.com*, 29 April 2009, http://www.wate.com/Global/story.asp?S=10274802 (accessed 10 May 2010).
2. Bill Hybels, *Just Walk across the Room: Simple Steps Pointing People to Faith* (Grand Rapids: Zondervan, 2006), 186–187.
3. Larry Bates, *The New Economic Disorder* (Lake Mary, FL: Excel Books, 2009), 20.
4. Frank J. Hanna, *What Your Money Means and How to Use It Well* (New York: Crossroad Publishing Co., 2008), 7–8.
5. Quoted by Ron Blue and Jeremy White, *Surviving the Financial Meltdown* (Wheaton, IL: Tyndale House Publishing, 2009), 38.
6. Federal Reserve Statistical Release, "G.19 Report on Consumer Credit," 7 May 2010, http://www.federalreserve.gov/releases/g19/Current/ (accessed 10 May 2010).
7. See http://www.crown.org.
8. J. K. Gressett, "Take Courage," *Pentecostal Evangel*, 30 April 1989, 6.
9. Martyn Lloyd-Jones, *Spiritual Depression: Its Causes and Its Cure* (Grand Rapids: Eerdmans Printing Company, 1965), 20.
10. Adapted from Luke Veronis, "The Sign of the Cross," in *Communion*, Issue 8, Pascha 1997, http://www.incommunion.org/2005/08/06/the-sign-of-the-cross (accessed 10 May 2010).
11. Thomas Giles and Timothy Johnes, "A Prisoner of Hope," *Christianity Today*, 5 October 1992, 39–41.
12. Quoted by Philip Yancey, *Where Is God When It Hurts?* (Grand Rapids: Zondervan, 1977), 119–120.

About the Author

Dr. David Jeremiah is the senior pastor of Shadow Mountain Community Church in San Diego, California, and the founder of the award-winning *Turning Point* radio and television ministries. *Turning Point* was launched in 1982 and today reaches millions of people around the globe through the Internet and publications, as well as by radio and television.

Throughout his more than four decades of preaching, Dr. Jeremiah has been a student of Bible prophecy, and the chapters in this book are the fruit of his study of the Scriptures, of numerous sources from experts in the financial world, and of current global events.

Dr. Jeremiah has written many award-winning books, including: *Escape the Coming Night, Captured by Grace, What in the World Is Going On?* and *Living with Confidence in a Chaotic World.*

While Dr. Jeremiah is an avid sports fan who has spoken at several professional basketball, baseball, and football chapels, he enjoys nothing more than spending time with his wife, Donna, and their four grown children and ten grandchildren.

3 Great Ways to further your study

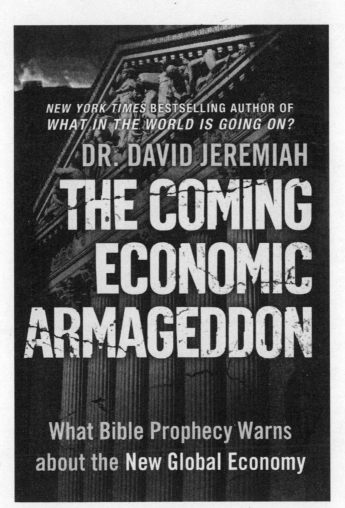

NEW YORK TIMES BESTSELLING AUTHOR OF
WHAT IN THE WORLD IS GOING ON?

DR. DAVID JEREMIAH

THE COMING ECONOMIC ARMAGEDDON

What Bible Prophecy Warns
about the New Global Economy

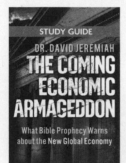

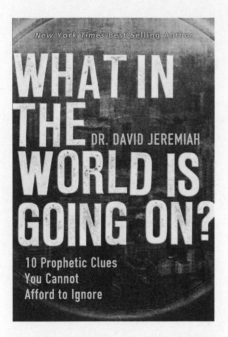

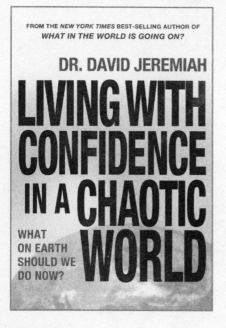

II OTHER TITLES
BY DR. DAVID JEREMIAH

CAPTURED BY GRACE   `A NEW YORK TIMES BEST-SELLER!`

By following the dramatic story of the "Amazing Grace" hymnwriter, John Newton, and the apostle Paul's own encounter with the God of grace, David Jeremiah helps readers understand the liberating power of permanent forgiveness and mercy.

LIFE WIDE OPEN

In this energizing book, Dr. David Jeremiah opens our eyes to how we can live a life that exudes an attitude of hope and enthusiasm . . . a life of passion . . . a LIFE WIDE OPEN! *Life Wide Open* offers a vision, both spiritual and practical, of what our life can be when we allow the power of passion to permeate our souls.

SIGNS OF LIFE   `A NEW YORK TIMES BEST-SELLER!`

How does the world recognize us as God's ambassadors? In *Signs of Life* you will take a journey that will lead you to a fuller understanding of the marks that identify you as a Christian, signs that will advertise your faith and impact souls for eternity.

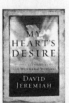

MY HEART'S DESIRE

How would you answer a pollster who appeared at your church asking for a definition of worship? Is it really a sin to worship without sacrifice? When you finish studying *My Heart's Desire*, you'll have not just an answer, but the biblical answer to that all-important question.

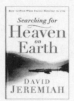

SEARCHING FOR HEAVEN ON EARTH

Join Dr. Jeremiah as he traces Solomon's path through the futility of:
• The search for wisdom and knowledge
• Wild living and the pursuit of pleasure
• Burying oneself in work
• Acquiring as much wealth as possible
Dr. Jeremiah takes readers on a discovery to find out what really matters in life, the secret to enjoying "heaven on earth."

WHEN YOUR WORLD FALLS APART

When Your World Falls Apart recounts Dr. Jeremiah's battle against cancer and the real-life stories of others who have struggled with tragedy. Highlighting ten Psalms of encouragement, each chapter is a beacon of light in those moments when life seems hopeless.

SLAYING THE GIANTS

Loneliness. Discouragement. Worry. Anger. Procrastination. Doubt. Fear. Guilt. Temptation. Resentment. Failure. Jealousy. Have these giants infiltrated your life? Do you need the tools to slay these daunting foes? With practical appeal and personal warmth, Dr. Jeremiah's book, *Slaying the Giants in Your Life* will become your very own giant-slaying manual.

TURNING POINTS & SANCTUARY

These 365-day devotionals by Dr. Jeremiah will equip you to live with God's perspective. These topically arranged devotionals enable you to relate biblical truths to the reality of everyday living—every day of the year. Perfect for yourself or your next gift-giving occasion, *Turning Points* and *Sanctuary* are beautifully packaged with a padded cover, original artwork throughout, and a ribbon page marker.

III STAY CONNECTED
TO THE TEACHING OF DR. DAVID JEREMIAH

Take advantage of two great ways to let Dr. David Jeremiah give you spiritual direction every day! Both are absolutely FREE!

TURNING POINTS MAGAZINE AND DEVOTIONAL

Receive Dr. David Jeremiah's monthly magazine, *Turning Points,* each month:

- Monthly Study Focus
- 48 pages of life-changing reading
- Relevant Articles
- Special Features
- Humor Section
- Family Section
- Daily devotional readings for each day of the month
- Bible study resource offers
- Live Event Schedule
- Radio & Television Information

YOUR DAILY TURNING POINT E-DEVOTIONAL

Start your day off right! Find words of inspiration and spiritual motivation waiting for you on your computer every morning! You can receive a daily e-devotion communication from David Jeremiah that will strengthen your walk with God and encourage you to live the authentic Christian life.

To request *Turning Points,* visit us online at www.DavidJeremiah.org and click on Magazine to begin your monthly subscription. To receive the daily e-devotional, select "Subscribe to Daily Devotional by E-Mail" when you visit the Turning Point website. These inspiring resources are available to you without cost or obligation—sign up today!

⬆ MAXIMUM CHURCH

READY! SET! GROWTH!
LET DR. JEREMIAH'S MAXIMUM CHURCH TAKE YOUR CHURCH THERE.

With a united vision to strengthen the Body of Christ and reach the community, your church can experience spiritual and fiscal growth through creative and compelling campaigns.

With over forty years of ministry experience, founder Dr. David Jeremiah now shares his passion for pulpit teaching and church leadership by offering solid Bible teaching campaigns designed to stimulate the spiritual and fiscal growth of local churches. Maximum Church campaigns are created for full-spectrum ministry including preaching, teaching, drama, small group Bible curriculum, and suggested Sunday school material—all supported by electronic, print, and audio visual files.

SIGNS OF LIFE
Lead your church to become one of Christ-like influence in your community as you take the five Life Signs discussed in this book and apply them to the lives of your congregation.

This campaign is based on Dr. David Jeremiah's best-selling book *Signs of Life*.

CAPTURED BY GRACE
Based on the best-selling book *Captured by Grace* by David Jeremiah, this ministry growth campaign will help your church and community discover the depths of God's unrelenting love and grace.

For more information on Maximum Church,
VISIT WWW.MAXIMUMCHURCH.COM